DIAMOND HEART

Book Five

BOOKS BY A. H. ALMAAS

For more information on A. H. Almaas and all of his publications, please go to: www.ahalmaas.com.

DIAMOND HEART
Book Five

Inexhaustible Mystery

A. H. Almaas

SHAMBHALA
Boston & London
2011

Shambhala Publications, Inc.
Horticultural Hall
300 Massachusetts Avenue
Boston, Massachusetts 02115
www.shambhala.com

9 8 7 6 5 4 3 2 1

First edition
Printed in the United States of America

❸ This edition is printed on acid-free paper that meets the
American National Standards Institute z39.48 Standard.
♻ This book is printed on 30% postconsumer recycled paper.
For more information please visit www.shambhala.com.

Distributed in the United States by Random House, Inc.,
and in Canada by Random House of Canada Ltd

Library of Congress Cataloging-in-Publication Data
Almaas, A. H.
Inexhaustible mystery / A.H. Almaas.—1st ed.
p.   cm.—(Diamond heart; bk. 5)
ISBN 978-1-59030-906-3 (pbk.: alk. paper)
1. Spiritual life—Ridhwan Foundation. 2. Ridhwan
Foundation—Doctrines. I. Title.
BP605.R53A46 2011
158.1—dc22
2010051838

TABLE OF CONTENTS

PREFACE

We live in a world of mystery, wonder, and beauty. But most of us seldom participate in this real world, being aware rather of a world that is mostly strife, suffering, or meaninglessness. This situation is basically due to our not realizing and living our full human potential. This potential can be actualized by the realization and development of the human Essence. The human Essence is the part of us that is innate and real, and can participate in the real world.

This series of books, Diamond Heart, is a transcription of talks I have given to inner work groups in both California and Colorado for several years, as part of the work of these groups. The purpose of the talks is to guide and orient individuals who are intensely engaged in doing the difficult work of essential realization.

The talks are organized in a manner that shows the various states and stages of realization in the order that occurs for the typical student, at least in our teaching method: the Diamond Approach. They begin with the states, knowledge, and questions most needed for starting the work on oneself, proceeding to stages of increasing depth and subtlety, and culminating in detailed understanding of the most mature states and conditions of realization.

Each talk elucidates a certain state of Essence or Being. The relevant psychological issues and barriers are discussed precisely and specifically, using modern psychological understanding in relation to the state of Being, and in relation to one's mind, life, and process of inner unfoldment.

Hence, this series is not only a detailed and specific guidance for the student, but also an expression and manifestation of the unfoldment of the human Essence as it reveals the mystery, wonder, exquisiteness, and richness of the real world, our true inheritance. Each talk is actually the expression of a certain aspect or dimension of Being as it descends into the consciousness of the teacher in response to the present needs of the students. The teacher acts both as an embodiment of such reality and as a channel for the living knowledge that is part of this embodiment.

It is my wish that more of my fellow human beings participate in our real world and taste the incredible beauty and integrity of being a human being, a full manifestation of the love of the truth.

Richmond, California, 1986

INTRODUCTION
to Book Five

This volume is the last of the five books in the Diamond Heart series. Except for the material in the last chapter in this book, the series is based on edited transcripts of teachings I imparted to my first Diamond Approach groups in the 1980s. At that time I gave talks, responded to questions, and clarified important points about the teaching and the practices of the teaching.

The Diamond Approach has evolved as a living, dynamic teaching that continues to develop and unfold. This unfoldment turns out to be an intrinsic property of reality. Since reality is alive and dynamic, and not simply characterized by an intrinsic primordial purity, it is in continuous unfoldment and evolution. Even realization and enlightenment are understood to be open-ended and continually revealing deeper and subtler forms of reality and its inherent spiritual purity. Thus the Diamond Approach does not subscribe to the position that either reality itself or the state of enlightenment is a final condition, but rather sees both as being in a continuous process of creative renewal. Such a radical view of reality and spiritual liberation manifests in the way this teaching has presented itself both to me and through me.

The talks in the Diamond Heart series illustrate this characteristic very clearly. We can think of the progression in the five volumes as indicating a gradual or progressive path, and this is partly true. However, the deeper truth is that this teaching has its own logos and intelligence, in which spiritual opening and liberation occur in many ways, and with many facets, reflecting various complementary views of reality. Liberation, then, becomes not so much a matter of realizing and actualizing a particular view or pure condition of reality—even if we recognize that reality as primordial, natural, or absolute. It is more a matter of realizing that reality has the freedom to reveal its various possibilities in our lives without limitations of mind, position, or perspective.

Many chapters of the books in this series address particular states or facets of reality that reveal specific ways in which reality manifests to us. Throughout the books, there is a natural progression of subtlety and depth in the facets described. This is not, however, due to any attempt on my part to follow a gradual path, but because reality's inherent intelligence expresses itself in my teaching in the most appropriate and digestible form of spiritual purity for those individuals receiving it at the time. We cannot receive subtle and profound truths of reality all at once, due to the many delusions that constitute our ignorance— both learned and innate—and the natural limitation based on the degree of maturity of our individual consciousness. Even when we are realized or enlightened, the aliveness of reality will at some point reveal, if given freedom of expression, that some subtle delusions still remain that have been unconsciously taken to be permanent features of reality. Some might take this to mean that one's liberation is limited, but the Diamond Approach sees it as a sign that reality is alive and dynamic, and hence never settles permanently on one particular condition as being the state of enlightenment. Every delusion that we discover simply points to a deeper and more inclusive enlightenment, thus moving enlightenment toward the freedom to unfold from realization to further realization.

As reality manifests its mysteries in various facets and dimensions, different types of realization and different kinds of enlightenment give us a much more detailed and complete understanding of the true nature of reality and the potential for being human. Even though some of these revelations can be seen as partial or transitory, the total picture that emerges is much more complete than that which results from one cataclysmic experience of, or breakthrough into, enlightenment. And it addresses more fully the various aspects of human life and the situations we find ourselves in every day.

The Diamond Approach views reality as inherently indefinite, and this indefiniteness lies at the heart of its aliveness and freedom. Even in its indefiniteness, reality reveals that it possesses a distinct purity—what I have termed at different times "true nature," "essential nature," or "being"—as the ground of all manifestation, as the irreducible perfection at the very heart of all and everything. I have described this ground as being composed of five coemergent dimensions—not as absolute givens but as a way of viewing and understanding true nature and its relation to the forms that we experience. These are universal love, pure presence, nonconceptual awareness, absolute emptiness, and creative dynamism. I have referred to these dimensions as boundless or formless because of their pervasiveness and omnipresence—sometimes conventionally referred to as the nonlocality of this purity.

Spiritual purity is indivisible, even though it is the nature of each and every thing. Without focusing on any particular dimension, Book One explores the reality of this purity, which pervades everything. Book Two of the series includes discussions of this purity as love, revealing that true nature is inherently heart, which gives us the capacity to feel and respond. Book Three explores in some detail this purity as presence, the immediacy of being, independent of the constructions of our individual minds. We find here that the dimension of pure presence reveals true nature to be inherently mind, and as mind it gives us the capacity to know and discern. Book Four further elaborates on the experience of true nature as pure presence, and how this purity of presence is the beginning of knowing. What is revealed here is that mind and knowing are different from, even though connected to, perception and experience, and that our capacity to perceive is due to the fact that awareness is inherent to our true nature. The fourth volume discusses in some detail how pure awareness is radically nonconceptual—that it is not only *not* mental, but is beyond cognition of any kind, even spiritual knowing, or gnosis.

The present volume, Book Five, introduces two dimensions of the purity of reality that complement those discussed in the previous books. It goes into some detail about how pure awareness can appear in a deeper and more mysterious form than nonconceptual awareness. This dimension clarifies in a most complete way the fundamental and paradoxical nature of emptiness. It explores how the underlying and inherent purity of reality is the source of all forms, manifestation, experience, and awareness, without these forms ever being separate from the expanse of this source. It shows how everything that is, is simply the forms that emptiness takes, as its radiance. True nature is inherently emptiness.

The understanding of emptiness in these talks and discussions is closest to the understanding of emptiness posited by the Prasangika Madhyamika tradition of Mahayana Buddhism—that of the absence of inherent existence of self and phenomena. However, this dimension, referred to as that of the absolute, is not simply emptiness. It is emptiness totally inseparable and not differentiable from presence, which is the fullness of self-knowing being. The realization of this dimension reflects the paradoxical nature of classical enlightenment, by which one recognizes that one has always been this unsullied, empty ground of luminosity; and this recognition resolves experientially the dichotomy of existence and nonexistence.

Some of the chapters in this book discuss this absolute dimension from the perspective of the heart—the absolute as the inner beloved, as the true essential home from which we have been estranged, as the mysterious night of stillness in which all suffering and strife cease. We come to see in clear relief that the emptiness of this dimension can be seen as its indeterminacy, but that this indeterminacy does not mean that it is unknowable. The title *Inexhaustible Mystery* refers to the paradoxical nature of our spiritual purity: that we can know it more and more, and we can discern ever deeper and more subtle realizations about its nature without ever exhausting its truth. We can know our spiritual purity, but we can never know it completely. We can never say the last word about it, because there is no end to what can be known, and no way to know it from its own perspective.

It is always through our individual consciousness that we know the mystery, even when we experience ourselves as its vastness, its expanse, its luminosity. It is *our* experience, not somebody else's. In other words, this perception is happening through a particular individual consciousness, even though we recognize ourselves as this empty vastness. This demonstrates the implicit presence of individual consciousness, of the individual soul. No experience or perception can occur without this organ of experience, so there is no way to know this mystery from its own viewpoint. There is no claim that the mystery knows itself in a way we cannot know it, for it needs our individual consciousness for it to know. But simply put, the mystery can only know itself through a particular individual consciousness, and hence it can never know itself absolutely without it.

The Diamond Approach takes the view that the teachings of different spiritual paths approximate the knowledge of this mystery in different ways, some definite and precise, others indefinite and ambiguous. However, we see no reason to take one as true and the others as false. Different teachings can each reflect objective truth about reality in its purity because of this indeterminability of the mystery.

The absolute ground of reality is always and continuously manifesting all its forms—all the forms of experience and perception. This points to the fifth coemergent dimension of true nature—creative dynamism—which is the second dimension that the present book introduces and discusses. This discussion is an inquiry into the inherent dynamism and aliveness of reality, which is always morphing and transforming its appearance. We learn that reality, which is always appearing in one form or another, reveals itself as the dynamic luminosity of true nature when perceived from the vantage point of the realization of the absolute. By presenting the understanding of this dimension, this book shows how our spiritual purity is inherently creative and dynamic, and is always displaying or manifesting all the forms of experience we encounter.

Some of the chapters use Christian metaphors, the sayings of Jesus, other passages from the New Testament, and various ideas from Christian mysticism in discussing the creative dynamism of the universe. These offer a way to understand the creative dynamism as the Cosmic Christ, the Logos, the Word, which is the firstborn of the Absolute. Creative dynamism can be realized as the living and dynamic creativity of the Absolute, and all of existence can be seen as the articulation of its revelation by this dynamic force. Hence, this dimension of creative dynamism can be experienced as the word, for manifestation is cosmic articulation.

We can also experience this dimension as the activity of speaking, for the dynamism is reality speaking out its forms, and this reveals the mystery of how our speaking can become a form of revelation of truth. We can further experience this dimension as the activity of thinking, for the creative dynamism is also indefinite reality thinking out its forms. Each form, each experience, is a thought, a word, a concept. But they are all a flowing continuity of becoming, a becoming that never establishes itself as fully existing, because it is never divorced from ontological emptiness, the nonexistence of true nature.

The final chapter is taken from more recent retreat

talks, material presented in 2008 and 2009. This teaching illustrates the inseparability of the five dimensions, but specifically focuses on the two dimensions that the book discusses—absolute emptiness and creative dynamism—and how they are inseparable. This chapter also exemplifies the living and evolving nature of the Diamond Approach as a teaching, for it points to the truth that enlightenment goes further than the realization of the boundless, empty luminosity and dynamism of true nature. The realization of the empty, boundless ground of reality simply functions as a way station toward a freedom that expands even further, opening up a much more inclusive view of the totality of reality—one that encompasses all realizations without needing to adhere to any of them.

As in previous volumes, I urge the serious reader to bring the openness of your total being to the material in this book. These talks were offered as a direct transmission of the purity of reality; hence the words are simply carriers for a deeper energy and consciousness. My hope is for you to learn more about the reality that we live in and as. Toward that end, you need to use mind—but it needs to be an open mind—as well as an open heart. For it is with an open heart that these talks were given. May they open more hearts in our world, and may more of us see the beauty and splendor of reality.

DIAMOND HEART

Book Five

Inexhaustible Mystery

ONE

Poor in Spirit

Today we will work with the well-known Sermon on the Mount, attributed to Jesus (Matthew 5:1–12, King James Version). I will first read it and then talk about it some.

> Blessed are the poor in spirit, for theirs is the kingdom of heaven.
>
> Blessed are they that mourn, for they shall be comforted.
>
> Blessed are the meek, for they shall inherit the earth.
>
> Blessed are they which do hunger and thirst after righteousness, for they shall be filled.
>
> Blessed are the merciful, for they shall obtain mercy.
>
> Blessed are the pure in heart, for they shall see God.

> Blessed are the peacemakers, for they shall be called the children of God.
>
> Blessed are they which are persecuted for righteousness' sake, for theirs is the kingdom of heaven.
>
> Blessed are you when men shall revile you and persecute you and shall say all manner of evil against you falsely for my sake.
>
> Rejoice and be exceedingly glad for grace is your reward in heaven, for so persecuted they the prophets which were before you.

We will focus on two lines from this sermon to illustrate an important stage of our approach to inner work. Jesus says:

> Blessed are the poor in spirit, for theirs is the kingdom of heaven.

> Blessed are the pure in heart, for they shall see God.

These two concepts, central to the Sermon on the Mount, are central also in our understanding of the inner journey, and in most spiritual teachings. It will be useful for us to have some appreciation of their meaning and significance. The first concept is that of poverty and the second that of purity. We want to appreciate how they relate to each other and how they relate to what we do. We need to understand them in a way that makes sense with our orientation to inner work, where we are not monks and nuns, where we are not renunciates, but rather lead ordinary lives in the world. How can we live the poverty of spirit and the purity of heart while we are living in the world? Jesus's words actually point to the answer. If he simply said we should live in poverty, we could not harmonize that with our work and practice. His understanding is so deep that it is applicable to any way of life, not only to the way of the monk.

The verse "Blessed are the poor in spirit, for theirs is the kingdom of heaven" goes to the very heart of a mature attitude toward spiritual work. What does it mean to be poor in spirit? And why would that mean we will have the kingdom of heaven? To be poor in spirit is not easy to understand and appreciate. It is not something that most people ordinarily seek or want.

Jesus does not say that we need to be materially poor in the world. He does not say that we need to be poor in ego or poor in mind. He says we need to be poor in spirit, and he obviously means something specific. Our spirit will need to be poor if the kingdom of heaven is to be ours. The concept of poverty is central in Christianity, and also in other traditions. In Buddhism, for example, the story of Gautama is well known—he renounces all his riches and worldly comforts and becomes a mendicant, begging for food, before attaining to Buddhahood. He established a monastic order where an important part of the discipline is that each monk has a bowl with which to beg daily for food.

Poverty is also a central principle in the Sufi tradition. The followers of Sufism are sometimes called dervishes, which literally means a person who goes around begging for alms. For the Sufis, being a dervish is an exteriorization of the spiritual poverty. Theirs is a path where they attempt to live the poverty both physically and spiritually, to accept poverty at all its levels.

Whenever they have something, they just give it away. The only thing they want is nearness to God.

Why is the question of poverty important? What does the kingdom of heaven have to do with whether we are poor or rich? It is not easy to see the truth of Jesus's sermon: that poverty is a certain condition or state that, when it actually happens, is better than all the riches possible. So what does it mean that we have to be utterly poor in order to be rich in everything? The Son of Man tended to say things that were very hard to understand!

To understand the poverty of spirit, we can recall the "dark night of the soul" that John of the Cross wrote about. He divides the "dark night" into two nights: the night of sense and the night of spirit. The dark night for him means the way of poverty. The dark night for him means the darkness, the unknowing, and the pain of poverty as the soul divests herself of all possessions and attachments. He calls it a dark night because it is dark emotionally—difficult and painful—and also dark mentally—lacking guidance and clarity about the process.

According to John of the Cross, we need to begin with the night of sense, the stage of poverty related to the external life, the material life and all its mental, emotional, and physical possessions. For him the night of sense is the stage of purification of the soul from her animal nature, from her sensual attachments and desires. When we are relatively comfortable with this level of poverty, we can move to the dark night of spirit, the stage of being poor in spirit, which is purification on the spiritual level, totally emptying the soul and getting her ready for her beloved, her God.

The core of the question about poverty is possessions, and more deeply the attachment to possessions:

possessiveness. Possessiveness is having to have: money, clothes, reputation, credit for achievements, essential experiences. To be poor means not to have these things, and this becomes a major part of many spiritual approaches because the need to have things is the support for ego-self, and leads to neglect of the inner life and the truth of spirit.

Having possessions is necessary in our normal life even for simple living; that is the way our society is structured. It would be almost impossible, or at least distracting, to live in our modern society and not have any possessions. Each of us needs at least clothes, a bed, a toothbrush, and so on, and without them life would become so difficult that we would not have the time or space to do what we need to do to live our lives, including spiritual practice.

However, having possessions naturally tends to become possessiveness, an important support for the sense of self, which is ultimately false. The more a person is selfish or egoistic and the less he is in touch with deeper reality, the more it is important for him to have things. Havingness is important for ego; having things gives us the illusory sense of safety without which the ego-self cannot live. Having things makes us feel protected, secure, more permanent, successful, important, and so on. Just knowing we have things—we don't even have to see or use them—gives this sense of security and permanence. It gives us a sense that we can fall back on them. Having things gives us a deep feeling of support that connects with the preservation instinct.

The havingness, the possessiveness, doesn't only manifest on the physical level, but extends to the mental and emotional levels, even the spiritual level. When people begin doing inner work, they come with the same attitude of possessiveness, wanting to have things and accomplish things that enhance the sense of self. They simply swap material objects for spiritual objects and are basically still functioning in the mode of possessiveness. The desired objects become experiences and insights, grace and realization.

Of its very nature, the ego needs an object to hang on to. It has to have something of its own; it has to own things. Often when we feel that we really love a person, we say, "I want you, will you marry me, come live with me, be mine." We want the person all to ourselves. If someone else touches them, we might lose them. The core of the nature of ego is that kind of possessiveness. The object could be a human being, money, furniture, books, fame, a position in society, an artistic creation, a boundless dimension. We might say, "I'm an artist; that gives me a sense of who I am, a sense of value, a sense that I am not just a nothing." The person who doesn't have much feels he is not important, and the more materialistic our society is, the more we look at things in this way. Havingness becomes not only necessary for survival and living, but for esteem, recognition, and significance.

Because havingness is a cornerstone of the ego-self and its life, spiritual traditions have seen poverty as necessary for realization, which is largely a going beyond the ego and its view of reality. Learning to be poor, to live without attachment, without havingness, becomes the way to empty the self and to move toward the truth of reality. Since it is almost automatic that possessing becomes possessiveness, many of the spiritual traditions teach material poverty as an effective method to counteract the tendency of havingness. Living a life of renunciation becomes the way to avoid the temptations of havingness. The world begins to appear as a temptress to be shunned and renounced at any cost. This strategy can help, but there is no guarantee for success. Most renunciates do not become enlightened.

In any case, this is not the meaning of being poor in spirit. Being physically poor does not necessarily lead to spiritual poverty; otherwise, all the poor people in the world would be saints. Havingness is not only about physical possessions. It is a psychological attitude, and the nature of the object is not what matters. We can have literary or artistic accomplishments, opinions, judgments, ideas, preferences, feelings, states, experiences, also family, friends, acquaintances, activities, interests, hobbies, and so on. All these can and do become objects of havingness. We are all rich with these things, even the materially poor among us. It is true that abundance of physical possessions tends to predispose us to an extreme attitude of havingness, but the tendency toward havingness is not fundamentally connected to the physical. Thus, the way of poverty includes nonattachment to all levels of inner possessions too. We can experience all the rich phenomena of our human, essential, and spiritual lives, and we can learn not to be attached to them, not to need them for our sense of self and value.

But poverty of spirit is still radically different from this. When we hear that poverty is actually the path, is something ultimately desirable and necessary for our realization, most of us cringe. We tend to think of the spiritual path the way we think of any other endeavor, as a way of gaining, a way of accumulation. We believe, directly or subtly, that to progress on the spiritual path is a matter of having spiritual things instead of material things. We believe realization is a matter of accumulating spiritual experiences, insights, visitations, inner riches, inner capacities, inner accomplishments, and so on.

Or, even more subtly, we believe it is a matter of

having more spirit, vaster spirit, more presence, more immense presence. We are bigger, vaster. But all this amounts to becoming bigger and vaster egos that are still full of pride, albeit spiritual pride. We even become attached to our emptiness, to our idea of emptiness as a spiritual accomplishment. We are still not poor; we are quite rich, quite full, with all kinds of things. We are actually full of ourselves, exactly what the path of poverty is trying to liberate us from.

The way of poverty is for us to be so empty, not possessing anything, that the Ultimate Truth, the inner Beloved will find us worthy of beholding it. The inner Beloved is a jealous beloved. It won't show itself unless there are no other lovers in our heart. When our heart is completely empty, then will it reveal itself as the mystery underlying all of reality. And the way to such inner emptiness is that of poverty, specifically the poverty of spirit.

Remember what Jesus said. You need to give up not only your clothes, money, furniture, books, lovers, ideas, prestige, accomplishments, achievements, creativity, ego, and mind, but your spirit itself. Poor in spirit means you haven't got spirit, just like poor in money means you haven't got money. What does it mean not to have spirit?

We are working here on essential realization, learning how to connect with essence, reality, spirit, soul—and now we have to give it up. You may think this guy Jesus expects a lot. You may think he was talking to poor people who didn't have much to give up materially, so they had to give up something else. I think he is talking to everybody. The attitude of possessiveness, the attitude of havingness, is a central attitude of ego. You are somebody who has things. Can you imagine yourself being somebody who doesn't have anything?

Not having in this context means not having to have. It's the willingness to be poor. It's not a matter of becoming poor, although that might happen too. If that is what it takes for you to experience that you don't have to have, then maybe you should not have possessions. So the easiest things to give up, to be detached from, and not to care about are the physical things—clothes, money, and so on. What is more difficult to give up is the inner domain.

To be poor within means to give up your thoughts, feelings, wants, desires, likes, dislikes, preferences, opinions, beliefs, ideas. Being poor within is not holding positions about what is good and what is bad. If you do that, then you still have preferences, you still are not completely poor. From this perspective we see that everyone is very rich. We are all rich in spirit—full of ideas, preferences, opinions, beliefs, goals, and ideals.

Surrendering our thoughts, feelings, judgments, preferences, and desires doesn't mean that these things disappear but that we don't have them in the same way. They just come and go. We don't hold on to them as possessions. They are not vital for us. Maybe we can learn to be that poor inside. But then, as we begin to have experiences of reality, of essence, of awakening, the ego wants to possess these too. We believe that essence, spirit, and inner states belong to us, that we accomplished them. Havingness is back again. We might even believe we have virtues like patience, humility, courage, and equanimity. On a spiritual path, the ego can become rich again, can come to possess a wonderful inner panorama, the panorama of spirit.

To be poor in spirit ultimately means that we need to be poor in the inner states themselves, the states of realization, the positive states. We need to be poor in love, poor in compassion, poor in intelligence, poor in truth, poor in awareness, poor in existence. But what does this mean? Clearly, as we open up to our nature we begin to experience these things more. Being spiritually poor does not mean that we do not experience spirit, just as being materially poor does not mean we do not have material things. Rather, poverty means that we do not possess spiritual experiences or material things. We realize that we don't own them; when they come, they come, when they go, they go. We do not have them, hold on to them, or take the position that they are ours. We treat them as visitors, as guests.

The moment that we say some experience is ours, we go back to the same attitude, just like the person who has lots of money. We feel rich again and we support our ego with that richness. To learn to be poor, we have to go very far. The attachment to realization has to go. The attachment to inner states has to go. Needing to have good states has to go, just as needing to have bad states has to go. We learn that our attachment to negative states also can make us feel full and rich with oceans of hatred and mountains of jealousy. We can be rich in envy, anger, and fear. These inner possessions support the identity in the same way that oceans of love and mountains of strength do. The ego says, "These are mine."

The perspective of poverty requires a continual letting go, a continual giving away, a continual disowning of all possessions, of all dimensions of experience. We have less and less. The less we have, the poorer we feel, and the more there is purity. Saying that we "let go" or "surrender" is not quite precise. It is more accurate to say that we discover that all of our states and feelings and inner experiences don't belong to us. We cannot sell them, we cannot trade them, we cannot accumulate them, we cannot store them, we cannot have them at will. They are not ours; they are gifts. These phenomena that pass through our souls are similar to the weather. Is the weather ours? Can anyone own the snow, the rain? What comes, comes; what goes, goes.

The evolution of the urge toward possession is connected to our physical survival. Ultimately, however, it has come to serve the survival of the ego, the false self. When we experience essence, essence doesn't feel it possesses anything. Essence never says, "I have strength. I have realization." It is you who says that. Essence is just there; spirit simply is. When you say you have something, essence feels compassion toward you. "Poor guy, he wants to be rich." Having to have is attachment. Attachment can be to anything: material possessions or emotional, mental, essential, divine, enlightened possessions.

For instance, the Buddhist tradition teaches that the last barrier to go as enlightenment is attained is the belief in attainment. When you feel you are enlightened and now you don't need to meditate, that's what has to go. Only when you see that you want to meditate even after you are enlightened do you know that you are enlightened. If you say, "I am finished," then your teacher tells you to go and meditate. That state in which you believe you are finished means that you are still rich; it means that you are not finished yet. The one who is finished never feels finished.

Since we are looking at this situation from our Western perspective, rather than viewing it from the perspective of nonattachment, we see it in terms of poverty. The notion of poverty, as we discussed earlier, is part of the Western spiritual tradition. Poverty is the Western counterpart of nonattachment. However, nonattachment is not identical to poverty. To be poor in spirit means to be completely nonattached, but the sense of poverty is a different flavor of experience from that of nonattachment.

Nonattachment means we have reached a place of realization of true nature or spirit, and we experience ourselves as the spirit, which is inherently nonattached. In the Western traditions, the question is looked at from the perspective of soul, not spirit, where soul is the individual total consciousness through which experience happens. It is useful here to recognize the distinction between soul and spirit. Poverty means the soul has learned to recognize that everything she experiences, everything she has, is not hers. All experience is a gift from true nature, from the source of all manifestation. In monotheistic language, the soul recognizes that whatever richness she experiences, whether material or spiritual, comes from God, a gift and grace from him. She owns nothing because there is only one owner. Even her actions and accomplishments are not hers, for without the capacities and qualities that God gives her, she won't be able to do anything.

The soul recognizes that the spiritual qualities and experiences are not hers; they are God's qualities, and are bestowed upon her, and just as easily can be taken away. She recognizes that even her very substance, her very existence, is a gift from God. She is nothing, possesses nothing, and can do nothing. This is the dark night of spirit, which is an actual experiential condition, and not only an insight or understanding. As the soul recognizes her truth—that as an individual soul she possesses nothing—she begins to experience the true condition of being an individual soul. And this is the condition of being totally empty, totally poor, totally incapable, totally lacking. This is the state of poor in spirit, traditionally referred to as mystical poverty.

To be completely poor is to recognize our true condition as individuals, which is that nothing we have or experience or accomplish is actually ours. It all belongs to the ultimate spiritual truth, the absolute ground of reality. We then experience a phenomenological emptiness, a voidness of all qualities, of everything, including being and existence. When this condition prevails, it becomes possible for the source of all manifestation to reveal itself in this voidness. This is a subtle point. When we recognize our inherent poverty, our sense of self is completely denuded, which makes it possible for the essence of divinity to manifest.

The state of poverty is not simply a lack, even though the soul cannot help but see it as such because we are looking through the veils of selfhood. Accepting our total poverty, and not asking for more, allows us to surrender whatever is left of our selfhood. This surrender reveals that the emptiness of poverty is simply the inscrutable darkness of the Divine Essence, which is obscured as lack because of subtle veils. Now, however, the emptiness of poverty reveals itself as the majestic and luminous darkness of the mystery of Being. The dark emptiness becomes a luminous night, the mystical midnight sun, the very essence of divinity, the divine darkness that is the source of all light.

From this place all manifestation appears as the grace and fullness of Being, as the resplendent beauty of the face of God. We find ourselves in the kingdom of heaven. More exactly, we recognize that all and everything is the kingdom of heaven, now revealed to us by accepting our emptiness. We perceive tremendous fullness and plenitude, infinite riches and abundance, but none of it belongs to any individual soul. It is all the body and heart of God.

By accepting our poverty we allow the essence of divinity into our hearts, and this reveals all of creation as the kingdom of heaven: "Blessed are the poor in spirit, for theirs is the kingdom of heaven." We are blessed with this vision, with this realization, by going through the dark night of spirit and accepting without protest our inherent poverty. By accepting our poverty we give up our self-centeredness, our egoism. This is the condition for the arising of true reality, reality as it is, reality not dependent on what our minds believe, not dependent on what we have learned, not dependent on our prejudices and histories. Reality, as it is, is one. Some people call this the experience of God.

Jesus, however, does not say we experience God. He says the pure in heart shall see God. He does not say you are with God or relate to God or will be God. He says you see God. What is significant is the matter of seeing God. You are not with God, because you are not; there is only God. You do not relate to God, because there is no other than God. You are not part of God, because God has no parts. You see only God. You are not created by God, because there is only God. God doesn't create anything else.

Is it possible for there to be God when there is something else? When we believe that there is God and creation, then there is God and there is us. What we are talking about then is not God. We are talking about an idea in our minds about what God is. We have not seen the true God yet. The understanding of poverty shows that everything is God's, and no one has anything, including existence. We only appear to have things, appear to exist as individual souls, but when we accept our poverty, and see the Divine Essence, we recognize that all and everything is the manifestation of God's Being.

When you are God, you don't feel you are God. If you feel "I am God," then the "I" is still there. You are not God; you don't relate to God; you are not part of God; you are not supported by God. If you believe any of these things, then you think there is something other than God. And when you experience something other than God, it is no longer God; it is your idea of God or something you learned about God. God becomes something you made up in your own image. But God is not made in the human image; it is the other way around. You are an image of God.

The experiences of devotion to God, relationship to God, union with God, connection with God, being part of God, being cells in the body of God, being God—all appear on various paths. But they all retain the sense of the presence of the self. When the self goes, there is only the seeing of God. You don't even feel "I am being God" because there is no "I." If you say, "I am experiencing God," there are two, not one. If you say, "I love God," there are you and God. When there is God, there is no one there who loves God; there is just God. There is the seeing of God and that's it. You don't feel that you are seeing God, that you are relating to God, that you are God; you don't feel anything that has an "I" in it. You don't feel anything. There is just the seeing of God, and God is all and everything. All that you can see and cannot see.

If for one moment you see that there is something other than God, whether separate from God or connected to God, if for one moment you perceive that God has parts, then what you are experiencing is not the absolute oneness. You are experiencing parts. As long as you are experiencing parts, there are ego boundaries, which bring a sense of separateness, a sense of richness of possessions, and a sense of impurity.

To be poor is to lose self completely. To be pure is to see nothing but God. There is no such thing as the devil and God. There are some religions that are based on the division between the world of light and the world of darkness. These two Gods of the light and the dark are always fighting. People generally choose one or the other. If you choose darkness, the soldiers of darkness will come and aid you against the soldiers of light, and vice versa, in an eternal and perpetual battle. But that level of perception has not yet arrived at the monotheistic view, where God is one, absolute, and eternal. God is simply what is, what has been, and what will be. God is all that can be experienced, all that can exist, all that can be conceived, in its original purity and pristineness, free from the veils of the ego-self. God is the one reality.

To even call it one is not exact; we say one to mean it is not many. So when the heart is completely unattached and pure, when the heart does not claim to know what God is, when the heart does not claim that it wants God or doesn't want God, when the heart doesn't have a wanting of anything, then the face of God appears to us. As long as we want, even wanting God, we are still not completely poor. There is a you that wants something. And the true God will not appear as long as you are there. As long as you take yourself to be a separate person, a separate entity that relates to other entities, there is something impure and unobjective about the perception. Reality, as it is, is not apprehended.

We see here that the concepts of poverty and purity are connected to letting go of ego, leaving behind the self that believes in impure or pure. To be pure means not to believe anything. Not to believe anything does not mean you have beliefs that are suppressed. To be pure means to have no reified discriminations, but that does not mean that you have discriminations that are repressed. To be pure means that you have no preferences, but that does not mean that you have preferences that you are avoiding. The detached person who does not feel anything, who does not feel his preferences, is not what we mean by pure. Such a person has many impurities, attachments, and discriminations, but is not willing to experience them.

The concepts of poverty and purity appeal to our hearts. They inform the path of the heart. They are things that you can actually feel. You can feel the poverty and the purity. Ultimately, poverty means letting go of all havingness. The final havingness is the self. Purity ultimately means letting go of all attachments, all preferences, all prejudices and personal beliefs and positions. When there is complete poverty, there is no self, no you; there is total purity.

Let's see if you have questions.

STUDENT: Is there a sense of loss in the path of poverty? And does it feel like pain and suffering, as John of the Cross wrote?

ALMAAS: Letting go of attachments and accepting poverty is a heart-wrenching process. We feel deep tears as we experience the continual loss of everything we love. We feel oceans and oceans of hot black tears. The tears of letting go and surrender deepen into an ocean of grief, and the ocean becomes darker and blacker, so black that at some point you don't even have tears.

What we are letting go of, what we are losing, are things we have cherished all our lives. You have to let go of your cherished beliefs, your loves and hates, your loved ones and your enemies, your ideas and philosophies, your comforts and consolations, even your mind and your heart. Most of us will protest, "How can I let go of my heart? What is life without my heart?" It is not a matter of not experiencing your heart or anything else; it is more a letting go of needing to possess things. The resistance and reluctance reflect the fear of the poverty. You think that if you let go of something, "That's it. It's going to be gone forever." But you have to take that risk. You don't know whether it will be gone forever or if it will come back again. That's the test of the poverty. You might feel that your self is going to go, your heart is going to go, your intelligence is going to go. And you have loved and needed all these aspects of yourself.

To accept your poverty is to see that none of these are yours; you never really had them—you just believed you did. Realizing this poverty, although painful for the heart, is actually how the heart is purified. Although it is a grueling process, as we come to the point of recognizing and accepting the truth, peace and a causeless contentment arise in the soul. The process is similar to that of accepting our inner spiritual aloneness. Aloneness is a matter of letting go of objects, of object relations. Poverty is letting go not just of relationships but of everything, absolutely everything. Inner poverty is a more comprehensive concept than aloneness. First you have to accept aloneness, which is not easy, but we do come to accept it as we feel the peace and purity it brings to the soul. Then you have to accept poverty. You discover not only that you are completely alone; you discover also that you don't possess anything. You are so empty, so poor, that you don't even have deficiency. It is not that when you let go of everything you will feel deficient. Feeling deficient means you still have something; it supports the illusion of separate existence.

If you have deficiency, you are still rich. Poverty is complete freedom. Poverty ultimately becomes completely pure, completely empty. This turns out to be the absolute state, the state of having absolutely nothing. Nothing is yours; you are beyond everything. The clothes are not yours, the feelings, the body, essence, God—nothing is yours. When you have nothing and you are absolutely poor, then you go beyond it all. But then you can have it all, since you don't need it anymore. So, ultimately, the letting go means letting go of the center that possesses. If the center that possesses is gone, then there is no you that has something, and then you experience everything.

Possession involves an entity that restricts you in space and time. If you have an experience or a state or a possession, then you must exist somewhere in space and time, which is a limitation. By being rich, you define yourself and make yourself exist in a limited way: "I am here now and I have something." And when you have nothing, completely, absolutely, then you are not in any place or in any time. If you are not in any space or any time, you are not a local phenomenon. You have all space and all time available to you. You are then an openness, a nothingness that has everything with no barrier.

That's the paradox to which Jesus was referring. If you become poor in spirit, you will be in the kingdom of heaven. If you are completely poor, you get nothing absolutely, which ontologically is the same thing as having everything. The switch point concerns the sense of an existing self, the feeling that there is a me who has or who doesn't have. The transition is that the sense of self goes. Before that goes, you have things or you don't have things. That central sense of self who is going to have this, who is going to be enlightened, who is going to experience God, who is going to get rich, who is going to have pleasure, is what ultimately goes.

Everything else will be left. God will be left, pleasure will be left, fun will be left, everything will be there without you. Then everything will be experienced purely. Pleasure will be pure pleasure because you are not there to contaminate it. As a separate self that possesses things, you are an impurity. Without that self, when there is love, there is pure love. It is not you who says, "I love you." Sometimes when you feel love you can actually sense a little, dark, murky cloud sitting somewhere and looking at this ocean of love. When you feel, "I'm loving and I'm going to save the world," the world needs to be saved from you. As long as there is a you that wants to save the world, the world needs to be saved from you. You are just making trouble for people by pretending to save them when in fact you are asserting your own deficiencies.

You haven't got anything to save anybody with anyway. And if you're fortunate, you will be saved someday by that love itself. It comes and melts you, and shows you it is not you who is going to save anyone. You can be saved, but only by everything being taken away from you. One thing after another will go, until you become completely poor; then you will be gone. The riches are your support; when you are completely poor, you have no supports, and then you just dissolve. You are gone. A wave of death comes and purity pervades.

STUDENT: So is it simply a matter of understanding that the ego-self does not truly possess anything because it itself is an illusion?

ALMAAS: Yes, if you are looking at it intellectually, or experientially but through the mind. But the path of poverty is the path of the heart. Intellectual understanding won't do it. The insight and understanding are important, but on the path of mystical poverty the soul must completely feel and live the richness, the poverty, the deficiency and fear, the loss and pain, the attachment and the longing for freedom. The more the heart leads the way, the more possibility for insight to arise.

You feel the poverty in your heart. You feel the pain of letting go of things you love. You experience the poverty as deep suffering and sorrow. It is not easy for the heart to let go and be poor. It lets go with a lot of pain, a lot of tears. When you think about it, your mind says, "Okay, let's do it. This makes sense. Let go now." But the heart doesn't work that way. Your mind can say, "Okay, I'm making a vow of poverty." That's fine and some paths do that, but it must come from the longing of the heart.

The Sufi dervishes, for instance, give away everything they have to their neighbors. If they get a gift, they offer it in a spirit of sacrifice. When they feel enlightened, they offer their enlightenment to God. It is a heart attitude, an attitude of generosity that is not easy to grasp. Of course, it has to be a heartfelt, genuine giving away. You cannot say, "I'm going to have less and less so I can be free." That is the mind talking and that does not work. It cannot be a strategy; it has to be a living longing. When the impulse comes from the heart, there is some kind of surrender, of giving up, of learning a lesson after difficult and painful experiences.

We are talking about mystical poverty because this perspective is needed in our work here. We are not working to get richer; we are working to get poorer. You might think you are coming here to get more realized, to achieve more essential states. The truth is you will have less and less. The heart and the mind usually do not hear this message for years and years. They keep rebelling, keep doing things according to what they have learned. "I don't want this. I want that." After some long time, the heart and the mind become wiser. The heart sees, responds, and moves toward poverty. The heart realizes that riches hurt, that they are not the real thing, not the truth, not the true Beloved. Also, the heart realizes that trying to get riches is not the heart's nature. Its nature is always surrendering, forgiving, disowning.

When you are poor, you don't feel, "I have achieved poverty." When you are poor, you don't have such claims. You don't come to conclusions about yourself. You don't say, "Now I am realized. I am loving. I have this or that." The heart is soft and humble. The soul takes the direction of poverty because she realizes that all that she has tried wasn't true. She has been pursuing possessions and achievements like a stubborn little kid who doesn't want to change. The soul comes to see the truth and finally recognizes, "Yes, that is really how it is."

If you are really maturing, you finally come to say to yourself, with sincerity and sobriety, "How many times do I have to hit my head against the wall? I don't want to hit my head against the wall anymore, not because it hurts but because it is a dumb thing to do. It is not my nature to do that; someone else told me to do that, and now I am fed up with such stupidity." You wake up; you grow up. This is an inner knowledge, a heart knowledge, an experiential knowledge, a taste, a feeling, an actual state. That's what the movement of poverty is.

STUDENT: What is a pure heart?

ALMAAS: Pure heart is what I also call the courageous heart. The courageous heart does not eliminate love when there is hatred and does not try to choose one thing above another. The pure heart is open to the presentations of Being regardless of what they are. It is happy to be with whatever God wills, and it asserts no position. The attitude of purity is the attitude of no assertion. You don't assert any truth. You don't assert any knowledge, any perspective, any position. You don't take a position; you don't have a position; you don't have a particular truth, opinion, belief, religion. You are absolutely poor. The attitude of purity is that you never close your mind and say that's it. You never close the door. You are open not because you are uncertain, but because it is not possible to assert this or that about reality in some absolute way. And also there is no need or urge to assert this or that view.

STUDENT: How is poverty related to surrender?

ALMAAS: Speaking of poverty is another way of talking about surrender, about generosity, nonattachment, selflessness. But the state of poverty has a sense of sacredness. Poverty is so absent of everything that it is absolutely sacred. There are no contaminations, no impurities, nothing exists in it absolutely. It is so empty of everything, all attachments, all objects, all qualities, that it is absolute sacredness. The sense is that poverty is where God comes from, the abode of God. Poverty is the condition before anything comes into being. It is completely, absolutely sacred because it has not been contaminated by manifestation. No creation has happened yet. Nothing has occurred. Nothing has been said.

Some people call poverty the great death. It is not just the death of you or your ego. It is the death of everything. The absolute cessation and annihilation of all that can be perceived, felt, experienced. It is preexistence.

For most people, the most recalcitrant attachment that we confront as poverty approaches is the attachment to the dual unity, the attachment to the good positive relationship, which is ultimately the attachment to the good mother. The dual unity is the early ego structure in which the soul experiences the self and the mother as one world with no other, usually characterized by the feeling of merging gold love. The dual unity transferences manifest as attachments to the people you love or attachment to your relationship to God. The attachment to the dual unity is the fantasy that we will be in blissful union with a good object.

We see here the connection to true, existential, objective aloneness. Aloneness has to be accepted completely for it to become poverty. But letting go of dual unity does not imply that dual unity will never happen, or that it is not possible for it to manifest, or that it is not real. Letting go of dual unity means there is no attachment to it. You don't feel you have it. It is something that might occur sometimes. If you are an individual soul, then the loving condition of the dual unity may occur sometimes.

The need for a positive relationship with another is very deep, and at the deepest level for most people it is unconscious. We don't normally feel the desire for dual unity directly. It is powerful and renders us extremely vulnerable. When you directly experience the need for dual unity, you can't sleep for weeks at a time. You wake up from your sleep terrified, or shivering from cold and fear. It is a tremendous challenge to bring to consciousness and let go of the good relationship to the good mommy that is in your mind. It is such a fundamental need of the individual soul, and so entrenched, that we live it without ever becoming conscious of its power.

When the need for the good object takes over, we are generally willing to forget everything—essence, reality, God, truth—and unconsciously, compulsively go for the dual unity. Its power is the final psychodynamic support for the ego identity itself. The following are intimately connected: the attachment to life, to existence, to love, to the good mother. It takes the state of absolute poverty to expose this deep attachment, to bring to consciousness the part of you that has not changed its mind and heart, and still believes it is going to get the perfect union with the perfect object one of these days. The soul might believe that the way to get the dual unity is to become enlightened, but she is still pursuing the perfect object.

To thoroughly comprehend this deep desire, you need absolute purity. Deep in the soul resides the primal longing for the good mother, where everybody feels: "I just want my good mommy and that's it. I want to sit in her lap, have her give me a big hug and kiss my neck. Then I will feel happy and complete." The terror of giving up this deep longing of the soul is one reason why poverty is frightening. When the state of poverty begins to arise, you find yourself running a mile a minute, terrified as if a goblin is after you, after your most cherished possessions, after your very life.

To comprehend what I am talking about, you have to penetrate deep inside, in your guts, where things are stuck and held, where you are too afraid to be truly alone and truly nothing. People die not wanting to let go of this deep desire, this hope and attachment. I am not saying that you should try to find this need for dual unity, for the good object, and relinquish it. The truth is revealed simply by exposing it, by looking at your attachments in your life. All the attachments come from this source. It is the foundation of all impurities.

STUDENT: It seems that once you give this up, life becomes so empty and you are so desolate and poverty-stricken, that there is nothing in life worth getting attached to.

ALMAAS: If you give up that longing for the good object, then you are truly poor. If you are truly poor, then you live in sacredness. If you are truly poor, you won't feel it is not worth it or it is worth it. None of that exists. You don't give up out of hopelessness. You give up because you know that is the way. No one can do it any other way. It's the objective truth, and you see it. Along the way you fight, you get mad, you disbelieve your teachers, you misinterpret the teachings, and so on. At this juncture of the inner journey, many people begin to doubt the teacher and teachings; in reality, they simply don't want to let go. So they may think that when it comes to this point, the teacher is possibly not right. That is one of the last doubts. In reality, unconsciously we are asserting, "I prefer Mommy over God." We pretend that we want God, but what we really want is Mommy.

STUDENT: You are talking about the desire for the dual unity, which is the longing for a positive merging kind of relationship. But how does negative merging fit into this?

ALMAAS: Negative merging, and the attachment to negative relationships, is produced by the part of you that doesn't want to give up. There is a tremendous mountain of hope supporting this part. This is what I sometimes call the libidinal ego, the ego infused with libido, full of energy, vigor, strength, and instinctual intelligence. Because it is always going after this wonderful object, and because most of the time it cannot attain it, it ends up in a frustrated, ungratified condition, which we call negative merging.

If we inquire into our various relationships, especially the object relationships we enact in the world, we find many varieties, but underneath them, much more hidden than most forms of relationships, is the libidinal relationship. This is the powerful part of the ego-self that embodies the animal soul and all her tendencies, which becomes constellated around the infantile desire, hope, and wish for the wonderful object, the libidinal object that will gratify all of the soul's needs and desires. The libidinal ego is the instinctual and infantile source of attachments and desires, and typically is split off from our conscious experience.

Under normal circumstances, when we experience this deep, hidden part of our soul, it does not feel negative. We actually feel full of life and full of vigor when we experience ourselves as the libidinal soul. We are strong, full of passion, full of energy, brimming with a zest for life. But we are not going to let go of what we want and what we believe we have. We passionately hold on, wanting the riches of life and all the objects that promise gratification. If you become aware of the deepest image that this libidinal ego is holding on to, you see the image of a luscious breast. This is the initial image, the core image that the libidinal ego doesn't want to let go of. It is a wonderful golden image, which we see full of all the essential qualities. At this early age, the spiritual and the animal forms of experience are not yet differentiated; they are interpenetrating.

We find we have a deep lust for this object of gratification. The lust has a sense of wanting. The wanting we feel is powerful, passionate wanting, strong and robust. Because it is such a powerful force, many spiritual traditions, like Sufis or Christian mystics, try to direct that wanting toward God. If you truly manage to direct the libidinal impulse toward God, then realization becomes easy. That's one reason why Sufi poetry talks about God as the Beloved, as though he is a woman or man with whom we are besotted. The soul is able to channel all that libidinal energy toward the transcendent reality.

This is the most suppressed object relation. The libidinal object relation involves the dual unity, which is the deepest way of attaining the yummy object. The state of poverty is a threat to this core structure. This is a realm into which we don't usually venture. When we approach that place where that libidinal energy resides, we may start having visions of devils and gods.

Remember the story of Buddha before his enlightenment? The devil Mara came to him, sending dark forces against him, in the hope of distracting him from finally letting go of attachment. First he threw spears at him and sent monsters to scare him, but Buddha didn't budge. Then he started sending wonderful, beautiful women with luscious breasts who tried to tempt him. The detached heart of Buddha didn't move. That is when Mara himself acknowledged the Buddha and was converted.

This state of poverty and purity, this depth and level of work, require that we really want the truth as it is. We have to be intimately touched and moved by reality, by truth, by essence, to be able to even contemplate venturing into a condition like the poverty of spirit. For most people, it is not their concern. Moving into this realm is not part of ordinary life; it is only needed when we are moving deeply into the truth of reality.

For those who are genuinely motivated, we need to realize that the poverty of spirit requires tremendous devotion and struggle. We must develop purity, nonattachment, understanding, love, and many other qualities, all the way to perfection, all the way to completion. Mystical poverty is the entrance into the Divine Essence, the window into the deepest mystery of reality, the absolute truth of Being. Only those with a powerful pull toward that most beautiful of all beloveds will dare to venture here. And of these, only those who love this Beloved to the extent of complete annihilation into its mystery chance upon this doorway.

TWO

The Guest Arrives Only at Night

Today I'll read you one of my poems titled "The Guest Arrives Only at Night":

Annihilate mind in heart,
Divorce heart from all relationships,
And then love,
Love passionately,
Consume yourself with passion
for the secret one.

When you are absolutely poor,
When you are no more,
Then the Guest will appear
And occupy his place,
In the secret chamber,

His abode,
The heart he gave you.

He is the Inner of the Inner,
He is the Secret,
He is the Guest,
And he arrives
Only at night.

There is much in this poem that we can discuss, but I will focus mostly on the theme expressed in the title, "The Guest Arrives Only at Night." I will use a specific terminology of the path of the heart, where the Absolute is variously referred to as the Beloved, the Guest, the Secret, the Inner of the Inner, and so on. We'll discuss some of these terms as we proceed, but now I want to get to the essence of this poem.

In our path of seeking the truth out of the love of the truth, we encounter many forms and dimensions of truth. At some point we discover the essential truth, the actual presence of spirit, which is our true being. We discover many aspects of this essence and realize that these aspects manifest on several dimensions. These dimensions are revealed as the inherent primordial structure of true nature, our essential being and the being of all existence. Each dimension reveals something fundamental to true nature and necessary for our life and experience. Our path unfolds these dimensions in a sequence of increasing subtlety and depth. The deepest and final dimension we find, the dimension that forms the ground of all dimensions, and of all manifestations, the ground of all grounds, is what I refer to as the Absolute.

The preceding poem is a faithful expression of the

path of the heart as it discovers and realizes this Ultimate Truth of reality. In our particular path the heart does not simply dispense with the mind; the heart subsumes the mind. Insights are not gone but are the outcome of the love of the heart, the sparks of the fire of passionate love.

The poem shows that the way of the heart is love. The inner journey is motivated and powered not by utilitarian needs, such as the need to be free from suffering, but by the self-sacrificing love of the soul for her source and for her true nature. The heart loves the truth; the deeper the truth, the deeper the love, and the deeper the love, the deeper the revelation of the truth. The Absolute is the true Beloved of the heart, whether we are conscious of it or not.

The mind cannot and does not know the Guest; it does not and cannot know the Secret. The mind does not know, really, what the heart deeply loves and desires. Only the heart knows the Guest because the Guest is the true possessor of the heart. Only the heart can know the Secret, can know the Guest. The heart will simply not rest unless it is occupied by its master. The heart is bereft without its owner.

The mind, on the other hand, has all kinds of ideas about what ought to fill this deepest emptiness of the heart, what ultimately will bring a final peace. The mind does its work conceptualizing the Beloved, creating many images and forms for the heart to love. These images, ideas, and beliefs that the mind creates in the process of its development distract the heart. The heart loses its way as it begins to long for and pursue the images created by the mind. In our ordinary experience, the heart follows the lead of the mind because we feel we should follow what we know to be true, and we believe it is the mind that knows truth.

The heart is what possesses the truth sense, not the mind. The mind can discriminate and know, but it is the heart that ascertains whether it is the truth. Since the Beloved is the Ultimate Truth, only the heart will know it for certain. And since the heart primordially loves the truth, the Ultimate Truth is inherently its deepest Beloved.

The heart's primordial knowing of what will fill its emptiness is intuitive, not conceptual, and usually unconscious. The heart's vacancy is the chamber where the Guest resides. That is the nature of our heart. Because the heart loses its way we spend a whole life wanting this and wanting that, needing this and needing that, searching for this and searching for that. Every time we acquire a new beloved, whether a person, a career, or a philosophy, for a while the heart believes, "I found it." After some time and a lot of disappointment and heartache, we realize, "No, that isn't it. My heart is still not contented." And everything we find, everything we achieve, everything we love, we eventually discover is not it. The heart remains dissatisfied and the emptiness still gnaws at us.

Ultimately, the heart cannot be deceived. As long as the Guest is not in its natural chamber, the heart is empty at its depth. That total inner poverty is not only the deepest emptiness of the heart but becomes the central void around which the ego personality forms, around which the most primitive structures of ego form. Ego activity is, in large part, an attempt to fill this emptiness, to cover up this complete poverty with all kinds of things we love and long for and want.

Our ordinary thinking mind knows only what it has heard from others, or what it has learned in the process of its own evolution and development. We conceptualize various objects as the Beloved of the heart, as what will bring true fulfillment and contentment. Throughout our attempts to fulfill the longing of the heart, the search for the Beloved is veiled by the concepts of the mind. Although the heart believes it is pursuing the true Beloved that will grant final peace and fulfillment, in reality it is chasing after impostors. The heart, as a result, finds many lovers, one after the other. The heart falls in love from time to time and is happy when it finds a new love because maybe the Guest has finally arrived. Maybe this is the one.

The heart conducts its love affairs one after another. The love object changes in form, depending on the stage of development, on the background of the particular individual, on the present circumstances and possibilities and so on. The love object can be another person, another toy, another activity, another job, another home, another car, another dress, really just about any manifestation in our life. The love object might be an inner state of one form or another, an idea of enlightenment, a concept of God, or a notion of the perfect relationship. We can pursue simply pleasure or love, even compassion. We accrue many lovers as we try to fill the gnawing emptiness at the depth of our hearts.

We all go through life moving from one love affair to another. And always we end up disappointed because at some point we discover that this is not the one. The latest beloved is not the final Beloved. Even though it seems wonderful for a while and we believe we finally have arrived, we keep finding out that our various love affairs are temporary fixes. And the search begins anew. The mind constructs new ideas, more refined conceptualizations of what it is we want.

This endless process continues as the mind creates increasingly subtle and increasingly sublime concepts.

Even when we feel we are following our heart, loving something deeply despite the counsel of the mind, we are actually following the mind in subtle ways, ways we still do not recognize as created by the mind. We might be moved by the inner promptings of the heart, but usually our longing is created by the mind's concepts. The mind veils our heart to a much larger extent than we know. We are appalled and humbled when we discover how thoroughly our mind controls even what feels like our deepest movement toward truth. This is most obvious when we consider the love objects we pursue in the world of manifestation. But even the inner objects we seek, such as essential states or various subtle dimensions, are forms and concepts constructed by the mind. The Guest is beyond all conceptualization, whether it is forms of the outer world or the inner world. The Guest is prior to all forms and all manifestations. The Guest is their ultimate source.

The mind, therefore, can never accurately conceptualize the Guest, for the Guest is beyond the world of concepts. The Guest is pre-mind, pre-conceptualization, pre-relationship. The Guest is not something that the mind can ever imagine. The Guest is the slayer of the mind. The Guest is the confounder of the mind, its annihilator, its death, even though it is also its bedazzler.

Now, the mind is not bad; it is not trying to deceive us. In fact, the mind tries all the time to be of help. It does its job as best it can. The mind is ultimately a servant. However, its function in our ordinary state of consciousness is to conceptualize, to create things through thoughts. The mind is effective and tireless in its concept-creating function. Furthermore, this function is useful for practical day-to-day living. The mind tells us how to take care of our everyday life and increases our ordinary knowledge. The heart, however, has an interest in something that is wholly outside of our everyday world.

So the mind's normal functioning is useless when it comes to knowing the Secret. The mind will never know the Secret, even though at some point it longs for it. Our mind loves and wants the Secret. The mind is always looking for the Secret but will never know it the way it ordinarily knows. The mind is relieved of its task only when it finds the Secret, when it finds its own death, which happens to be its deepest rest. The mind will be able to function after such realization, but only as the faithful servant of the Guest, expressing it out of delight in its ineffability.

We see here that the mind is in quite a dilemma. Because our ordinary experience is so dominated by mind, it seems as if the mind is the only means we've got through which to search for and know what we are seeking. For a long time, the mind is the only instrument through which we know what to do and how to go about doing it. Without the mind, we usually cannot discriminate differences in our perception and experience. But in following the path of the heart through the inner journey, we discover that the mind's role ultimately is to know that it cannot know the Secret. Only when the mind finally realizes that it doesn't know the Guest, cannot know it, and will never know it, is it possible for the mind to quit and for the heart to take over. Then it is possible for the heart to follow its own guide, its own inherent promptings. Instead of the heart being guided by the mind, the heart will be guided by its own desire that expresses its love for the Guest.

That is why the poem says to annihilate mind in heart. Once our usual mind gives up the search for the Beloved, we can allow all thoughts, ideas, beliefs, or concepts about what it is that we're looking for to dissolve in the heart. We need to focus the mind in the heart and let it go to sleep. We need to let the passion of the heart take over and consume the mind. The mind needs to cease guiding the heart, needs to quit telling the heart what it should long for and love.

This is not simply the cessation of mind but also cessation in the heart. In other words, the mind drowns in love, words drown into the passionate love of the heart. Conceptualizing ceases and love takes over.

As the mind is allowed, or allows itself, to acknowledge its own poverty, to recognize that it is not what can know the Secret, it will slowly accept not knowing. We discover that we cannot know the Secret in our usual way of knowing. The mind begins to learn that not knowing is the way, and becomes willing to rest, to surrender, to die.

As the mind begins to relax, the situation of the heart becomes clearer. We begin to see that we don't feel the true longing, the true wanting, the true loving of the Secret. We've been loving other things, wanting other things. Our heart is full of unreal lovers. When the mind is out of the way, we see that the heart is full of various lovers, idols, and impostors standing for the real Beloved. We find all our attachments residing in our heart, everything that we think we should have; all our physical, emotional, and spiritual possessions crowd our heart. We find our heart preoccupied, filled to the brim with things of the world, things of the mind. The mind is still present, but subtly and in the hidden recesses of the heart.

As long as we want something that we can think

about, it is an attachment and not the true Beloved of the heart. As long as we long for something that we can relate to in a relationship, it is an attachment and not the true Beloved of the heart. These objects of attachment are still not the true passion of the heart. The true Beloved is not an object we can relate to, for anything we can have a relationship with is an object made by the mind. That is why the poem says to divorce heart from all relationships. I do not mean to abandon all human relationships; I mean to abandon the mode of relating when it comes to the search for the inner Beloved. Relating to something implies a duality of lover and Beloved. The true Beloved simply does not admit such duality. Relationship, as any form in duality, is within the realm of the mind, and the Guest is pre-mind, transcendent to mind.

Furthermore, all the issues we have in doing our work as we're going through our search will have to be seen only as distractions. Issues, difficulties, conflicts, mental and emotional, are to be recognized and understood, so that they stop distracting us from our real search. We understand our mind and resolve our emotional conflicts not for their own sake but to reveal our true love. As long as we don't understand our issues, our mind and heart will focus on them and we will be distracted from our true love. Ignorance, conflicts, assumptions, beliefs, and so on obscure our true love and veil the face of the Beloved.

We need to see that all of our inner work, all the understanding and insight we gain, is a matter of recognizing what distracts us. Each time we understand something new, we need to sacrifice it, to let it go. We need to learn not to be attached to any object, any form, any insight we can know in our minds. We need to learn not to be attached to anything we can remember, whether it's an issue we're exploring, part of our personality, or an essential state. Everything is to be explored, to be understood objectively, and, at the moment it is understood, to be sacrificed completely, absolutely, and willingly at the door of the heart.

That is exactly what understanding something means. To understand something means ultimately to sacrifice it, to let it go, to be done with it. If we do not let it go, if we keep holding on to it, we have not fully understood it. When we thoroughly understand something, it's gone—whether it's an aspect of the personality or an aspect of essence. We're attached to it only when we haven't completely understood it.

The path of the heart shows us that everything we become attached to remains in our heart, filling the abode of the Guest. Our attachments become idols filling the sacred space of the Kaaba, the holy place of the absolute Beloved. We need to recognize all our attachments, even to spiritual states, as distractions. All the levels of realization—even though they're good, wonderful, and useful, and inevitably we fall in love with them—are ultimately seen to be distractions.

As long as we can conceive what it is we realize, as long as we can remember it, as long as we have a relationship to it, even if it is a deep realization, it is a distraction. That still is not the Secret. And anything we realize, anything we understand, will stop being a distraction and the attachment to it will fall away the moment the relationship to it disappears. When there is no duality of subject and object, when you and what you realize become one, only then is it sacrificed, only then is it gone. In that very second of complete understanding and realization, you go beyond it. Understanding is the last step toward transcendence.

You cannot hold on to something unless you don't

completely understand it. Because of this we can say that the search, or the work, is a process of continual disappointment. You find something, and then you realize you haven't found anything. You get something, and then you realize you haven't gotten anything. Whatever we find is not it, whatever we have is not it, whatever we get is not it, and whatever we love is not it. As long as the subject remains separate from the object, it's not it.

And we know it's not it because deep in our heart remains some kind of emptiness and longing for its true owner. The heart isn't made for all these other things, for anything we can know or hold on to. On this path the heart is divested of its attachments, one by one. The path of the heart is a process of breaking all idols, of sacrificing all loves and desires, until the true love of the heart shines forth, pure and undivided, faithful to its only Beloved. The Guest is the complete annihilation of the lover, of the subject.

As the heart is divested of its attachments, we become more and more aware of its empty chamber, a process that is identical to the soul's realizing her poverty. We realize with full feeling and cognition that we truly do not have anything, that we never had anything, not only objects of attachment, but also spiritual qualities or realization, attainments or accomplishments. We do not even possess existence on our own. In other words, when we quit filling ourselves with false loves, we realize we are totally empty, totally lacking, totally indigent.

More accurately, when we first encounter the empty chamber of the heart, we feel it as lack, as poverty. We need wholeheartedly to accept this poverty; otherwise we will fill it again with idols and impostors. We need to realize that we are totally poor as long as the

Guest has not arrived, that we are completely bereft without the nearness of the Beloved. To pretend otherwise means that our love of the Beloved is still not complete, is still divided between the Beloved and our own selfhood. We are still in the stage of worshiping idols; we have not arrived at true monotheism.

As we progress on the path, we discover and experience many things, both painful and wondrous. We discover how we are living our mental structure and how essence can increasingly characterize our experience. Such movement and progress will usually make us think that we're working hard, and because of this hard work, because of all the devotion and sacrifices, we are moving toward the Guest, toward the Secret. We will ordinarily think that we are choosing to move toward it or not choosing to move toward it, that we are orienting ourselves toward it or longing for it. We believe we love it and, because we love it, we go toward it. But in time, as the Guest draws nearer, we realize that this way of perceiving what is happening is not accurate; it is an illusion tantamount to denying our real poverty.

This is one of our illusions and delusions about what is going on. We believe that without such motivation we won't progress on the path. In the beginning of spiritual work, we recognize our suffering, and our mind wants to find the Secret to relieve ourselves from suffering. After a long time we realize that the wish to eliminate suffering is not the true motivation. We begin to feel that to love truth for its own sake is the true motivation of the heart. Our heart begins to recognize its love for truth as the truth unfolds and the heart loves every form of truth that appears.

Yet even this is still not the true objective perception of the situation. We do not move toward the

Secret because we love it. That's how we see it at some point, that's how our mind formulates it, but that's not the truth about what's happening. When the heart moves toward the Secret, when you move toward the Guest, it is because you are pulled. You are attracted, as if by a magnet, the most powerful magnet there is. From within the heart itself, from the depths of the heart, from the innermost chamber of the heart, the pull originates.

It is not that you feel, "I want to go there," and through your work and devotion you move nearer. That might be how you feel it sometimes, but that is only the mind feeding you more stories. In reality, there is an inner attraction, something is pulling you from deep within, and you cannot help but experience that as your devotion and love. The mind does not know about this inner attraction.

You are not aware of the inner pull because you are distracted by all the external pulls, by the gravitational pulls of the debris that fills the inner space. You are normally pulled by so many things external to the Secret. External to the Secret includes both outer and inner attachments. All of it is external to the Secret. The less you are pulled by these distractions, the more you will feel the real pull. The more you feel this inner attraction, the more it penetrates your consciousness. The more the Guest penetrates your consciousness, the more the heart annihilates the mind. You will see your attachments as just that—attachments.

The more we drop our attachments and abandon our inner idols, the more we are filled with grief and loss and sadness. The whole universe will turn into an ocean of tears. As our heart empties itself of its idols, it sacrifices too its yearning and its longing, and even its love. You don't feel you long anymore. You don't even feel that you love anymore. There remains only the direct condition of being consumed by an ocean of hot tears. This is some taste of nearness of the Guest, but we experience it for a long time as the grief over the loss of all the things we are shedding and sacrificing. We willingly sacrifice everything, but we cannot help but feel such deep sadness and tears.

However, this again is another story the mind tells us, trying to explain something it does not and cannot comprehend. The mind cannot see that it is the Secret drawing nearer and beginning to melt us, to dissolve us. We can say that it is the heart passionately longing for and loving the Secret. But we can also say it is the Secret touching you, completely and passionately burning you up.

For a long time you do your work from the outside, by seeing the distractions and letting them go. As that happens, it is as if the Secret, as if the Guest, is coming closer. The nearness of the Secret is not like the closeness of any other lover you've ever experienced. The Secret will burn you up from within, will incinerate you. It will boil you to total evaporation through passionate heat.

This Secret, the ultimate Beloved, is not like any other lover. It will not appear in the heart, it will not come to its abode, as long as there is anyone else there. As long as you have another lover, it won't arrive. The true Beloved is the most jealous of all lovers; it is absolutely possessive. It either has you completely or it will not even bother to show up.

The poem says the Guest arrives only at night, when everything is gone, when all that you love is thrown away, detached from, sacrificed. The inner poverty, the inner destitution, becomes so complete that there is total darkness, nothing left to see at all. Even you are sacrificed, dissolved, gone.

This situation cannot be conceived by the mind. Even the heart does not know it until it finally experiences that the fire of this love does not lead to a union. The arrival of the Guest does not mean that you, the mind, or even the heart will finally behold the Guest or be with the Guest. That's not how the meeting will go. The nature of the Guest will not allow anything else to be present beside it.

This love affair will be final. The Guest is the slayer of the mind. The Guest is the bedazzler, the incinerator. Its slaying and its incineration does not happen through melting you in sweet love. It doesn't go that way. The Guest is not gentle. When the Guest arrives, it doesn't make you feel nice and wonderful and loving and cozy. That might be your experience of previous lovers. This Beloved has something else up its sleeve. Just feeling its closeness, you begin feeling your mind, your heart, and your body all burning up. And if you stay with it a few seconds, and do not run away out of fear, you'll be completely annihilated, totally dissolved. The process of being annihilated by the Guest is hot, the most intense passion, a passion that burns, a passion that eats up, a passion that consumes, a passion that kills, a passion more powerful than thermonuclear reaction.

We find out that the passion of the heart for its true master and the annihilating intensity of the nearness of the master are one thing. It is not two approaching one another but one recognizing its singlehood. By the act of passionately loving, you are being passionately consumed. By the act of intensely longing, you are being intensely annihilated. This passion does not take you anywhere; this passion erases you. This passion is nothing but the heart's limited experience of the annihilating power of the Beloved.

Only when the heart is completely burnt, completely incinerated, completely annihilated, completely gone, will the Guest arrive. It is like being struck by lightning. As the nearness happens, the soul holds on for dear life. She begins to think, "I didn't know what I was getting into. I thought I was getting someplace. Uh-oh, look what I've done to myself." She will try to run as fast as possible, trying to find the safest place there is. Where can she hide now? This is no kid's play; it is serious business. She might feel, "I don't even want to look. One look and that's it for me. So what should I do?" Most likely you will want to hide in your mommy's lap.

Why is the soul running away so fast? Why is she so terrified when she sees the night approaching, when she sees the brilliance of that night, when she glimpses the countenance of the Guest? She becomes terrified because beneath her fear lies an ancient, primordial longing. She is terrified of what she truly and most deeply wants. She somehow knows, although not consciously, that there is nothing sweeter to her, nothing more desirable to her, than to completely vanish, to completely burn and never be heard of again. Her love and desire for the Beloved is identical with her love and desire for total annihilation. The Guest ultimately is her nature and self, beyond being and nonbeing, a mystery where all ceases. The truth of the situation is that the perception of separation is unnatural, and the natural condition is absolute identity. This absolute identity, perceived through the unnatural duality, appears to us as passionate love.

You see, the Guest is not something you will get,

not something you will attain. The Guest is something that will erase you, that will make you disappear. The Guest is something that will burn you up completely. You can't even call it who you truly are, because it is before you were. You can't call it the nature of the universe, because it is before the universe was and will be there after the universe goes. When everything is gone, "you" is gone, everybody else is gone, the universe is gone—when everything is night, that will be the Guest. When the night is pure, when the night is before there were stars in it, when the night is pure night, complete night, nothing but night, then the Guest has arrived. Then the Secret has no other—there is simply the primordial potential.

The only glimpse you can get of the Secret is not the Secret but the beginning of creation, the thunder and lightning filling the universe. The Secret of the universe turns out to be its absence, its vanishing, its nonbeing. The universe is, but in its isness lies the deep Secret that this being is only the appearance of nonbeing. By vanishing, the soul clears the way for the Beloved. Now the Beloved takes its rightful place, the throne it made for itself, the heart it gave you.

What do you say at such times? There can only be saying without knowing there is saying. There is living, total involvement in living without the slightest consciousness that you live. Then all that is you is there. Nothing, absolutely nothing is held back. All the veils of light and darkness are gone. What you are is all that you are. In other words, to live as the Guest is the experience of what was the back being the front, nothing else remaining behind. The Guest is like the back of all existence, while all manifestation is the front. When the Guest has arrived, when the

Secret has moved to the foreground, then the back is the front. There is no more back, for the back is right there at the front.

One way of seeing this is to recognize that the Guest is all and everything. There is no more front and back, for there is only the Secret, and the Secret admits of no other. Such truth manifests in many subtle ways, from seeing that there is only the singlehood of the absolute truth to seeing that all phenomena are ultimately nothing but this selfsame truth. Then you are facing the world not with your front but with the front of your back. You are all back, all Secret, all mystery and darkness. This means you're absolutely naked, completely, for there is nothing in front of your back. Your most inner Secret, the Inner of the Inner, is now right there at the surface. Your backbone is exposed, your spinal column is revealed. Not even that, but the potential for everything that animates your spinal column has shown its face. You're so naked you cannot even know it.

When your back is your front, then there are no intervening layers between you and what you face, the world you experience. Everything is totally direct, and you are totally yourself, with no intermediary or holding back of anything about you. Because of this complete immediacy and directness, your action can only be total spontaneity, with no hesitation whatsoever, not even the slightest consciousness of hesitation. Your action is totally spontaneous because you no longer have a back to look back to, no inside to check with, no inner self to make you self-conscious. In this condition of realization, when you act or interact, it is the Secret of the universe making the contact.

There is certainty in action because there is no hesitation, no doubt. How can there be doubt when the back is the front? There is no other than the back. Everything else is gone. Your presence then is not a sense of being present. There is no sense of being present, and there is no sense of being absent. There is just a totally unselfconscious fierceness. You cannot be seen by others, for what can be seen are only the veils, whether of darkness or of light. When there is no darkness, and there is no light, what is there? What is it? What are you? This is the mystery that has intrigued and confounded poets and philosophers.

As the Guest begins to reveal itself in the cavity of the heart, we see an amazing brilliance, pure luminosity like lightning that bedazzles you. As it approaches, the brilliance reveals a luminous blackness so absolutely black that it is the most luminous thing you can ever experience. The night of poverty suddenly changes to a luminous night, a radiant vastness so dark it is absolutely black, but so purely black it is luminous. We behold an immense majesty, an emptiness so void it is total transparency. Yet its beauty dazzles, its power intoxicates, and its intensity totally annihilates. To know it further, we can only reappear as the world, for there is no farther to go back. It is like arriving at the edge of the world and there is nowhere else to go. Our inner gaze simply switches to outer witnessing, the silent stillness witnessing all manifestation unfolding as its own bedazzling radiance.

The Guest is pure unknowingness; there is no mind, no darkness and no light. There is no consciousness, nothing to be known and no one to know it. The Guest is pre-everything. Let's say you become the absolute potential for all there is. But these are just words. We can say that you become the source of all you see. That's a nice idea, but again the words fail to capture the reality. We can say you are before there was the word, but we're still thinking of the word, the first word.

But before the word, before you heard the first news, what was there? What was that like? It's an absolutely unselfconscious spontaneity. When there is only the back that is the front, then there is only spontaneity. Spontaneity is blocked only when there are two. One says this, the other says that. When there is just the one, it is just spontaneity, without even knowing it. What is said is said completely. What is done is done totally, without an afterthought. And whatever is done or said is, by its very saying or its very doing, absolutely consumed, absolutely finished.

When I say the Guest appears in the heart, I don't mean you see something or someone in the heart. The heart becomes like a window that opens to the night. The heart opens to the world of absolute mystery, to the prior of time and space, the prior of light and knowledge. The love affair with the Guest is of a different quality, a different character. We can say that the usual love affairs are the love affairs of the day. The love affair with the Guest is the love affair of the night. It's the secret love affair, the most intimate. It is so secret your mind doesn't know it. And your heart knows it only by being absolutely consumed with passion.

A human being has two faces. Most people know one face, what is called the face of the day. Human beings also have a secret face, the face of the night. The Guest has arrived when the face you face the world with is the face of the night, the face of mystery, magic, and passion. The Secret, the Guest, will not arrive unless everything kneels in prayer to it. Everything has to kneel in prayer—your mind, your heart, your body, your soul, your essence, the universe, God. Everything has to kneel, ready to be vanquished. And you don't pray to it for anything for yourself; you can only pray to it absolutely. You pray only for annihilation. That is the only prayer. The prayer is a passionate love, so passionate in its sweetness that it will burn you up completely.

Even the nonconceptual universe is a shell around the Secret. The nonconceptual is a way station. First you experience reality without concepts, which is enlightenment. And when that happens, when the nonconceptual nature of reality is experienced, you sacrifice that, you go beyond that, which is not actually going anywhere. It is simply annihilating whatever remains.

The journey is not toward anything. The journey is toward the obliteration of everything. Only when everything, absolutely everything, is seen as a veil, has the Guest arrived. Obviously this is not an easy journey, because of the many distractions. There are millions of them; the mind is ingenious at creating distractions of all kinds. But at some point you will feel the consuming passionate love and realize that passion is not just love, it's the source of love. Love is nothing but an emanation from it, one of the veils. That passion is itself annihilation, an intensity that burns from within, a dynamic and intensely active void. It is the secret one, and it is the Secret of the universe. Only something this immensely powerful will allow the heart to become completely poor and totally empty. That passion is itself nothing but the Secret touching your heart and incinerating it. This fierce, passionate love is capable of dissolving the deepest attachments and cleansing the heart to utter purity.

The Guest has been given many names, but the names are irrelevant. It's called the Absolute, the self of God, the Divine Essence. It's called the Secret, the Guest. It's called the unmanifest, the mystery, the Inner of the Inner, the divine darkness, the transcendent, and so on. All these names are in relation to other things, other concepts, but the Guest is not in relationship to anything. You can't give the Guest a name. So even though I use various words like the Guest or the Secret to point to it, ultimately we can't give it a name.

Nevertheless, I have various favorite names for the Absolute, depending on how the Guest is manifesting. Today my favorite name is the Secret. Two days ago it was the Guest. A while ago I called it the divine ipseity. Ipseity is a very good name for it. I like it because most people don't know what it means. It's good to give it a name that nobody knows, because if you think you know what it means, that's not it. Ipseity is a name that was used in the past for the same reality we're talking about. The dictionary defines it as something like the final selfhood. The word "ipseity" was used by early Christians. In Arabic the Sufis refer to it as *hawiyyah*. Ipseity is not exactly identity and not exactly self, but both and also something between the two meanings; it can also mean nature or self-nature.

"Ipseity" means it is its own nature and it is its own self. Hence it is both self and the nature of self. "Ipseity" means the nature of all things, but also the self of all things. It is a nature, a reality that is the self. So, it is not the self in the sense of being an entity or identity or having a sense of self. It is the self in the sense of being the actuality of what is. It is both the thing itself and the nature of the thing. It is both the gold and the lion in the golden statue of a lion. The gold is the nature, the lion is the self, but the ipseity is both; it is the golden lion.

So, if you say the Absolute is the nature of things, that is not exact. If you say the Absolute is the self, that too is not exact. But when self and nature are one thing, when ultimate reality and ultimate self are one thing, then you go beyond dualistic approaches. There is not a self that has a nature or a nature that is expressed in a self; nor is it both self and nature. The two are simply one thing, absolutely. "Ipseity" refers to the fact that the Absolute is at once the nature of the universe and the universe itself, at once our self and our nature.

Our contemplation needs to be very subtle here. What is the self that is the absolute nature? What is the self that is not really a self, but you can't say it is not a self? If you say it is the nature of things or the absolute reality of things, you make it more impersonal than it is. If you say it's a self, you make it more personal than it is. The self that is the absolute nature is neither of those but has both as its potential. It's like moving my hand, but my hand is not different from who I am. So I and my hand, the mover and the moved, are one thing. There is nothing within the hand that moves it. It is total nonduality, absolute singlehood.

We can say "I" to refer to the self that is the absolute nature, but it's not an "I" in the sense that it has a feeling of "I" in it. It doesn't have a feeling of identity. It is "I" because there is nothing else to refer to when I speak. It is what speaks, and it is what does, and it is what is. When you say "I" but there is nothing else but that I, what do you say? You can't say it isn't "I," because there's nothing else. That's the back being the "I." You can say "I" without a feeling of "I" and without this "I" meaning some entity or circumscribed reality. I can say "I move," "I talk," but there is no sense of there being me talking, feeling, or doing anything. There is no self in the normal sense of the word.

The Absolute is not a nothing in the sense of complete voidness. It is not passive. It's true that it is a complete nothing, nothing there, but this nothingness has an annihilating power. It's like explosions in every cell. So we can't say it's a nothing. Yet we can't say it's a something, for its annihilating power is that it is pure voidness, absolute absence. It is not present and it is not absent. It's both at once. It is absolute absence and it is complete presence. So the presence of the Guest is the complete presence of absolute absence, without the presence and the absence being two things. You see what I mean when I say it's beyond concepts? The way I am talking now no longer has rational meaning. You can have the understanding only if you get the direct sense of what I'm talking about. If you just go with your mind, with my words, no way, nothing will happen except maybe a headache.

Okay, let's have questions now.

STUDENT: I've been noticing how full I am with myself, how there's just no space for anything else to be there, and how much I really don't care about the truth. I'm wondering if this is just coming up or I'm becoming aware of it because of the aspect that you're talking about.

ALMAAS: Anything and everything may arise as the absolute truth nears our consciousness. The Absolute is the center, the deepest ground of our consciousness. So any and all issues, all ignorance and positions, may arise as a barrier to it. That is why in the path of the heart, whatever you experience, good or bad, you just sacrifice it, you simply give it away. Whatever it is, you give it away by thoroughly understanding it. I say by understanding it because without understanding, it will be quite difficult to give it away. So to understand it implies not to judge it as good or bad. It doesn't matter what it is. The Guest is nothing but total, continual giving away, whatever it is. Even if you think it's the Guest, give it away.

As I said, the Guest is pre-anything. So whatever you conceptualize it to be or think it is, give it away, sacrifice it. This path is actually very simple. Whatever you've got, give it away. It doesn't matter what it is, what you realize, simply give it away. Give it away in the sense of not being attached to it, not in the sense of rejecting it.

If you are in a continual process of giving away, the good and the bad, then you are harmonizing with the Guest. The Guest is the source of everything, the infinite potential of all reality. It is inexhaustible, and it is always manifesting everything by giving away its treasures.

Whatever you've got, give it away. You don't need to think of it in terms of which level it is, what's going to happen, where you are going. Just understand it, sacrifice it, give it away, forget about it, and leave room for the next one to come. And whenever the next one comes, whatever comes, understand it, realize it, and sacrifice it, and do the same with each one that follows, forever.

No holding on to anything, good or bad. You don't hold on to evil, you don't hold on to enlightenment. The path of the heart is very direct, very simple. If you find yourself attached to anything, give it away—whatever it is you're attached to, even if you think, "Oh, that's my true self, oh, that's God realization, now I have the Absolute." Forget it, give it away. It's only your mind starting to hold on here and there.

The Guest cannot be seen as an object to hold on to; otherwise, it is nothing but an image or form the mind has created. We need to give this image away or we will be disconnected from the Guest again. Because of this we cannot have something to hold on to as the Guest. Realizing the Guest is continual sacrifice.

STUDENT: Is there a reason, other than my personal reasons, that the perspective you have discussed by working on this poem sounded really sexy? It sounded quite sexy the whole time.

ALMAAS: It is pretty sexy. In the old days people talked about this path only in love poetry, erotic love poetry in particular. It's passionate love poetry, the story of the soul as lover and the Absolute as the Beloved. When I wanted to introduce the Absolute to you for the first time, what came up was a poem. The poem I read is one that arose at the time of my discovery of the Absolute as the true Beloved of the heart. I was following the passionate love of the heart for its secret Beloved, which led directly into the mysterious luminous night of the Absolute. Poetry simply poured out at that time; it was not because I was reading classical mystical poetry. The images, words, and impressions were quite poetic, and very sexy because of the passionate intensity and the sensual immediacy of the process. I realized that the tradition of speaking of this discovery of the Absolute in poetry is not simply a following of tradition; it originates in the immediate quality of the experience.

We can hear the poem again, hopefully with more feeling and understanding.

> Annihilate mind in heart
> Divorce heart from all relationships,
> And then love,

Love passionately,
Consume yourself with passion
for the secret one.

When you are absolutely poor,
When you are no more,
Then the Guest will appear
And occupy his place,
In the secret chamber,
His abode,
The heart he gave you.

He is the Inner of the Inner,
He is the Secret,
He is the Guest,
And he arrives
Only at night.

THREE

Sinking Your Boats

Since today is Easter, I have decided to give you a gift. It is a small gift: the view I have developed from my personal experience about the true human being. It is a straightforward, simple talk about you, about being a human being.

This work and all other schools of spiritual work, all religions, all methods and philosophies about enlightenment, liberation, God, spirit, true nature, and so on, should not be necessary. I do not mean they are not necessary; I mean they should not be necessary. They are attempts to describe what a human being is actually supposed to be, and how to go about being that. They all ask the same questions: What is a human being? What is a real and complete human being? What is the real human life? What is the human life that has actualized the full human potential? What is it that we are all about, and how do we go about being that?

In actuality, the human being is much bigger than the vision of any of these teachings; no teaching can encompass the totality of what is possible for a human being. We ultimately do not need any of these teachings, which are nothing but ideas and concepts created by the mind. Although genuine teachings reflect and express reality, they are nevertheless in part cultural creations that have been developed throughout history. Many of them faithfully reflect real facets of reality and, as such, are good and helpful, but they remain excess baggage to reality.

Reality is beyond any teachings that can be formulated and promulgated. Reality simply is. Everything we say about it is extra, a creation of the human mind. We cannot adhere to teachings as if they are reality. We use teachings and benefit from them, but then we discard them, we drop them. To carry teachings with us after we learn to live in reality is to carry an extra load. We need only reality, and the teachings are simply vehicles through which to reach and live in reality. Reality is beyond tools, methods, and helpful perspectives. Reality is innocent of it all.

The point is not to be enlightened or to be God-realized. Rather, we are to live the way we are supposed to live. That is all, and simply so. We are to live reality the way reality actually is. Teachings approximate, and at best express, what that means and suggest how to go about it. Ultimately, teachings have no objective validity but are conceptual tools created by well-meaning individuals to help us live our life in the most natural and complete way possible. Once they have served their function, teachings are to be dropped. Otherwise, they will remain addendums to reality, a weight for us to carry.

I am not saying that teachings are inaccurate, or are empty fabrications. The real ones are accurate and express reality faithfully, but they are still an addition to simply living reality.

Understanding this dynamic allows us to recognize that reality is beyond any formulation and vaster than any teaching. We learn to be natural, simple, and truly autonomous. We live our lives without concepts and ideas. Otherwise, we end up becoming primarily Buddhists, Christians, Hindus, Jews, and so on, which is extraneous to being simply true human beings. Concepts and beliefs bind us, whereas reality itself is beyond any framework and experience. Reality is natural and totally true when we live without any ideas about it, when we spontaneously live without any self-reflection.

Teachings are boats with which to cross a river. You are not supposed to carry the boat with you on the other shore. If you carry the boat with you, you will end up with a greater load than when you started. Teachings help us see how our experience is limited and bound, and offer us ways to liberate ourselves from such unnecessary boundaries. Once we are free, to keep on looking at reality through the same lens will again bind and limit us. Once we are free, teachings become artificial, extraneous, and unnecessary. To be free is to be free from all concepts, all formulations, all views.

Furthermore, a teaching points toward reality, but it is not reality and will not give you reality. No teaching, on its own, gives you certainty about what reality is. Who decides ultimately what is real and what is not real? The final and ultimate judge is you. Is any teacher, philosophy, or religion going to decide for you? All of these teachers, religions, and work systems will be happy for you to find out for yourself what life is all about and how to live according to the truth. You cannot be certain of reality in any other way. A teaching points toward the truth, but you need to experience it and find out for yourself that it is reality. You have to find your own certainty; you cannot borrow it, not even from the highest teachings.

If we are to mature into real human beings, we need to recognize and come to grips with the extent to which we ordinarily do not want to be fully responsible for our perceptions, our truths, or our life. We are largely ignorant: we do not know much about ourselves, reality, or life, and what we do know is often not true. We lack true certainty. The combination of not knowing and knowing falsely makes us feel scared and uncertain. As a result, we constantly seek some kind of view, some kind of school, some kind of teaching, some kind of belief to follow. We search for something to support ourselves. This is not bad; it is simply our normal condition.

In the beginning of the work, we don't know what is real, we don't know what is not real, and we have no idea how to find out the difference. We are scared, we are small, we feel as if we don't know. And if we did know how to go about it, we still wouldn't actually be able to do it. So the teachings are necessary. But these teachings are boats to cross the river of ignorance; they are not the other shore. Their descriptions of some of the features of the other shore are not the same as the shore itself. In order to get to the other shore, we need to abandon our boats.

If we stay in them, we will never get to the shore.

We need, at some point, to sink our boats. This point is as subtle as it is important, as tricky as it is necessary. We need to sink our boats exactly at the right time: If we do it too soon, we will drown in the deep waters of the river, but if we do not do it at all, we will never arrive.

There is one story that it took thirty years for the first of Buddha's disciples to be enlightened. When the disciple finally saw and realized the truth, saw and understood true nature, he felt a little disconcerted. The disciple avoided Buddha because he was feeling ashamed and guilty. Finally, Buddha asked him what was going on with him. The disciple said it was hard to talk about but finally told the Buddha: "Now that I see the truth and I realize it, I see that all that you have been saying is bullshit. It is not necessary." Buddha asked him not to tell anyone. He said: "I'm glad you know the truth, but people need to think that what I say is true so that they can find out what you found out." In effect, Buddha was saying, "Don't tell anybody, they'll kill you and me, and then they will have no chance of finding out what you found out." The idea of letting go of attachment to teachings is also found in the Zen koan "When you meet the Buddha on the road, kill him."

But it is not easy to abandon our beliefs. It is not easy to be completely responsible and to stand absolutely on our own, to forget all that anybody has ever said and to find out directly what we are and what reality is. We will at some point need to find out for ourselves whether there is enlightenment or not. And if there is, what is it?

Is there God? Is there truth? And if there is, what kind of truth is it? Is there such a thing as self-realization, ego death, rebirth, and so on? We hear about them. We read many books written about them. But what do we actually know about them? And do we really need all these ideas? If so, when do we need them and for how long?

I am not saying that these ideas are not true. The formulations of spiritual teachings are ways to say what we are all about. My own experience has shown me the reality of the concepts of enlightenment, self-realization, freedom, rebirth, God, love, and so on. All of this exists. However, I also know that we come to see that they are not important. Truth does not end there.

The jig is up when you realize that even though your notions about reality may be true, you haven't discovered them for yourself. Maybe you deeply believe all or some of these things. But what does it matter that Buddha said something or Christ said something? That in itself does not give you the certainty, let alone the real knowing, that it is true. You believe because you need to believe, not because the beliefs are true. You are scared and helpless and need to believe in something. You don't know yourself well enough to live without beliefs. When I say that we don't know ourselves well enough, I don't mean only in terms of our realization; I also mean in terms of beliefs about who we are, what we are supposed to do or to be, whether we are good or bad.

In actuality, all beliefs are in the same bag: whether they are about God and enlightenment, or about whether you are good or bad; whether about timelessness and eternity or about your being a person who was born at a certain date, the son or daughter of such-and-such parents. Beliefs are all in the same category. In your mind they are the same thing; they probably come physiologically from the same part of your brain. There is no difference, ultimately, between one belief and another.

Of course, it is terrifying to think, let alone accept, that these beliefs exist only in our minds. They may not be true or completely true, or true the way we believe they are true. What if after all these years we find out that Buddha is wrong about emptiness? Or that Moses never spoke to God in the burning bush? We read the stories and we believe them. Maybe the stories are not true, or maybe they were true but things changed. Maybe reality does not remain static and changes even its nature and structure. How do we know that this is not the case? Who says that things don't change? Who says that what Buddha said then should be true now? Do we have any proof that it should be so? We don't; nobody does.

The stories we have been told may be true or not. We cannot be certain until we find out the truth for ourselves and, ultimately, until the truth is relevant for us. We have to be bold in order to ask these questions and to confront ourselves in this way. If we are to reach certainty and true autonomy of realization, we need to be willing to be heretics. What's more, we need to become universal heretics, not believing anything that we do not know from direct experience, beyond stories, beyond hearsay, and even beyond the mind.

To have a free mind is to be a universal heretic. You don't believe in the ultimate reality of any concept. You can assume any belief you find useful and attractive, but you don't need to hold on to any of it. Without being captured by your beliefs, you are strong enough and confident enough to throw away any and all beliefs and perspectives, each and every philosophy and story. You can stand totally alone, completely independent of all that comes through the mind, through time and space. This station of realization is difficult and rare. Most of us don't have the nerve to lose our minds. Although terrifying, it is necessary for true freedom.

We have to risk that we may be wrong. We have to risk the aloneness and the terror of being totally on our own. We have to risk cutting all of our supports, burning all of our bridges, destroying all of our boats. They are all ultimately and fundamentally concepts that come from hearsay or, at best, from our own past experiences. Even the concepts and knowledge that have come from our own immediate experiences cannot be relied on. That knowledge is like Buddha's words—old, unless corroborated in this moment.

Maybe a week ago you had an experience of realization, but how do you know that will be the same today? Who said that God won't change or that self-realization should continue being the same today? In other words, we cannot hold on to any concept past our direct experience of it; otherwise, what we're doing is believing a story. Whether someone else's or our own, a story is a story, not true reality here and now.

To be truly independent and autonomous, we need to be free from the concepts acquired from others as well as our own past experiences. Our minds hold on to concepts, memories, and stories. When we truly are ourselves and live in reality, we do not need concepts for support, we do not need memories to know who we are, and we do not need stories to be naturally at ease. We are who we are not because of what we believe, not because of what we remember, but because of what we are now and, ultimately, because of what we are truly.

Being real is a risk and an adventure. What will be

left when all of the concepts are gone? Who will we be? How will we see the world? What kind of feelings will we have? How will we see other people? We do not really know, and there is no way to find out until we do. We can see it as a movement toward ontological independence or autonomy. However, even these are approximations, familiar concepts from the past that we are now applying to something that we still do not know.

It is difficult to talk without creating another boat. We destroy one boat, and the moment that we say another word, we create a new boat. It is difficult to be and not think of being, to really forget our entire mind, to take our mind and put it into one of our pockets and zip it up for a while. But this is precisely what we need to do if we are going to find out the truth for ourselves. Such freedom and such boldness are not easy.

The boats cannot be sunk all at once. Usually we sink a few boats at a time; otherwise, we may get overwhelmed, flooded, totally disoriented. To sink all of our boats we have to confront all possibilities. We are completely and absolutely at sea then: nothing above, nothing below, nothing to hold us from any side. At this juncture, we cannot expect anyone or anything to help us. It is useless even to think that Christ will be your guide, or an angel will descend, or a bodhisattva will help. These are some of the boats that we need to abandon.

Work schools have been created to help us reach this juncture. They are useful for most of the way, for almost the totality of the inner journey. We need the boat to traverse the course, but not to finish it. We have to be completely alone at some point, absolutely independent, not simply from other people's minds but also our own. Our own mind is the juncture where other minds hook on to us. It is our mind that holds on to concepts, whether our own or others'.

The work is necessary to teach us how to build boats. But a genuine teaching shows us also how to destroy these boats, and then how to create better ones and destroy them, until we learn that we don't need boats at all. In this respect, work schools deal more directly with the situation than do world religions. Work schools rent you temporary boats, whereas religions sell them to you for life. While the boats may keep you afloat, they will never permit you to reach the other shore. In order to cross the river and reach the other shore, you have to abandon the boat at some point.

The course of the work is a learning process. It has been described in many ways: enlightenment, freedom, liberation, realization, union. There are countless ways to go about doing the work: through the will, the heart, the mind. But, ultimately, it is a matter of learning, of growing up. The simplest way to describe this is as a process of learning to mature.

The inner journey is a matter of each of us coming into our own. What does it mean to come into our own? From the beginning, we must allow that we don't know what it means. We are not necessarily going to be bigger or better persons than we are now. Growing up might be a completely different thing. A child cannot grasp what it is to be an adult until adulthood arrives. Even if the child witnesses adulthood all the time, which is what usually happens, it does not mean there will be understanding. Understanding and real knowing of what adulthood is will have to wait for adulthood.

What we usually consider adulthood is not real adulthood; it is a case of arrested development. It is not easy to mature on our own. Our difficulty with maturation stems basically from two kinds of ignorance: what we have forgotten and what we don't yet know. Inner work is a process of remembering what we have forgotten and learning what we still don't know. We can't do one without the other. If we only remember what we have forgotten, it won't be enough. If we simply learn what we don't know, it's not enough. There has to be an interaction between the two.

Remembering what we have forgotten largely means working with the personality, the ego structure of the soul. Knowing what we don't know involves learning about essence, being, reality, and truth. Some teachings view knowing as a type of remembering, which in some way it is. For the purposes of this discussion, though, it is useful to distinguish knowing from remembering.

In doing our work it is important that we do not develop some kind of religion or belief system. We want to be free from all conceptual boxes. Ultimately, the point is not to become a Buddhist, a Christian, or a Jew but to be a true human being, to realize the truth, whatever the truth is. When we start on the path, we do not know what we will realize. Our work emphasizes love of the truth, wherever that may lead. I do not say we are trying to find enlightenment, or God, or a true self. These terms are sometimes useful to illustrate certain points, but the love of the truth is what fuels the work. If there is God, you will find out; if there is enlightenment, you will find out; if there is a true self, you will find out.

The way to actualize the truth is to love it, which then becomes a process of learning and education. You discover then what you take yourself to be and why. You take yourself to be who you think you are because of the truth that you have forgotten. Your emotions, feelings, beliefs, patterns, and conflicts determine your experience and perception. You need to delve deeply into them and investigate them in order to discover what objectively exists. You can't see the truth objectively as long as your mind is influenced by these things that have become part of the unconscious of your personality. Your fear, anger, hurt, hatred, vulnerability, and doubt all need to surface.

Inquiring into these elements of your mind allows you to discover your unconscious beliefs about reality, enlightenment, God, yourself. What you believe is supposed to happen and what your dreams and hopes are need to emerge into the light of awareness and understanding in order for you to examine their truth. This is not easy to do. No one experience that you are going to have will get rid of all of these beliefs. No single experience of enlightenment will dissolve your unconscious. You will have to deal with and come to terms with the specific forms and content of your mind.

Some teachers do seem to say that one day you will be struck by lightning and your unconscious will burn out. Although wonderfully comforting, this is an infantile belief. If it were true, we would have many more mature human beings by now. My own investigation reveals that it simply does not happen in this way. In my experience and understanding, the person who has no unconscious lives a very normal and simple life. Even after people have the experience of enlightenment, they still have to integrate their ego and their unconscious. The process of integration of the ego and personality does not happen automatically and takes longer than the realization of enlightenment. You need to absorb and metabolize the ego in order to live as a mature human being. There is no way around confronting yourself, your unconscious, your fears, your doubts. I myself haven't found any magical way around this. We each have to confront ourselves. We cannot simply practice a spiritual technique like meditation or prayer, have some deep experience, and expect it to totally transform us. The experience, regardless of how profound, simply cannot erase all the false influences on your consciousness.

If we thoroughly investigate the matter for ourselves, we see that we have to confront ourselves in very powerful and deep ways. Those persons who have arrived at the balanced maturity of humanity have done so in the form of renunciation, discipline, friction with teacher and community, pursuit of practical tasks, following lessons given to them by their teachers, and in so many other ways that the various teachings have developed. In this work we do it through inquiry into our everyday experience.

Becoming a mature human being doesn't happen easily or instantly. Although there is grace and there is blessing, it is only to help you confront and deal with your situation. Grace won't do the whole thing for you. It will give you more confidence, more trust, but you will still have to deal with yourself. The help of the school, the teaching, and the teacher are small things compared with what you need to do yourself. This is part of the educational process of the inner path. The path requires the clarification and the transparency of all that determines your experience and perception of yourself and of the world.

Whatever questions you have, whatever you do not understand about yourself, you have to pursue. If you have any dissatisfaction, any discontentment, you need to pursue it. Teachings and teachers provide help, guidance, and orientation so that you don't spend too much time dealing with the wrong issues. The teacher saves you time, energy, and effort. But the teacher can't do it for you. The teacher gives you guidelines to help you do the practice and to help you deal with yourself.

Doing it yourself does not mean twisting reality's arm. You might find out that you can't do it yourself. Maybe that's part of the education. You might find out that you are just a little kid floating in a huge ocean. If that is the case, then you need to find out that you really don't know or maybe you can't do it. Or maybe growing up happens in a way totally different from what you thought. Maybe you find out that you have been wrong to start with, that the whole world has been a figment of your imagination. Maybe you thought all this time that you had to do things and then find out that they are done by themselves. That will be a big relief, but you still need to find out for yourself.

You can't take my word for it. I can tell you all these things, but it doesn't mean much. When I tell you, it gets you all excited for a week or two, you might meditate more intensely for a while, but it doesn't last long. You forget, and after two weeks you don't do anything. You fall asleep again and come back here hoping some new approach will work. This continues until eventually it hits you that you have to be responsible, that ultimately you are the final arbiter of the truth of your own experience and life. You are the one who needs to determine what is real. How can anyone convince you of the truth if you don't see it for yourself? People get convinced by the teachings but not fully, because usually underneath that conviction there are fears, vulnerabilities, and helplessness. The conviction does not stand on solid reality, but rather covers up ignorance and inner conflicts.

People use beliefs and convictions for comfort, for

safety, for security, for support, as crutches. Following the conceptualization of developmental theorist D. W. Winnicott, we can call these beliefs and convictions transitional objects. Transitional objects are the little things, like blankets and teddy bears, that babies and toddlers use to feel comfortable and safe. These objects are called transitional because of the belief that children outgrow them by internalizing the functions that these objects provide. So the objects are transitions between the stage of total dependence on the mother and the stage of psychological independence.

But this independence that we acquire as we grow up from childhood is limited. Still dependent on concepts and beliefs, this independence remains on the level of ego. True human maturity, according to the inner teachings, is a much more radical autonomy, one in which we become independent of belief systems, philosophies, even concepts themselves. Simply recognizing the possibility of this radical maturity allows us to see how we have not yet actually outgrown the need for transitional objects but have merely exchanged physical objects for emotional or mental ones.

A person who grows up in a Christian community believes in Jesus or the Virgin; a person who grows up in a Buddhist community believes in Buddha or enlightenment; if you grow up in a Muslim family you believe in Muhammad and the Qur'an. Regardless of the truth of these things, people mostly use them as transitional objects. They use them as security blankets to go through life because it is very hard to go through life on your own. Your blanket might change throughout your life, but in some very deep way you always have one. You internalize the feeling of comfort and safety, carrying it around as your mother image in your mind. Ultimately, religion, God, and enlightenment become symbols indicating that you are too scared to be completely on your own. In some very deep but real way, you are still that little kid holding on to the blanket. Whatever the blanket may be—mommy, career, God, husband, Buddha, reality, essence—it is the child who needs to be seen and understood. We need to recognize that child, understand her fears, acknowledge her needs, respect her desires, and hold and comfort her directly.

This child within you, which is the core of what we call the ego or the personality, feels totally alone without these comforting objects. This child comforts itself with all kinds of blankets, transitional objects, teddy bears, and soft things to help it feel that things are okay. The ego-self, or the inner child at its core, is not enlightened; it does not know it is okay to let go of the blanket. This part of your soul is scared, angry, hurt, and full of doubt. This inner child needs to be educated. Your essence is the educator, the teacher. This perennially infantile part of the soul will not listen, let alone learn, unless there is enough compassion, love, and acceptance. The child is scared and doesn't know whom to trust. It doesn't know whom to turn to. So when it hears you or me talking about ego death, it thinks, "Uh-oh, now they are going to kill me." This deep part of your personality doesn't understand what ego death means; it hears death and gets terrified.

In other words, a deep and central part of you thinks like a child. Rational things neither reach nor touch it. We need to approach this part of us with love, gentleness, kindness, and understanding. We need to understand its helplessness, fear, vulnerability, hatred, anger, dependence, and ignorance. Ultimately, the inner child isn't real, but it doesn't know that. You know that, but it doesn't. The inner child takes for granted that it is you. It feels terrible about itself, angry, guilty, but it doesn't know how else to be. This is a real dilemma. We each have an inner child that is ignorant, scared, and disconnected from the real essence, that is not touched by our lofty and transcendental experiences, that still needs to be cared for and loved.

We cannot try to get rid of it, nor does it simply vanish because of our enlightenment experiences. Trying to get rid of it is both impossible and the wrong way to go. If we try to get rid of it, the inner child only becomes more obstinate and more scared. We need to educate it gently and lovingly. Then, in time, the inner child will dissolve, mellow out, and become softer. It will naturally melt into essential nature and get integrated. But it will allow itself to melt only if it feels loved and secure. If we reject it and judge it, it will tend to isolate and protect itself.

The inner child is a deep structure of the person you take yourself to be, the image that you have adopted to form you. Of course, you do not always experience yourself as a child. Sometimes you feel like a child, sometimes like an adult, other times somewhere in between, and sometimes even like an infant or an embryo. The image changes all the time; it does not stay exactly the same. Sometimes it is just a little thing floating in space, sometimes it is the image of a man or woman, sometimes a teenager, sometimes grandiose, sometimes helpless. The image structures the soul into an ego-self, which we end up believing is who we are, all that we are, while it is actually only one form that the soul assumes. But it is important to understand that the inner child is simply an inner structure, a construct of history, and neither exists on its own nor has to continue existing as a formative structure in our experience.

All of the manifestations of essence, truth, and reality are needed to deal with this infantile part of us. True nature, with all of its qualities of compassion, love, acceptance, will, strength, and so on, ultimately needs to become the teacher for the immature part of our soul. We understand and accept this ego structure and immature part of the soul by allowing it to feel whatever it feels and think whatever it thinks, without judging its feelings or thoughts or needs. We don't reject it because it has a bad thought; rather, we look and see what is happening. If it is angry, let it be angry, even if you can't understand why it is angry. Most likely, there is hurt under the anger. If it is grandiose and proud of itself, find out why, because it probably feels deficient and scared. If it is scared and terrified, it needs your compassion more than anything else. It is important to understand this infantile part emotionally and psychologically, not only epistemologically as a construct, for it to yield to being integrated into our maturity.

Allowing this infantile structure to be exactly where it is usually involves dealing with the superego. The superego criticizes and abandons this immature part precisely because it can be affected in this way. Your essence, your true nature, doesn't feel rejected or judged, nor does it give a damn about these manifestations. Our essential nature doesn't have an ear for these things. But this immature part of you, the ego-self, has just the ear for these things. And it is this part of you that needs to be educated, to mature little by little, through a gradual and gentle process of learning.

Allowing the immature part does not mean letting it run amok or letting it destroy your life. So when I say accept and understand the child in you, I don't mean give it license to act out all its feelings and impulses. I mean accept its feelings, its state. Accept how it is, how it experiences itself, but don't accept actions that may harm you or others. For example, sometimes that part of you might feel like it wants to hang itself, but accepting it doesn't mean that you go out and do it. Certainly you let it feel these things, which will give you the opportunity to understand why it feels this way. You listen to that part of yourself sympathetically. "Ah, you want to hang yourself, you must be having a hard time. What is it, what's bothering you?" You try to find out what is going on with it. It must be really scared or hurt, or something is bothering it terribly, otherwise why would it have such violent urges?

You don't just say, "Oh, terrible, bad," and spank it and send it to its room. But you also don't let it go hang itself or harm other people, mess up the house, or be lazy and lie on the couch for years without doing anything useful. You have to be firm with it, just as you need to be loving and gentle, otherwise it won't grow up. This balanced attitude and guidance is what will finally help it learn.

Ultimately, not only the inner child but all of our thoughts, fantasies, feelings, and dreams need to be understood, not judged and rejected. The immature ones continue to arise in our experience because of a lack of knowledge and understanding and, ultimately, because of ignorance. No thought or feeling should be prohibited in you. Every feeling, every thought, every idea, regardless of how wonderful or disgusting, should be allowed. There needs to be absolute freedom to think, feel, desire, imagine, and dream. These things, however, should be allowed within the context of understanding and not indulgence. We cannot be free of the power of concepts if we are not open to them and their emotional manifestations.

Understanding the ignorance of the ego, the ignorance that results from what we have forgotten, is necessary in order for the immature to mature. The soul, our individual consciousness, is much more than this immature ego part. However, she does not grow, or grows with various imbalances, when she does not deal with this immature part of her. In most cases, she does not grow because she identifies with this immature part and believes it is the totality of her. Only by becoming liberated from this inner child and integrating it into a larger context can she grow. She grows, then, as this part grows, with it and inseparable from it. In those cases when the soul develops without dealing with this immature part, the development is askew, not balanced, and usually leads to oddness and strange behaviors and attitudes, common in many spiritual circles. There is no real maturity here. The only way for the soul to move toward true maturity is by coming to terms with this immature part in a genuine way, integrating it, and including it in her development. Then the soul grows as a whole, with balance and grace.

The other kind of ignorance, on the side of our being and our essence, is what we don't know. Essence is what is needed to teach and transform the soul. To live a true human life means the integration of what we have forgotten and what we don't know, of ego and essence. It is the coming together, the harmony, of the surface with the depth. We, ego and essence, become one. We become one through and through. We mature as a nondual soul. This won't happen easily or in a limited amount of time or with a limited amount of work and understanding.

You are going to have to put everything you've got into it. You are the object of your work, not some abstract ego and essence. You are dealing with your life, your situation, your mind, your heart, and your nature. You can use all the concepts and ideas available from the outside, as I have said, but use them intelligently. Use them as vehicles, as boats, not as the truth itself. Use them to find out what is true, not just to comfort yourself with what might be true. Use them to confront the truth of yourself, not to avoid certain truths.

This way, little by little, we learn to become more autonomous, more independent. Not in the sense that we don't need people, but in the sense that we learn to find out for ourselves by ourselves. Ultimately, the only thing that will free us is our own experience, our own perception, our own understanding. We have to be converted by our own experience. We have to attain our own certainty.

It is inherent in the dignity of the human being that you can do this. You can become a real human being. It is possible to be real beyond ideas, beyond boats, beyond books and teachings. You can walk on your own feet; you can be your nature beyond words, beyond concepts, beyond teachings. You can simply be, and that will be the greatest teaching, the greatest testament to humanity.

To be truly a mature human being you have to go beyond all content of mind, yours and others'. Reality is what is, not what we call it, not what we think about it, not what we say about it. Reality is beyond all creations of mind, regardless how sublime and spiritual.

There will be more creations in the future. Our mind will not stop creating concepts, and we will never stop hearing stories. But we can now, with maturity, know how things work, and take stories and thoughts as such, for we are directly living reality as it is.

One thing I am implying here is that we can experience and know reality beyond concepts and history, independent of concepts and history. Recognition of this radical maturity indicates that it is possible for us to live with absolute fearless spontaneity. The fearless spontaneity will manifest as love, truth, confidence, and goodness. We are usually afraid that if we are spontaneous and fearless we will do bad things, we will make mistakes. But we need to learn why we think this way. What are you afraid of doing? What do you think is going to happen? All these doubts need to be thoroughly looked into and understood, for such fear and uncertainty only point to some undigested material in our mind. We probably have not seen and understood something about our motivation even though we might dimly intuit it. This lack of understanding appears as uncertainty, as fear of spontaneity. As I've said, we need both to learn and to mature on the path. There is no end to it. There does not come a time when you completely mature and you finish. I don't think that is possible. As long as you are alive, you mature. You can be awakened, but this does not mean there is no further process of maturation.

Our potential is infinite, inexhaustible; hence there is always realization after any realization. You'll have all kinds of experiences, states, and conditions that may feel like an ultimate state of realization, but then that too keeps changing. The moment you say this is it, you will get stuck with a concept, and tomorrow there will be something else to be realized. So the true state of realization is actually a lack of attachment to realization.

When you are really autonomous, you are truly mature. You don't need boats; you don't need to think even that you don't need boats. You don't need to think you are enlightened. If you need to think that you are enlightened, you still need a boat. To be a truly mature human being, you don't need to think anything about where you are. Enlightenment is an idea that was created because people forgot how to be themselves. If human beings never forgot their original state, there would be no idea of enlightenment. No one would know there was anything like that.

Imagine that all human beings from the beginning were free and no one lost their freedom. Would anyone have an idea of God or enlightenment? No, people would go about their business being happy. They wouldn't need any boats. The boats exist because we need to get free, because we are broken and lost, because we are separated from our Beloved, because we are split from our true nature. As a result, we have many ideas about how to get what we have lost. But if you are really free, you don't need to think about it. And since there is no need for it, the concept will simply not arise.

This is true about any concept; we have the concept because we lack something, because we think something is absent. Even the concept of love would not be there if we did not lack love. People make a big deal about love because it is missing, because it is rare in human societies. But imagine all human beings, from the beginning of all time, always feeling loving and always feeling loved. Do you think there would be an idea of love? Nobody would ever have thought of it. It's just like air—people only think about it when it is missing, or polluted. If love is there all the time, people wouldn't even have the notion that anything like love exists. People have the notion about love because it is lost, because we get separated from it. But when love is completely realized, the person who loves does not feel she is loving, the person who gives does not feel she is giving. They do it and they don't think of it. There is no need for these ideas. We need these ideas because we are still not complete. We are still ignorant about reality, about the truth. We need these concepts because we are immature and incomplete.

Today I find myself using simple language, straightforward and down to earth. I think it is much better than using language like "enlightenment," "God," "divine guidance"—all these big concepts that actually scare the hell out of us. They are words that somebody created to correspond with certain experiences, but if you use these words, you unconsciously attach all sorts of ideas and feelings to them. You hate them, you like them, you are confused by them, you are bored with them, you are conflicted about them, you judge yourself with them, you judge others with them, you do not really know what they refer to, you do not know for yourself whether they refer to anything at all. Much of your history with these words has to do with your relationship with your father, your mother, your church, your teachers, the books you read, the experiences you had in the past, and so on. The original meaning of these words is most likely completely lost to you. So I think it is better not to use them. Instead, go simply, tread lightly. Find out what is the truth, what is really here beyond teachings, beyond concepts. Find out who you are.

So really the message of peace in Easter is peace with ourselves. At least that is where we need to start. Let's see now if you have questions.

STUDENT: There is something you said that I have a problem with. How can I love the truth if I don't know what it is? And how can I love all truths? That animals have to kill each other to survive is the truth, and I just hate that.

ALMAAS: This is a very good question, and pursuing it can lead us to subtle places. Loving the truth does not mean loving a particular statement that happens to be true or a particular manifestation or event that happens to be true. That is not what I mean. To love truth points to an attitude toward investigation: You love finding out the truth. Of course, some of the truth you might encounter is somebody killing somebody else. Loving the truth doesn't mean that you should love that.

But what you love is that you want your eyes to be open and to see. You want to know if something like that is happening, instead of pretending otherwise. You don't love closing your eyes; you love to know what the truth is. Loving the truth does not refer to loving the object of investigation; and, in fact, loving the object would not be loving the truth, but loving something in particular. To love the truth doesn't mean that you love what is negative, or even what is positive, for that matter. For most of us, it would be impossible to love the negative.

To love the truth is an attitude toward finding out, toward investigation. The heart is involved in the process of learning. The heart loves the learning process. So some of the things you learn are difficult and some of them are enjoyable. But to love the truth means that you don't care whether what you are going to see is painful or pleasurable, for these are not the truth you love. What you love is the actual process of education, the actual process of inquiry and discovery.

When we stay the course of loving the truth for its own sake, we find out at some point that there is an element of truth that manifests each time we discover a particular truth. This element of truth is not the particular event, but a certain state or quality of consciousness that arises as we discover the truth. When we investigate that consciousness, we discover that it is the essential aspect of truth, which is not a particular truth but the fact of truth, now experienced as a presence of true nature. In other words, to love truth is to love our true nature, for our true nature is the element that makes it possible for us to discern truth. To put it differently, the attitude of loving the truth, of finding out the truth, turns out to be loving the essential truth. We do not know that for a long time, not until we discover our essential nature and recognize it as truth that is not an event or a statement.

Therefore, ultimately, the truth is something positive, but it is really beyond good and bad, for it is the ground of all reality. But that is not in the differentiated realm of our lives. In this realm what is true can be harmful or useful, but to love finding out the truth is to love our true nature, the truth that makes it possible for us to discern truth from falsehood. We love the nature of truth and not necessarily the many forms it takes.

On deeper levels of realization, as on the boundless levels of Being, where everything is a manifestation of true nature, loving the truth becomes even more subtle. Here we feel we love everything, but that doesn't mean that we love crimes and diseases and so on. We are aware of the reality that pervades everything and that reality is what we love.

At the level of the boundless dimensions, we do not love an individual form but rather the immaculate nature of the wholeness. As we go deeper into our journey of discovering truth, we will see the meaning of truth change. At the beginning, truth is finding out about relative phenomena and space-time events: our emotions, our feelings, the world, conflicts, and relationships. But that is only one kind of truth, where the love is not of these elements but of the process of revelation of the truth, for this revelation is the essential truth penetrating our ordinary experience.

In the next stage, essence becomes the truth. The various essential states are truth, various manifestations of truth. Here, we love both the process and what we discover. However, it is tricky to love the essence itself, because this can lead to the reification of essence and to the attachment to experiencing it, which is antithetical to loving the truth for its own sake. In the following stage, we go beyond essential aspects to something that is beyond essence and personality, the truth that is the essential ground, transcendent true nature.

As you see, we need to investigate even our love of truth. We need to apply the love of truth to our love of truth and find out what it means to us. We need to find out what love is and what truth is. In the beginning you probably do not know what truth or love is. Who said love and truth are good? You need to find out for yourself. Truth is one of the elements of reality that, like a thread, goes all the way through all of the levels of reality because truth is what is actuality, what is present. If you really want to find out the truth, you can find out everything. So truth becomes the guide. Truth becomes a light that can guide you everywhere.

I say loving the truth instead of seeking it, because if you are seeking truth you might seek to avoid feeling pain. You might seek truth for another purpose, which will then make you not see the truth. But if you really love truth, then you will automatically want to see all of it, not for any particular reason but because you like seeing the truth. So loving the truth is not exactly seeking the truth, even though it might include seeking the truth sometimes. Loving the truth is the attitude of the heart. The heart falls in love. It falls in love with the truth, with an aspect of reality.

The heart falling in love with the truth is one of the most important realizations, the most important change, that can happen in a human being. The heart really turning toward the truth is the most far-reaching realization because if you really love the truth, you'll realize everything. However, if you love one particular state, then you might realize that state and not others. The truth is not just one thing. The truth is all that there is, whether or not you know it. Loving the truth does not mean you love the truth because it is going to help you realize everything. That is an ulterior motive. That is not included in loving the truth. You don't care if it is going to lead you to this or that. You just like it. You can't help it.

STUDENT: What do you see about the role of prayer?
ALMAAS: The question of prayer is profound and vast, and many traditions are built upon it. I can only address it partially here, as it relates to our exploration today. As long as you take yourself to be a separate

ego, prayer is good. Prayer could help you to eliminate the separateness. Prayer, then, is not for you to be
blessed or rewarded by God. The objective of prayer
is for you to be taken in, to dissolve in God. Prayer
is obviously a powerful method for bridging that gap
of separateness. Some people could use it more than
others, depending on their background. But not everybody can use prayer. You need the right attitude;
otherwise, it is just words. Prayer needs the involvement of the heart, indicating that you are willing to
surrender, to let go.

Ultimately, prayer is like any other method: it is
a boat that at some point you will need to abandon.
Your life itself will need to become the prayer, or the
meditation, or the inquiry. You may practice whatever
works for you—pray, meditate, inquire, take aims—
until you realize that it no longer works. At that point,
continuing to do that practice means you are acting
from the perspective of nonreality. Any of those methods assumes that you are a separate individual who
needs to get someplace. At least that's how most people begin these practices. The practices have deeper
bases in the truth of reality, but that is difficult to see
until we actually arrive at this reality.

When you realize the truth, however, you see that
you do not need a boat, for you have already arrived
on land. You need a boat only when you have not yet
reached land. But the boat cannot get you all the way
to the shore. You must get wet. You have to leave the
boat at some point before you can reach the shore.
You have to get your feet wet.

These practices teach all kinds of things. You grow
and develop, but you have to see that they are based,
at least in part, on an unreality, on a perception that is

not yet completely objective, because objective perception is a perception of the oneness there is. In reality there is no person who needs to be enlightened; there is no river, no boat, no other shore. But you can't from the beginning act from this perception, because you can't see it yet. You have to use the boats; you have to pray, with utmost humility, for a long time. You have to meditate with total dedication, and you have to do it all the way. You can't sink the boat until you take it as far as it can go.

What I mean is that you can't take my words when I say, "Sink your boats," and think, "Okay, I will sink them all as of now." No, you can only sink them after you have used them fully, after you have found out for yourself that things do not work this way. As long as you have the slightest hope they can work, you have to keep using them. You can't trick yourself when you hear that they don't work and say, "Okay, I will sink all the boats now." You must realize that the question is not simply the boat of the teaching; it is a matter of all boats, any concept or crutch. You need to see that you have millions of other boats floating all the time, like "I'm a good person," "One of these days I'm going to get rich," "I am a Republican," "I am devout," "Compassion is necessary for enlightenment," and so on. These are boats too. To sink the boats means to sink all boats, not just prayer and meditation.

The spiritual methods are really nothing but using ego activity itself in the service of the truth—at least for the first stages of the path. The ego starts working from the moment it is created. Everybody is working on themselves all the time, way before they join a work school. Everybody is trying to make themselves better: more loving, stronger, smarter, more successful, more helpful, better-looking, and so on. The work simply directs this compulsive tendency of the ego toward itself. You can be working to attain happiness, wealth, fame, somebody to love you, enlightenment, or God. It's all the same thing. It's all the same person trying to do it, trying to get someplace.

Why do you want to pray or meditate? The moment you sit and say you want to meditate, you already have a hope that something will happen. You are working on yourself. The same person and the same attitude sat quietly so that Mommy would love you, so that Daddy did not hit you. You want the same thing, to be left in peace, to be happy. When you were a little kid, you tried to be good by pleasing your mother; now you try to be good by meditating. But the people who created the meditations are clever because through the meditation you will see, at some point, that what you are doing is a hopeless activity.

More precisely, what separates good spiritual methods from normal ego endeavors is that they are set up to self-destruct at some point. Ego activity is endless and not self-reflecting. Spiritual methods help you see what you are and the absurdity of trying to get enlightened.

When you get to this point, then you are ready to sink your boats. Then, by simply living, you are meditating, praying, and loving the truth all the time, without knowing that you're doing it. The realization has become unselfconscious. As long as it is self-conscious, there is attachment still. The moment you are conscious of what you are doing and you want it to be good, you know that you still need that boat. It is a deep and difficult journey to get to the point where realization is unselfconscious.

Human beings are lucky if they have flashes of that true naturalness once in a while. To really sink our boats and become mature, we will have to go through some big doubts and big fears. We will need to understand how our mind works, the true dynamics of experience. We will need to stand in the universe alone. Very few human beings actually do it. But it is possible, and it reveals true human dignity and maturity.

FOUR

Suffering and Its Cessation

Today we will spend some time discussing suffering, since it's on our minds much of the time. The deepest understanding of suffering involves the most complete understanding of our work, including all the levels of knowledge that appear in the process of realization.

It's natural that human beings don't want to suffer. Everyone wants to feel good. Not only human beings, but all living beings want not to suffer; they want to feel good, to feel safe. It is obvious, a given. Many people approach our work with the motivation to be free of suffering. This is one of the main attractions of work like this: we hope that it will help us with our suffering, our pain, and our difficulties. Most people come to the work because of suffering and dissatisfaction, because of some discontent or other with their lives.

But what is suffering? Why do we suffer? And why do we sometimes suffer more when we start paying attention to ourselves? We know that suffering is universal, that a large part of everyone's experience is suffering, pain, discontent, difficulty. And most of the time we don't know what to do about it. We have no idea why there is so much suffering or what we can do to alleviate it, although we always do want to alleviate it. To really penetrate this issue, to have a thorough understanding that will relieve our suffering, is no small thing.

People tend to be optimistic about their suffering, and about their chances for happiness and fulfillment. Especially when we are young, we have all kinds of dreams about how we will attain happiness. As we get older, we might realize that it hasn't happened. So although we might start out optimistic, full of enthusiasm, youth, and energy, our dreams tend to collapse, and we realize that happiness is not as easily attained as we thought. Most people live entire lives never understanding or resolving their suffering.

Many traditional teachings tell those who are interested in unraveling the question of suffering to work diligently on it for thousands and thousands of lifetimes. The relief, the final resolution, is called enlightenment. This notion of needing to work through our suffering through many lifetimes indicates how difficult and complex the issue is.

Understanding the complexity of suffering might help us to become more patient and tolerant rather than discouraged or cynical. When we understand the nature of suffering, we might be more compassionate with ourselves, working with our difficulties more patiently instead of hoping that they will disappear in a year or two. If we do this work hoping that our suffering will soon disappear and then we'll have some kind of magical enlightenment, we are going to be thoroughly disappointed.

This disappointment might make us more cynical, and could even make us abandon the work. But that will only compound the suffering. It's better to start with a more realistic attitude from the beginning, so that when our disappointment comes, it won't be devastating and won't stop us from continuing on our path.

Human beings don't actually have to suffer psychologically. Suffering is not inescapable. It is possible to understand ourselves and our mind enough to stop all the unnecessary suffering. But what is the most effective path toward relieving our suffering? What will bring us some happiness, some peace, some satisfaction, some contentment in life? And how about total peace and contentment?

We see that there is a lot of suffering and that it's not easy to be free of it. We see that resolving our suffering requires a lot of work, a lot of time, and a lot of energy. We see that it is better to start with a realistic attitude about suffering. Being realistic does not mean that you will be less dedicated; in fact, it's just the reverse. The more you are informed and realistic about the situation, the more you are willing to work to actually resolve your suffering. There is no alternative to actually resolving the situation. You can't trick suffering.

Today we will come to understand why there is no magical cure, no shortcut to resolving suffering. Not even killing yourself will necessarily end your suffering. Killing your body could actually increase your suffering. So when we squarely face the situation of suffering, we realize there is no easy way out. If we study the situation objectively and calmly, we will see that there is only one way to approach suffering.

There are different methods of actualizing that one way, but there is only one way of fundamentally leaving suffering behind. That one way is dictated by the nature of suffering.

To eliminate suffering you have to eliminate the causes of suffering. If you resolve one instance of suffering without dealing with its causes, another situation will arise that will bring more suffering. You can't eliminate suffering in one situation and expect it to disappear from all situations. The difficulties will simply change form. Suffering persists as long as the underlying causes continue to be there.

The reason suffering is so complex and such an entrenched part of our experience is that the causes of suffering lie in multiple dimensions of reality. Today we'll look at the different dimensions in which suffering appears.

One of the first things we notice is how our suffering is generated through our history. Toward the beginning of our work, we often realize that a lot of our emotional difficulties, and the pain that arises from them, are connected with what happened to us in childhood. Our childhood environment was not completely understanding and hospitable, and the resulting pain and difficulty are present now. Psychotherapy works with this initial level of what causes suffering, dealing with our personal history and its effect on us in the present. If we were rejected then, we now are afraid of being rejected. If we were frustrated then, we now experience being frustrated. Anger, insecurity, fear, hurt—all began in childhood and persist to this day. This is the emotional life of most people.

We learn in our work that the way to deal with suffering is to understand it. You need to be awake to your situation, and you have to discover what is actually happening. You might feel miserable without knowing why, but when you inquire, you might realize that you are living through certain patterns and having certain reactions. You might discover that habitual, unconscious reactions to situations in your life generate all kinds of suffering. In the course of becoming conscious of those patterns, you might trace them to your childhood and see what started them. Understanding the patterns and experiencing the original situation that created them tend to loosen their hold and relieve the pain.

So here we see the causes of suffering that have to do with the inadequacies of our upbringing. But we come to see that the childhood events that caused our suffering continue to do so now because we haven't completely understood them. When we do understand them, the suffering seems to lessen and some of the patterns die out. When you understand the causes of suffering, the causes are often eliminated. The profound understanding that arises here is that the cause of suffering is lack of understanding. You suffer because you don't know what is moving you, what is making you react in one way or another. The more you know what triggers your reactions and your behavior, the better chance you have of resolving those issues.

Our work exposes the extent to which we blame our parents for our suffering. When we delve deeply into the matter, we realize that the lack of understanding is more basic than what happened with our parents. What happened in childhood caused the suffering in some sense, but not knowing those causes, forgetting about them, not understanding them, is what perpetuates our suffering. Our work is based on the insight that understanding the causes of suffering is the best way to relieve it.

Understanding, knowledge, and awareness are the tools, are the method, are the path. All our methods are ways of actualizing self-knowledge. As our knowledge develops, as we understand the historical causes of our suffering and the patterns generated by them, different energies and qualities are liberated in us. Our potential is freed as those causes dissolve. Some of what is liberated is beingness, the presence of essence. Qualities that were closed off because of our lack of understanding become open again. And these energies, these qualities, support us in looking further, opening more, understanding our situation more deeply. We begin to experience things that we never imagined. It's not only that we didn't know about the actual negative events from childhood that caused our suffering; we realize that part of the situation is that we didn't know fundamental aspects of our being. And this turns out to be a large part of our suffering: that fundamental aspects of our being were cut off, suppressed, and forgotten.

The process of inner work has two threads: seeing the negative causes of suffering, and seeing the positive causes of suffering. The negative causes of suffering involve the negative experiences, often from childhood, that created suffering. What I call the positive cause of suffering is the actual blockage of our potential, our essence. The positive cause is the alienation from true reality. After a while the process of understanding involves these two threads working together. You understand personality and you understand essence. You understand your history and you understand your nature. You understand your mind and you understand your beingness. These two threads are inherently intertwined in our work in the Diamond Approach.

When the essential qualities of your being are cut off

and your bodily energies are suppressed or distorted, the suffering caused by your past cannot be touched by the real potential of your beingness. This is why our work on the liberation of our essential nature is crucial to addressing our suffering. Our essential nature is the joy, the contentedness, the pleasure, and the peace of our soul necessary to resolve our suffering.

It's not easy to understand how these two categories of the causes of suffering are actually both perpetuated by the lack of understanding. Until we inquire into our experience, we don't consciously know about the patterns, identities, and reactivities that govern our life. Until we explore presence, we are not naturally aware of our beingness, our essence, our essential nature. So, again, the primary cause of our suffering is ignorance. We suffer because of the absence of awareness, the absence of understanding. The knowledge, the awareness, the understanding are primary in doing our work. Self-knowledge is not simply a matter of understanding your personality, your mind, and your history. Self-knowledge also means understanding your potential, your nature, your essence. Self-knowledge means coming to realize the nature of reality, the nature of truth.

As we go on, we discover that true understanding requires much more; it requires compassion, acceptance, forgiveness, love, clarity, strength, and will, among other things. Although these aspects of our being are cut off by the patterns of our personality, when we work in the dimension of essence, we begin to see things in terms of the interaction between ego and essence. We see that the work of liberating our essence involves understanding both our ego and our essence. This process ultimately leads us to the actualization of the true self, true individuality, true consciousness, and to the actualization of all the essential aspects.

But even opening to essence does not end the suffering, which many experience as a disappointment. It takes a lot of stamina and dedication to continue the inquiry regardless of this disappointment. But if we stop at this stage, our suffering might even increase. This is because the experience of the aspects of essence, such as love, joy, strength, or fulfillment, brings more light to our personality conflicts and ego deficiencies. So we might start to experience suffering we didn't even know we had, simply by seeing the contrast to our essential experience.

Our new experiences of essence and being are expressions of the truth and tend to bring to light previously hidden truths. As we continue in our inquiry, further causes of suffering are revealed. As our essential experiences naturally put pressure on the ego-mind, we begin to understand even deeper levels of our suffering. Most of us think we can be liberated without fundamentally challenging our identity. But as we become comfortable with essence, it begins to exert pressure on who we think we are. Inevitably, we must begin to question our very identity.

Our essence doesn't have beliefs and concepts about what is real and what is not real, what is us and what is the nature of reality. In doing our work, a subtle new suffering is revealed: We experience essence or being but don't allow it to transform our identity. So people say things like "I realized essential love today," or "I have actualized my essential self." They are talking as if the personality owns essence. This is another, more subtle form of suffering caused by lack of understanding. It involves both reification and attachment.

When you say, "I have a true self," who is talking? There is a deep contradiction in this assertion. Saying "I have a self" means that there is an "I" and a "self" and they are different. Isn't "I" supposed to be a self? As we go on in the work, that sense of duality becomes more and more obvious. We see, increasingly, that although we can experience our beingness, we still take ourselves to be something else. We still identify with something. Those identifications are challenged by our new experience, and we increasingly realize that the deeper causes of suffering have to do with those identifications. We suffer because of what we take ourselves to be, because of what we take reality to be.

Now, what we take ourselves to be and what we take reality to be are linked with what happened in our childhood. A lot of what we believe has to do with our relationship with our mother and with our childhood environment. However, on the level of essential reality and on the level of identity, the issues that arise are universal; they don't depend on childhood specifics. Wherever you go in the world, everyone has certain fundamental levels of suffering, regardless of how happy or miserable they might be. The very identification of oneself as an object among other objects makes us suffer at this deeper level.

Fundamentally, we don't suffer because our mother didn't love us or our father was mad at us, although these things might have made it worse. The problem is much more universal. The fundamental notions about what a human being is and what reality is constitute a universal social phenomenon, although it does vary in different cultures. These notions lead to suffering because they are not true; if they were true, they wouldn't lead to suffering. So again we notice that seeing the truth is the way to freedom from unnecessary suffering.

When we work at the level of questioning our identifications, we realize that even the suffering that we have so far explored is based on these fundamental beliefs about what a human being is. These concepts, which are shared by all humans, are the basis of all our emotional conflicts and difficulties, and of the patterns that generate our mental anguish. For instance, when someone rejects you, you are likely to feel hurt and angry. You might understand that it has to do with your father rejecting you, not liking you, being away a lot, and so on. Therefore, you are always feeling rejected; the feeling of rejection lives deep inside you. You might understand that when someone rejects you in the present, it activates those feelings of hurt and anger, and you suffer. But you might not be aware at this point of the assumptions your reaction is based on. For example, you assume that you are the same person now that you were as a child. That assumption is part of the pattern. For childhood to affect you now, you must assume that who you are now is the product of what happened to you in childhood. You need to see that your belief about who you are, your very identity, is the result of your past. And this is more fundamental than simply the dynamic of past history affecting your experience in the present.

However, if you don't simply take yourself to be the result of your past, then the past has no influence on you. Who says that what you are now is what your father rejected? You might feel that your mother or father rejected your body. What body? The body that your father rejected is not the body you have now. The atoms themselves are not the same. Literally, the cells of your body are the product of food you have eaten in the last seven years. So your father and mother didn't reject the body you have now. But you continue believing that they rejected your body and that now everybody rejects your body. Which body are you? Are you still that little kid from all those years ago? We often feel, "If I do such and such, Mommy will hate me." Your mother might be long dead, the body you felt was rejected is completely different, and still the identity, and all the feelings that come with it, are there.

We continually identify with something in us that isn't there any longer; we are identifying with a memory. Our identification is so strong that we might even feel insulted if someone tells us that's not really what we are. When I show students that who they think they are is not really who they are, some of them actually get mad at me. They say, "You don't see me! You don't see that I am a suffering little thing." It's true; I don't see that. The student feels, "You're just like my father. He didn't see me either." But we are talking about two different things. The student is talking about the father and what he didn't see, and I am talking about who the student is now.

We each take some part of our identity from the past and live our life as if we are that object in our memory. We have a powerful, entrenched belief that we are our history. This belief is a much deeper cause of suffering than what actually happened in our childhood. If you just stop believing that you are your history, if you really let go, if you see that that's not you, all that happened in your childhood will be gone. You will be completely new. What happens now might cause you suffering, but what your mother did, what your father did, whatever depression or war you lived through, is gone. They exist only in your mind. So we realize that a deeper cause of our suffering is that we hold on to the past, and we hold on to it in a certain way. We use the past to determine what we are. The past generates our concepts, our beliefs about who we are and about what reality is.

However, as we continue exploring and experiencing new dimensions of being, we see more clearly what needs to be explored. When we understand that holding on to the past, allowing it to determine who we are now, is a deep cause of suffering, that pattern tends to dissolve. This allows us to be more open to the experience of being as a timeless presence that has nothing to do with the past.

Our understanding of the conditioned mind supports the revelation of new aspects of being. We see that even though the causes of suffering keep becoming more subtle, one thing runs through all of them: ignorance. We just don't know what is real. As our exploration and inquiry deepen our awareness, understanding, and knowledge, we begin to penetrate the ignorance. The new understanding might inevitably make us aware of much more suffering than we were conscious of before the exploration. We might even begin to experience our suffering in a previously unimagined but actually beautiful way: the sense of the "dark night of the soul," the sense of being in hell.

Everyone who does the work goes through this. If you haven't been through this dark night yet, you can count on its happening if you continue on this path. The time will come when you will have to struggle with deep suffering as you confront deep beliefs about yourself and about reality. And there is no one you can blame for this suffering; it is not a matter of history. It is a matter of beginning to see reality and beginning to confront your ignorance. This is a great struggle because the mind is deeply habituated, and it is hard to let go of those entrenched beliefs and attachments. Suffering and conflict will become intense for all of us. Although there is no way around the suffering, it helps somewhat to know that it is a normal part of our work.

Now we're getting to the nitty-gritty of the cause of suffering. Most people balk when they come to this point. They say, "Uh-oh, I didn't know it was going to come to this. I thought I was going to get happier." But to erase suffering does not mean that you are going to be happy. In fact, you begin to realize that you are not even going to enjoy the fruits of your work. At this point people tend to get mad at the teaching, the work, truth, reality, God, and all of that. We feel duped. We have in some sense been tricked by the truth. We see that there was no way for anyone to tell us in advance what the situation really is; we never would have believed it.

In the course of coming to understand reality, we confront increasingly deeper concepts about who we are, concepts that form the foundations of our suffering. Our belief that our body is the same body as the one we had in childhood generates all kinds of suffering. But the deeper problem is that we take ourselves to be our body at all. You think you are your body. Or you think, "If I am not my body, at least I am inside my body"; or "I am the mind that goes with the body"; or "I am a soul inside the body. It is my body, nobody else is in it, so don't tell me I am not my body." But as you approach actualization of the deeper aspects of being, this idea will be challenged.

If you are essence, what does that mean about your body and your mind? You will have to slowly, perhaps even begrudgingly, come to know that you are not a body that has essence. You are the essence that has a body. Most people don't like that. You will want to be the body that has essence. You will want to be the self that sometimes has good experiences. What dawns on you little by little is that those essential and subtle realities really are you. And you begin to see that the long stretches of time when you believe yourself to be the body, or a separate individual self, are the transitory experiences.

The belief that you are contained within the body, bounded by the body, related to the body, part of the body will be wholly challenged. You will come to see that belief as one of the major sources of suffering. At some point in our work we realize that our true nature doesn't have boundaries, that who we are is not bounded by physical partitions. If we continue believing in the solidity of those partitions, then we are trying to compact our true nature to fit into our idea of ourselves. This will bring a lot of tension!

We begin to feel this tension in the body, sometimes as prickly, or like iron or leather all around the body. This is inevitable if we take the whole universe, our actual nature, and try to compact it into our little body. No wonder things are heavy; no wonder we have a hard time. And really, that is what everyone is doing all the time. Our identification with the body, with the shape of the body, with the size of the body, brings us deep suffering.

Even our desire is yoked to our identification with the body. When you want someone, you want his or her body. When people are falling in love, it's important that they get the body involved. It is not enough that the person says, "I really love you." Our response is, "So? When are we going to get in bed? What difference does it make whether you love me or not?" You have to get the body. The body becomes of utmost importance. This is a strong instinctual reality.

The physical and emotional desires are not a problem as long as you remember that you and the other person are not simply the body, are a lot more than the body, are bigger than the body. We can disidentify from these subtle concepts about who we are, including the concept that we are the body. At some point we might realize that we are not the body, but we still continue to think that the body is the most important reality. Even realization of essence, or self-realization, might not remove our belief that the body is the most real and fundamental reality. Typically we believe that the body is most real, then the emotions, then our essence—essence, our true nature, is a final luxury.

But when we are awake to the truth, we know that it is completely the other way around. We discover that we are the essence of Being and that our suffering will not stop as long as we take ourselves to be anything else. As long as we are creating duality, separating ourselves from Being, taking the surface to be what we are, we will suffer. It is as if you are saying, "I am my skin; the heart is not important—the heart is extraneous to the skin." But the heart and the brain are actually more important than the skin. When you believe that your body is more fundamental than your essence, you are in trouble. That trouble will generate all kinds of emotional difficulties, bodily tensions, states of suffering, fear, helplessness, and deficiency.

So to really deal with the issue of suffering, we need to understand reality. We need to go all the way through the process of realization. The process of realization, of understanding the truth, is a process of understanding and relieving oneself from suffering. There is no shortcut; there is only one way. What's causing suffering cannot be surmounted, cannot simply be dropped, cannot be ignored, cannot even be erased by some essential awakening or realization. Suffering is a fundamental factor in our lives that has to be dealt with. We need a lot of study and understanding; we need to go through all the dimensions before we can exit the realm of suffering. Many of us hope we can exit right away, hope we can transcend our problems through spiritual experience. But unless we actually penetrate our beliefs and identifications, our life will always involve suffering.

As we continue, we will come to challenge even deeper notions than the belief that we are our bodies. We can realize that we are not our body but are our essence; we can realize the essential nature of the world. Although this realization and actualization fulfills much more of our potential, and brings creativity and knowledge, still our suffering hasn't vanished. If we remain where we are without continuing to deepen our realization and expand our understanding, our suffering might increase again. Ever more fundamental beliefs and concepts about reality will arise and be challenged.

We confront not only our belief that we have a body but also our belief that we are a person. You believe that ultimately you are an individual separate from other human beings. Although you have realized that you are your essence, you remain certain that it is *your* essence, and other individuals have their own essence. You are proud of your individuality, proud of your uniqueness, proud of your independence, even proud of your essence. A subtle spiritual pride tends to arise at this stage. This ego pride signals the belief in one's separateness, in one's individuality, as ultimate.

You are real now, and the ego can be very proud: "I am not only myself, I am real ego now." It is true that you are the true ego at that time. Now the ego has an ultimate kind of pride. "I used to be fake," the ego says, "just an idea. Now I am real presence, and I exist as me. I am a unique individual with my own will, my own consciousness, not conditioned by the past." And it's true that you are not conditioned by the past any longer. But that truth becomes a source of suffering if you are attached to it, if you take pride in it. The pride will have to be challenged, which means that you will have to confront the idea of separateness. You will have to confront the sense that you are an individual, separate from other individuals.

So beyond the identification with the body rests the belief of being an individual separate from other humans and the rest of the universe. This is the main issue of ego. Most spiritual traditions deal specifically with this issue, addressing the movement from ego to non-ego. The transition from ego to non-ego is letting go of the belief in your individuality, your sense of separateness, your sense of uniqueness. This is an enormous transition and a big challenge. After all, you have worked all this time to achieve your reality, your unique reality. You have extricated yourself from your parents, your past, your identification with body. Finally you are real, and now this? Now you have to let go of this great accomplishment? We don't like this at all. Many of you will recognize this place: you might begin to argue with your teachers, reject essence and reality that is beyond you, fight with God, assert your independence in various ways. You want to do things your own way, to have your own creativity. But that pride and attachment, the belief that you have to have that independence, are simply subtler forms of suffering.

The issue of ego pride is the attachment to the belief that you are a separate individual. The ego is deeply invested in its separateness, its uniqueness. Our problem here is with God, with what is beyond our separate self. Who's going to be here first, you or God? At this stage, human beings want to be a little god. It's easy to feel, given some essential realization and development, "I'm a god on my own. I'm real. I'm eternal, not the creation of my mommy and daddy. I do my own thing. I work it out by myself. I develop myself. It is all done through my own efforts." That is true in some way. You have done it through your own efforts.

But the issue here is not reward or punishment, accomplishment or failure. The issue is truth. Individuality or the belief in uniqueness is not bad, but ignores fundamental aspects of the truth. Ignorance causes suffering, and truth relieves it. Since there is a deeper ignorance in the belief of separate self, a deeper mode of understanding needs to arise. The movement from ego to non-ego, from the individual to the cosmic, requires a profound understanding.

Most of us put up a big fight at this stage because we believe that if we let go of our separate individuality, we will lose it forever. There will be no boundaries, no person, no entity. "What's so good about that? Then I'll be inseparable from everyone else. The world is full of all kinds of pain. Why be a part of that? At least now I experience myself as a full, wonderful presence, eternal and full of joy and happiness. Why should I be part of everyone and go back to all that suffering?" We might begin to experience a lot of resentment, anger, and hatred at this stage because we want to protect ourselves. We have certain ideas about what will happen as we cease to identify with our separate individuality.

But you don't really know what will happen. What you expect to happen is wrong. If you let go of your individuality, you don't experience everyone's suffering, because the suffering only exists on the level of individuality itself. The belief in individuality, the belief in separateness, the belief in the ego boundaries, is what causes the suffering. As a separate individual, you can't help but be insecure, one individual in contrast to other individuals, always surrounded by forces beyond you. Even though you might have true will, a separate individual is always insecure. As you explore the actual condition of being a separate individual, you will inevitably encounter fear and helplessness. Experiencing the insecurity, fear, and helplessness of being a little, separate entity in a world of greater forces is the condition of every individual.

This belief in separate individuality is universal, and generally not even questioned. Even our sense of God often includes a sense of a separate individual. Since the Bible says that God made us in his image, and given our identification with our body and sense of separate self, we tend to think of God as a person like us, only a lot bigger.

Right now, you might believe that you are in this room because your body is here, because the separate individual contained in your body is here. Getting through this deep belief of being a separate entity is one of the greatest hurdles of the work. Some people take years to see through it or never see all the way through it. The ego pride, the fear of the loss of the sense of individuality, is deeply entrenched, and it takes a lot to go through it.

This belief in separate individuality creates enormous suffering for us. If you have emotional conflict, it is because you perceive yourself to be a person. If you were not a person, what would it mean to have emotional conflicts? What would it mean that someone is rejecting you? All the emotional conflicts that you've worked through are based on the belief that you are a separate individual; otherwise, what does it mean to be rejected, what does it mean to be scared, what does it mean to be successful, or to die? If you don't believe in a separate individuality, all of those problems disappear, completely. But if you continue to believe that you are separate, these issues keep coming back because their cause remains intact.

Even in the context of serious inner work, the belief in separate individuality tends to distort the truth. You might believe, for example, that there is a God somewhere who is taking care of you, who is guiding you. But that perspective is a subtle continuation of the ego view. You implicitly believe that you are a person, a separate entity, in relation to some bigger force. This is nothing but the personality's need for Mommy being reinstated in the relationship with God. True spiritual disciplines say the relationship with God should be dissolution in God. Death in God means dissolving the personality, dissolving the sense of separateness. You are not, ultimately, someone who prays to God. You are somebody who dies in God. Praying to God, surrendering to God, gets you closer and closer to God until there is no separation between you and God.

Alternately, you might believe you are somebody who got true nature, who has realized true nature. But the same dilemma arises here again, for the truth is much more subtle than this.

The resolution of the separateness has to do with going from ego to non-ego, from individual to cosmic, from human to divine. We realize that our deeper nature is God itself. Realizing divine nature means not being an individual; it means being totality, universality, infinity. Nothing is excluded from your sense of self. You realize then that whenever you talk to someone, you are talking to yourself. True love, true compassion, and true generosity arise now because there is no separation between you and the other. You could still feel yourself as an individual who sees how you are unique, but you know too that you are fundamentally connected. At a more intrinsic level, that separateness is not there.

The moment you go from ego to non-ego you experience not only that you are one with all human beings but that you are one with everything. You realize that the consciousness that has been compacted within boundaries has no boundaries. It is everywhere. Consciousness is the basic substance and nature of everything. The truth you realize, then, is that who you are is not the product of your childhood, is not your body, is not a sense of limited individuality. You are something that is everything, and you are seeing now the nature of everything, not only on the essential level, but on the level of Being itself, on a nondifferentiated level, a nonseparated level.

This does not mean, though, that you are no longer an individual. You will not lose individuality in the way you might imagine; the individuality will simply be one facet of who you are. It's like the example of the hand. In the beginning you think you are the finger, moving around, doing things. When your knowledge goes beyond the individual, beyond the ego, you find out you are the hand. You don't lose the fingers by being the hand. The fingers are still there, the individuality is still there operating; however, it is part of something larger. And you are that something larger. At the same time, you are also the individual. Your attention is sometimes the finger and other times the totality of the hand. Then you live as what is called a cosmic individual.

We see, then, a fundamental truth about our suffering. If we are a cosmic individual, if we are the totality, if we are the vast oneness, isn't it obvious that taking ourselves to be a small, bounded person is going to cause a lot of suffering? Isn't it obvious that this misunderstanding is the basis of most suffering? We don't need to reject the sense of being an individual, or the true self. Nothing is rejected; simply more is included, until everything is included.

In the process of development, we never lose anything. We think that every time something new is being realized, we are going to lose something. But nothing is ever lost. You don't lose your sense of humor; you don't lose your body; you don't lose your mother. My mother is still around; I talk to her when I want to. Even if she dies, I won't lose her. My father died two years ago, and he is still around as far as I'm concerned because he is part of that big fullness. He is me and I am him. How can I lose him? So there is no loss at all. Always there is more inclusion.

But in the course of our realization, we always face the fear of loss. You feel, "I am going to lose myself. I am going to lose my boundaries. I am going to be eaten up." But that's like saying that the hand is going to eat up the finger. What do we lose, actually? You lose certain beliefs that make you smaller, less than who you are. As the belief in separateness dissolves, you don't lose the finger but gain the whole hand. You don't lose your body but gain the whole universe. By letting go of the notion that your body contains a separate individual, you become the totality of the universe, which includes your body. No loss at all. There is only gain in going from ego to cosmic.

We imagine that letting go means losing. We feel that everything we've accomplished, everything we possess, all our relationships, all our knowledge, will be gone.

But despite this fear, when we understand the truth of our condition, we have no choice but to let go. Although we expect a certain kind of death, our transformation reveals a bigger, more universal life. Nothing is actually being overwhelmed; awareness simply expands.

We lose everything we have and gain everything there is. What you think you have is nothing, a droplet, an atom of the universe. That's what you lose. What you gain is the totality, not of this universe, but of all the universes that can exist. You become the totality of everything. You realize that totality is you. Sometimes you become an individual and walk around as a person, but you are the whole thing all the time.

We are not different individuals who are going to be separately realized. We are one organism. Sometimes we call it the cosmic amoeba, one infinite cosmic amoeba, with myriad protrusions called pseudopodia. So when someone is born, a pseudopodium arises, does its thing, and when it retracts again, we call that death. Pseudopodia come out when something needs to be done and retract when they are not needed. The organism continues being the organism. We could call it God. It is who we are ultimately. We are not a little pseudopodium; we are the totality of the amoeba.

So we could say that one of the deepest realizations is to realize that you are a cosmic amoeba. When you become a true individual, you are the cosmic pseudopodium. When you become your true self, a true essential personality, you become a pseudopodium of the cosmic amoeba. Going beyond that to non-ego, you become the totality of the amoeba. And when you become the cosmic amoeba, which is the state called Godhood, God-realization, cosmic individuality, or oneness, you realize that you not only move your body, you move everything. Nothing moves in the whole universe without your moving it. This cosmic amoeba *is* the universe, *is* one organism.

But it's not quite right to call it an organism, because we usually think of an organism as something bounded. Actually, there is one beingness, continuously transforming itself. The transformation of that beingness is the evolution of the universe. So the totality of the universe is what is called God. In my view, we can say that God is nothing but the universe and the movement of the universe. God is nothing but the universe at all times. When you realize the cosmic amoeba, you realize that all time—past, present, and future—is now. Right now. That is who you are. And given your ultimate nature, it is no wonder that you suffer when you are attached to the idea that you are a little finger. Resisting the totality of the amoeba does not relieve the pressure of this totality pushing against you.

In the life of that cosmic individual you can be that amoeba, living as an amoeba, or you can be one of the pseudopodia, an individual connected to the larger cosmos. In that station, you feel you are what is called a true individual. You feel you are grounded and you are an extension of the universe. You don't sit on the ground; you are a protrusion of the ground. That is the true experience of being a true individual. True individuality is not separate; it is a wave of the ocean. You are a wave who remains aware of the ocean. The personality tries to eliminate the ocean, leaving just the wave. This is a deep cause of our suffering.

The true work happens in the movement from ego to non-ego. It takes a lot of capacity and willingness to learn not to fight this movement. Seeing from the perspective of the totality, of the ocean, helps us to realize this movement. We realize that it has never been our own efforts doing the work, or doing anything. The totality was always doing everything. When we are separate, we think that we are doing everything through our own efforts. When we realize the nonseparateness and perceive the totality, we stop working.

Why would we work? The whole universe is working, is in constant transformation. There is no death and there is no life—there is only transformation. The fear of death, even the concept of death, is gone. The notions of life and death are based on the belief in being a separate individual. The moment you go beyond that belief you realize there is no such thing as death. How could you die? Simply one of the pseudopodia is retracted. That's all. Another pseudopodia will form. You don't die. Nothing dies. It is simple transformation.

As we realize that the form of the universe is in constant change, one of the main insights of all spiritual work arises. We understand that holding on to things, not wanting things to change, is a major source of our suffering. From the perspective of the totality, change is neither bad nor good. From the perspective of our separate entityhood, we consider certain changes good and other ones bad. We call some of them death and some of them life, some of them pleasure and some of them pain. This perspective necessarily and always involves suffering because it ignores the truth of the constant transformation of the totality.

We are included in the transformation of the cosmic totality. Contemplate the amazing movement from when you begin the work to when you actually realize yourself as the cosmic individuality. Contemplate how much has been learned and understood. The learning is not simply mental—you actually change. The whole transformation is a matter of expansion of consciousness, a matter of discovering the truth.

The truth changes form as we proceed. The first concepts that are challenged by the discovery of essence bring to light our mistaken sense of identity. We realize the essential nature of who we are. We know that it is not true that we were born and are our mother's child. It's not even true that our mother and father actually exist in the way we have thought. There is a Sufi saying that encapsulates this insight: "I am the father of my mother." You are the father of your mother in the sense that you are the nature from which your mother and everyone else comes. You are the father of everyone. The mother of everyone. The source of everyone.

The second movement of truth exposes our sense of boundaries and separateness as an illusion. We come to see that the cosmic existence is the real existence of the universe and the individual, even though sometimes we are not aware of it. Oneness is there all the time and sometimes we perceive it, sometimes not. When we realize the cosmic individuality, when we realize we are everything, we have conquered space. When we remain in the cosmic individuality, we realize after a while that the nature of that cosmic reality is eternity. It feels eternal in the sense that it has nothing to do with time. Cosmic reality includes all time, which makes it feel eternal, but, more precisely, it is altogether outside of time. Eternity is outside of time and perceives it. Now arises a freedom from time.

We come to realize that the totality, what we call God or the cosmic individual, is not only a oneness of space but also a oneness of time. The cosmic amoeba is all time. So we have a four-dimensional space here. This is called Einsteinian space. The cosmic individual is neither in space nor in time. You are eternal presence, in the sense that you are now, in this very moment, all times, all places. Realizing the state of God, or the cosmic existence, is realizing that eternity. There is a sense that you are seeing time passing, but time passes within the totality, within God. In the totality, it is all now, and time and space pass within you.

Within that timelessness, space and time pass. Space and time do not disappear; people do not disappear, but live, grow old, and die. But all of that passes through you as the totality. Eternity is not contradictory to time but includes it. This reality is hard to conceptualize if you are in the dimension of time. Time can only be linear. In the totality, there is no difference between time and space. They are coordinates, like the length and depth of one thing. At the stage of cosmic totality, we have gone beyond space and beyond time. And still there is more to understand. We have not yet reached the deepest, most basic insights.

Realizing our nature as essence and the nature of existence as cosmic oneness gives rise to an even more subtle understanding of reality. A more final stage will appear first as a deep longing and subtle suffering. A longing to disappear, to vanish, will arise. The concepts that are questioned are not a matter of whether you are an individual or oneness, whether you are human or God. The question is whether you exist or not. The fact of existence is questioned. We become uncomfortably aware of a sense of existence, even though our sense of this existence has no limitations.

The final limitation is the attachment to existence. You don't want existence to end. The suffering here is usually not a big deal. It's not as difficult as the suffering in going from the personal to the cosmic. At this stage, we suffer not because we are afraid of death but because we love existence. We love God. We love everything. The attachment to existence appears as a contraction, and this contraction is suffering. If there is love for anything, you are bound to be attached to it. The attachment will have to go if suffering is to be completely gone.

This is the transition from existence to nonexistence. At this stage there is nothing to do and no one there to do nothing. The cosmic existence has to go to sleep sometime. As an individual, don't you go to sleep every night? And when you go to sleep, are you an individual? Do you know anything? Do you feel anything? It's the same thing with the cosmic individuality; it has to go to sleep. When the cosmic individuality goes to sleep, what's there? Nothing. Not only are you gone, but the whole totality of the universe is gone. Complete nonexistence. We discover that the sense of our own nonexistence is relatively tolerable as long as we feel that the universe exists. We believe that when we go to sleep and disappear, we will wake up the next day and the universe will be there. But what are you going to come back to when you experience that the entire universe is gone?

At the beginning of the work, the question of existence is irrelevant; we don't think about it. But at some point we realize that attachment to existence underlies all of our suffering. Because we are so identified with the content of the mind, we are utterly convinced that we are questioning existence itself, that what we really are is threatened with disappearance. Even though we have seen at every stage that our process involves questioning and eliminating concepts in the mind and not losing anything real, the attachment nevertheless feels real.

So, little by little, the concepts go away. The concept of being the body, the concept of being an individual, the concept of past, present, and future, the concept of space—all dissolve. The last concept to go is existence, the notion that something is there. Awareness of existence is called consciousness. We are attached to the sense that there is beingness. And even when the sense of beingness goes, there can remain a sense of consciousness. If the sense of presence or existence goes, there will be just consciousness. Pure consciousness is awareness without content. In Zen, this is often called fundamental reality. There is no sense of existence, there is just awareness. There is knowingness, but not knowingness of anything in particular. Nothing can be said about it. But even this open knowingness has to go at some point. It doesn't go and never come back, but we discover that knowingness is not final, that consciousness is not final.

As the sense of knowingness and consciousness dissolves, the soul is in cessation; it has no sense of being or existence. We call this the Absolute. You realize your final nature is not that cosmic existence, but the source of cosmic existence. You discover that the nature of the human being you have taken yourself to be is ultimately the source of everything. This is the deepest mystery, unknowable by mind or by consciousness. You realize that the universe is simply a robe that you wear. When you take it off is when you go to sleep. The Absolute is like the sleep of the cosmic existence; the cosmic existence is like the waking up of the Absolute. The cosmic existence is the day; the Absolute, the night.

Losing the notion of existence doesn't mean you cease to exist. But the desire is exactly for that: absolute cessation. You wish that you would disappear, that you would cease to know that you had ever appeared. This is the deepest wish, the wish for the most fundamental dimension. And the deep love is a deep fear too, because of the attachment to existence.

You realize that your nature can be neither described nor known. You can't say that you exist, and you don't know that you don't exist. If you know that you don't exist, you exist. Complete nonexistence is complete cessation of consciousness, of knowingness. It is the cosmic sleep, the cosmic night. It is the deepest peace. This is not a permanent state of realization, but a phase for the deeper realization. What is called the divine coma, where there is no experience of sensation or perception, becomes the rite of entry into the realm of mystery, the mystery of the Absolute. To wake up from this divine coma without leaving the mystery of the Absolute is total peace and cessation of suffering. You realize that the end of suffering is not happiness but peace. From that peace arise happiness, fulfillment, love, and all the qualities of being.

Some of you might already see a problem that arises here, another source of suffering. We have not yet arrived at the final resolution. It is true that our mind can go, our consciousness can go. Our sense of things goes from being to nonbeing. But there remains a duality in the mind, which will create a subtle suffering or longing. That duality is between existence and nonexistence. We believe that existence and nonexistence are two things. How can that be? How can we be the totality of everything and then become something else?

The heart becomes perplexed at this point. That perplexity can lead to profound sorrow. In my own process, I didn't understand this issue for a long time. I would experience the state of the Absolute, and then experience the state of cosmic existence or the sense of being an individual. And there was sadness so deep that it filled the whole universe with deep, dark sadness and longing. It was hard to know what it was about. I felt, "I know who I am, I know my ultimate self, and there is still sadness." Some time passed before I finally said, "What is this sadness all about?" I realized that in going from existence to nonexistence, there is a sense of loss of the existence. The sadness was connected to my love for that existence.

To go to the Absolute brings a sense of losing everything. Even though I am becoming my truest, innermost, secret nature, I feel I am losing the totality of existence, which I love. For a long time I wondered, "Why do I love it? Why don't I love my deepest self more?" So in the state of existence, whether cosmic or individual, there would be the longing and love for the Absolute, for absence, for complete peace, for unspeakable reality. And in the state of the Absolute, there was a subtle longing for the existence that I loved. I realized at some point that I loved both equally, and this seemed to be a big problem.

The resolution that happens is nothing the mind can conceptualize. Logically, we can see that the resolution is for the existence and nonexistence to become one, for beingness and nonbeingness to become one. But no logic can prepare us for the realization that we are the cosmic existence that is completely, absolutely not there. We completely exist as everything and at the same time there is absolutely nothing there. There is no duality whatsoever, no loss whatsoever. Not only are you all existence and no existence, but you are both at once.

As you see, the understanding and resolution of suffering is not simple. It involves a fundamental transformation, a transformation that does not mean going from unhappy to happy. Understanding suffering requires transformations that we ordinarily don't think about and that our minds can't easily conceptualize. The causes of our suffering are so intrinsic to how we

10-27-21

live that once we recognize them, we can no longer believe that it is unfair that we suffer. How else could it be? Suffering is simply a symptom of incomplete knowledge. Suffering is a symptom of lack of realization, lack of complete awareness. We experience lack of awareness, of realization, and of knowledge as suffering.

As we begin to understand this, our attitude toward suffering changes: it is no longer something bad happening. We realize that there is simply something that we don't understand, that remains to be seen. Our suffering is a symptom, a sign coming from our nature, which is the deepest guide. Our suffering beckons us closer to the truth, shows us the way to peace. Through our suffering, our true self tells us that there is more to realize. Our suffering is connected with our guidance, and it's better not to try to silence it. The only approach to suffering is to understand it. Suffering is silenced in the final silence, in the Absolute.

Our perspective today reveals how our subtle conceptualizations create beliefs that cause us to suffer. The most fundamental conceptualization is the duality between existence and nonexistence. Within that fundamental conceptualization we make further differentiations: pleasure and pain, individual and cosmic, past and future, space and time. We differentiate still further: love and hate, happiness and misery, physical and spiritual, mental and physical, and so on.

The final outcome of all these differentiations is what we call our mind, our personality. The resolution of suffering is to eliminate false ideas, to abandon the belief in those differentiations. Some traditions teach that we need to free ourselves of the discriminating mind and go to the state of no-mind. The state of no-mind means no discrimination. The moment there is discrimination, the moment there are two things, the possibility of preference arises. The moment there is preference, there is attachment. The moment there is attachment, there is suffering.

So we can say that the ultimate cause of suffering is duality, or, more precisely, attachment to differentiated phenomena. If we can abide in our knowledge that the fundamental reality is nondifferentiated, then we might not prefer one thing over another. If our mind does not prefer one thing over another, then there is no attachment. Whatever happens, happens. Death, life, good, bad, you, other, are all one thing. We know they are ultimately conceptual differentiations; they don't absolutely exist. So there is no attachment to them at all. No attachment means no suffering.

Letting go of attachment is difficult until you truly know nondifferentiated reality and perceive the true status of asserted differentiations as conceptual structures. If you believe duality is absolute, attachment will always be there. If your world is carved into existence and nonexistence, life and death, individual and God, self and other, good and bad, then you cannot be nonattached. Attachment is one of the final challenges on any path of realization. Even after you realize cosmic consciousness and the Absolute, even after you realize that existence and nonexistence are concepts in your mind, attachment remains for some time. Attachment is habitual, and those habits will have to be metabolized as you become aware of them. That takes time. But once you truly know nondifferentiated reality, you have the insight that will dispose of attachment. The rest is a matter of time.

The final dichotomy is between the Absolute and the cosmic existence. The Absolute is the final subject and the final object is the cosmic existence. But when that union happens, when that dichotomy is erased in the understanding of nondifferentiated reality, there is no subject and object, no inside and outside. So the person who is completely nonattached, who knows reality exactly, will not assert anything. If someone is completely real, that person will not say, "I exist." He will not say, "I don't exist." He will not say, "I both exist and don't exist at once." He will not say anything like that. He will not say there is God. He will not say there is no God. He will not say there is both God and no God at the same time. Ultimately, reality is not any of these differentiations. Reality, whatever it is, is simply there. Whatever it is, it simply is.

Working as we have today to understand the nature of suffering might help us work in a more informed, more balanced, more optimistic way—optimistic based not on fantasies but on our realization of reality. When we know that ultimately we are everything, what's the point of trying to get one thing and not another? Even before we encounter the Absolute, knowing the cosmic reality begins to dissolve our attachment to asserting distinctions. You don't care whether you are rich or poor, big or small, old or young, pretty or ugly—you are everything.

Differentiation still exists in the sense that there are people, there are colors, there are objects, there are different states. But the differentiations are not ultimate or isolated or asserted. They are one reality. They are like different colors of one medium, like different threads of a single fabric. When the attachment to differentiation dissolves, it is not like you don't see people or trees or things happening. Everything appears as usual but, because you see the connecting fabric, there is a luminosity all the time. There is a transparency. You see through things. You look at a person and you don't only see the body; you see everything—all the essential aspects, all the energies, all the way to the mystery of the Absolute.

FIVE

Absolute Absence

Today we will have questions.

STUDENT: Is there such a thing as the experience of absence of consciousness?

ALMAAS: It can happen that a person's consciousness ceases for a period of time. In this absolute silence, there is no conscious experience.

In order to understand cessation of consciousness, we need first to understand consciousness itself. We can understand not only the experience of being conscious of one thing or another, but also the experience of pure consciousness, the underlying sensitivity that makes it possible for us to be consciously aware of anything at all. Sometimes pure consciousness is referred to as cosmic consciousness, but I think this makes it more difficult to understand. Pure consciousness is consciousness that is experienced directly and purely, instead of being inferred through the objects of consciousness. Since consciousness includes everything you know, you have nothing with which to contrast it except the absence of consciousness, which is a rare experience.

When I say "consciousness," I don't mean anything strange or unusual. Everything you experience is in consciousness. Ordinarily, our consciousness is full of objects: my body, the table, people, all that I see and hear, and all of our inner experiences. As we explore our experience, we discover finer and deeper states of consciousness until we know more specifically what pure consciousness is. As we become open to new modes of perception, through exploring presence and essence, we come to realize that Being itself is pure consciousness.

And it goes further. As we become more established in pure consciousness, we see that the things we have left behind are also consciousness. We are amazed to discover that our body is made of consciousness; our sensations are consciousness. We see that what our anger and love have in common is that they appear in the ground of consciousness.

Once we learn that our being is pure consciousness, it becomes possible for all discriminations to disappear. We abide in pure consciousness so fully that we do not differentiate between essence and ego, between physical and not physical. Consciousness is simply consciousness, independent of all objects, essential or otherwise. In the beginning of the work, our discriminations are so opaque that we need to refine our perception to penetrate that opacity. When we have our attention on the ground of the mind, and at the same time become aware of it without completely identifying with the content of the mind, the objects in the mind become more transparent, until there is only transparency. This transparency reveals to us the state of pure consciousness in which all objects that we have deemed coarse or impure, all that we have felt we had to leave behind, we perceive to be of the nature of consciousness itself.

But for the purpose of our discussion now, when I say "consciousness" I don't refer to any refined state. I mean simply the fact of being conscious of something. For example, when you pay attention to yourself, you notice sensations in your body. These sensations are actually consciousness. The presence of sensation indicates consciousness. If you have sensations in your knee, you are conscious of your knee. If you shift your perspective from a consciousness that is conscious of the knee and consider the sensations themselves as consciousness, the experience undergoes a subtle change. You become aware that a sensation is itself the consciousness of the sensation.

This is a glimpse of pure consciousness. The sensation of the knee, which is the consciousness of the knee, is the shape that consciousness takes in this location. If you suspend your differentiating mind, you will see there is no knee really. Only the sensation that we call knee exists, and that sensation is consciousness. You regard that lump of sensation and decide it is a knee. That is the name you call that part of consciousness. But really it is simply consciousness.

STUDENT: How is this related to the absence of consciousness?

ALMAAS: I am getting to that; it is important to understand consciousness to appreciate what its absence means. Total absence of consciousness is much deeper. The cessation of consciousness means no knowing. It is the absolute darkness of consciousness. In this condition, no sensation of anything and no consciousness of anything can endure. If you are in the state of absence of consciousness, you are not aware of anything in yourself. The state of absence possesses no awareness of absence. You are simply absence. Since there is no consciousness, there can be no consciousness of its absence either.

Absence is very difficult to describe. Imagine the absence of all the sensations you experience in your body, all your thoughts, images, and perceptions. Absence does not mean numbness, because numbness is still your consciousness sensing numbness. Neither does absence mean blockage, because blockage is your experience and sensation of blockage. Numbness and blockage can include an awareness that something is missing. In absence there is no sense that something is missing. Absence can be the total nonexistence of awareness, or it can be absence with an awareness of surrounding phenomena. The former I call cessation and the latter absence. I will make this distinction more clear as we proceed.

In the state of absence you are completely spontaneous without knowing that you're being spontaneous. The reflective capacity is not there. This seems improbable because we cannot imagine being aware without some self-reflection, without some consciousness of ourselves.

But no consciousness of ourselves is fundamental to the condition of absence, because we are not there! We are aware only of what is actually there, namely, our environment. We reflect neither on the environment nor on ourselves as the perceiver. No consciousness of self remains, because instead of self there is absence. As a result, we do not experience emotional self-consciousness; this is why absence is a condition of absolute spontaneity.

STUDENT: Is there any value at all to this state of complete absence of consciousness?

ALMAAS: No, it is not good for anything of a practical nature.

STUDENT: I ask because I've experienced absence, and the only way I recognize it is that when I come back to consciousness I realize that I have lost track of a period of time.

ALMAAS: That's true, but you are talking of the first kind of absence, what I call cessation. When we consider it in terms of conscious experience, cessation is a lost period of time. Because no experience or perception of anything exists in the condition of cessation, it has no practical uses in life. It happens to be, nevertheless, the total concentration of awareness on the ultimate reality. The ultimate reality, though, is not useful for anything practical.

STUDENT: It's a very odd state.

ALMAAS: It is. I agree.

STUDENT: There was nothing there at all for a while.

ALMAAS: That's true. Nothing is there for a while and then you come back and you realize there is something. So what happened? There is no way of finding out what happened because you were not present there. You were absent. Nobody was there who can tell us what happened.

STUDENT: Is it possible to lose daily life in the state of cessation?

ALMAAS: It certainly appears so. You have in a sense lost a portion of your life span because there is a gap in your conscious experience. However, total cessation is transitory. You let go of the self and all

of its supports for this period of time. Cessation is .
complete state of ego death, where even the consciousness of experience is gone. Some people call this aspect of absence divine coma. But cessation is only the
beginning of the capacity to experience the condition
of absence, which subsequently can occur within perception and action.

Actually, we are always living daily life from the place
of cessation, without being aware of it. Cessation is the
underlying ground of our experience all of the time. We
are always living from the state of absolute absence.

Because, you see, nothing else is. The ultimate reality, the ultimate nature of everything, is absence of
being, or nonbeing. Everything that you experience is
an expression of nonbeing. If we are to think of the absence of being as useful, that is its usefulness—it makes
everything arise and underlies all existence. Without
absence, traditionally referred to as emptiness, nothing can exist. Absolute absence is the source of all that
is. Practically speaking, you cannot get anything from
absence. Absence does not make you feel good or bad.
It does not help you make money or win an argument
with a friend. What absolute absence does is give you
presence, which you might consider useful or not.

STUDENT: I've asked other people about it, and everybody thought I was crazy when I said I'd experienced this state.

ALMAAS: It does sound crazy to people who do not
know it.

STUDENT: It feels like sleep.

ALMAAS: Deep sleep without dreams is similar to
complete absence. Cessation does not have consciousness or awareness. It is unknowable. In its completeness,
cessation exists without the presence of anything else.
Nothing is there and nobody is there to see nothing

being there. You can only know absence by being it. And as I've said, when the awareness returns in the state of absence, one can be aware of one's environment but without any self to be aware of it. This is a more subtle state than cessation.

STUDENT: Sometimes when I sit [in meditation], I resist "nodding out" or going to sleep. When you go into that place, is it like "nodding out"?

ALMAAS: No, absolute absence does not feel like going to sleep. It is much more crisp. Sometimes getting sleepy can be a way of entering it because the consciousness cannot tolerate being aware of absence. The usual experience is more like: There is something and then there isn't. It is also possible to know absence through consciousness. I am thinking of the condition in which both absence and consciousness arise at the same time. This experience is not easily accessible; it generally requires the realization of cessation first. In this intermediate experience between cessation and absence in action, consciousness knows absence by coming in contact with it. This experience is mysterious and paradoxical. You don't know absence in its entirety or in its absoluteness. You know absence from the perspective of consciousness as presence. But because conscious presence is in touch with absence, there is not complete absence.

In this state between cessation and absence in action, consciousness knows absence in an incomplete way. Consciousness is aware of itself as presence, and this awareness stops just at the edge of consciousness.

There is a drop, a falling off into nothing. You're walking along and suddenly there is a drop, and the drop is one hundred percent infinite. There is nothing there. You put out your hand and it disappears. It's not like you do not see it. You lose touch completely with your hand. So consciousness can know absence in this peripheral way, as the perception of the end of the field of consciousness, as the abyss beyond consciousness. Consciousness knows absence as its own ending. And if consciousness focuses exclusively on this absence, consciousness will completely cease.

But it's not possible to understand this intellectually. The cessation of consciousness is a radical kind of condition, different from anything you have known or can imagine. Usually, we are aware of a state of consciousness but not aware of the state of cessation of consciousness. I am talking about this not because I think that you will get it by listening to me, but because I think it will be useful to know that such an experience might happen to you at some point. So if you have already had the experience, you now know what it is, and if not, then when it happens you won't get too freaked out, you won't think you've gone completely bonkers. Absolute absence is a real condition, an advanced stage of the inner journey.

STUDENT: You were talking about an absence of self-consciousness that might still allow awareness of surroundings.

ALMAAS: Right, that's what I said. Absence and consciousness can exist at the same time. But in that case, I would call consciousness "awareness," because it is a consciousness that is totally empty of inner sensation.

STUDENT: So you exist as a body but sensation disappears?

ALMAAS: The world exists but without you. Just like that. The world and the experience of the world exist, and yet in your location there is nobody perceiving or experiencing the world. The world is the perception of the world, that is, the perception of the world is identical with the presence of the world. No sense of self or individual is needed to perceive the world. I don't mean that there is no physical body, but rather that the physical body is perceived as part of the world, not as you.

The experience of absence is complete freedom. You are completely not there, completely absent; you don't come and you don't go. You don't think of dying, for dying doesn't make sense anymore. As there's nobody there to die, there's also nobody there to live. There is awareness of the world, but that awareness of world does not belong to anybody, does not belong to a self or any kind of center. Universal consciousness becomes the world, and absence is the emptiness that underlies consciousness, that is beyond consciousness without itself being anything at all.

STUDENT: So this is a separate experience from what you were describing as cessation?

ALMAAS: Yes. The condition of absence can be absolute. When the absence is so complete that even the world disappears, I call it absolute absence, cessation, or annihilation. But in that absolute absence the world emerges, which means that consciousness emerges. Consciousness emerges as the ground of the world, containing the world. After the cessation of consciousness that is absolute absence, consciousness returns as the awareness of the world, where the awareness of the world is identical with the arising of the world.

We are so trapped in our usual way of thinking and of perceiving things that we don't allow the possibility that we are the perception, that we are the awareness of phenomena without being separate in any way from the phenomena. We firmly believe that reality is the physical world that we see, the same world that our mother saw. That is to say, we think the world exists on its own as a solid, basic, and fundamental reality. Everyone believes this.

In truth, however, the world is simply consciousness that arises from absence, from nothing whatsoever. But realizing this is a radical experience that arises as part of the culmination of one's work. One way to realize this truth is to understand consciousness. As long as you make discriminations in consciousness and take these to be true, self-existing realities, it is difficult to realize absence. Going from one state of consciousness to another, you're simply trapped within consciousness. You go from the painful to the pleasurable, from hate to love, from love to clarity, from this to that, through all of the various kinds of states and objects of consciousness.

Once you realize that all of these things are consciousness and allow yourself to be there as consciousness without needing to make discriminations, you become the presence of consciousness. Beyond any of the forms arising within it, this conscious presence will at some point spontaneously dissolve.

STUDENT: Can absence be described as the disidentification from consciousness?

ALMAAS: Yes, absence is absolute lack of identification with anything. Usually, though, we do not know what this means if we have not yet experienced absence. That is why I prefer to refer to it as the cessation of consciousness. Although I can describe it pretty well, absolute absence is difficult to imagine and understand. We can relate it to the experience of clarity, when your consciousness sometimes feels as clear as transparent glass or crystal. Now take that clarity and make it more clear, absolutely crystal clear. Then make it clearer and clearer and clearer and clearer and clearer until it is so clear that you can't even feel it. As the transparent medium of consciousness becomes so smooth, so clear, and so fine, it becomes thinner and more subtle and transparent. At its limit, absolute clarity is so fine, so clear, so subtle, and so thin that there is nothing there. The medium of consciousness is then absolutely erased. Complete absence is a state of complete lightness and openness because there is nothing there, not the slightest sensation, to obstruct the openness.

Usually some dullness or opaqueness, some thickness or heaviness, is attached to sensation. Because our normal inner experience is that of sensation, it is difficult for us to understand the fineness that is absence. We know how to contrast mild sensation with intense sensation, subtle sensation with dull sensation, but we do not know how to contrast sensation with absence of sensation. As I mentioned earlier, absence does not mean the usual absence of sensation in the sense of being blocked, numb, or not feeling anything. In each of these cases, you might be aware that you are not feeling anything, whereas in absence, there is no awareness that you are not feeling anything. Absence is absolutely clear, transparent, light, and empty. Absence is so complete that it is not possible to reflect on it, even if only to confirm that there is nothing there.

When we experience absence, we can't help but fall in love with it. Although it's certainly not what we imagine as lovable, absence is the most lovable condition. We think we love things or conditions that are pleasurable and sublime, but when we really experience absolute absence, we completely love it because there is no barrier whatsoever between our heart and this completely free condition. In the absence, your heart is so light, so open, so empty, that the sense is that your chest is not there. In fact, all of you is not there. What you have always experienced and taken yourself to be is absolutely absent. No remainder is left after you are gone. Such absence is so fundamental, so radical, so absolutely clear and exact and real that you can't help but be passionately in love with it.

STUDENT: Does the love continue after you're out of it?

ALMAAS: Yes.

STUDENT: Who loves it?

ALMAAS: The love is before and after absolute absence. If you are absence, you don't love it. We are always coming from absence but are not always aware of it. Similarly, our love and longing always ultimately have to do with the absence, even though we are not aware of it directly. After we have the experience of absence, we're generally more clear about our longing and love, as some sense of the taste of absence remains with us.

We are more used to thinking of our love and longing as having to do with what we call the Absolute. This is more obviously the Beloved of our heart. It is more difficult to see how the love is for absence. But absence is actually the essence of the Absolute. And when we experience absence, it is so unexpected and unfamiliar that at first we don't associate it with what we have thought of as the Absolute. Loving the Absolute involves a separation from the Absolute. If you are separate from the Absolute, or if you are not totally the absolute absence but are aware of it, then you might love it. If you separate more from the Absolute, you long for it. If you withdraw even further from the Absolute, then you forget it. That's how the journey of return or discovery goes: forgetfulness, discontent, longing, love, complete cessation.

STUDENT: I can imagine hating absence because it sounds like death.

ALMAAS: It does sound like that. Because many of us believe that death is the end of experience, the Absolute can seem like death. But absence is actually beyond death. Death is still the knowledge of death, the experience of death. Death is a space we can experience, whereas absence is so transparent, so absolutely not there, that it doesn't make sense to talk about it as death. Death is a gross experience, a coarse approximation when compared to the Absolute. It is hard to sense what I mean when I say absolute absence, crystal-clear absence. It is what is called the void, absolute ultimate reality, divine essence, the mysterious self of God.

STUDENT: How can you describe absence if you didn't exist to know it? How can one have any memory to either love or describe?

ALMAAS: As I said, it is possible for absence and consciousness to be there simultaneously. The first step of experiencing absence is total cessation. In this total absence that excludes everything, it is not possible to know it. Absence is not knowable in its absoluteness. Because absolute absence is not aware of itself, no consciousness or knowingness can exist in this condition. You only become aware of this total cessation as you come out of it. You do not remember anything about absolute absence because there was nothing to remember and nobody to remember it. Only in the coemergence of consciousness and absence is it possible to know absence.

Let's look at it this way. Absence is the sky and consciousness is the cloud that arises in the sky. The cloud is a conscious cloud and is aware of the sky, which is the absence of the cloud. Consciousness can be aware of absence as the absence of consciousness, but if the clouds are completely gone and there is only empty sky, then there is absolute absence. Since no consciousness of it exists, the sky is not knowable.

Now, it happens that absolute absence is the ultimate reality, the final condition of existence. It is the beginning and the end of all there is, of humanity, of the world, of creation, of consciousness, of everything. If a person moves toward absolute absence, everything will go right because they will be free in their life, and if a person doesn't go toward it, everything will go wrong because they will be living in the prison of illusion. It's that simple.

Ultimately, everybody loves absolute absence whether they know it or not. You know you love it when you become aware of pure consciousness. Before you become aware of pure consciousness, you are trapped within the differentiating consciousness, discriminating, rejecting, and prizing one aspect of consciousness over another. You want sweetness and merging or are angry because there is pain; you reject this person because they don't like you, judge that person because they're different from you, and so on. Within the differentiating consciousness, you are busy within the knowable world, trapped within your own mind. To go from consciousness to absence is to break out of the cycle of birth and death, to escape the trap.

STUDENT: Do you need to know about this condition and seek it in order to be able to find it?

ALMAAS: No, you only have to be oriented toward the truth. Before my first experiences with absence, I didn't know there was such a thing. I actually didn't know. Nobody told me. I didn't have a teacher who told me that absence was the Absolute. I read about emptiness but never imagined it to be such absence of presence. I was simply oriented toward the truth, and I investigated whatever arose. And one day, things disappeared. I was surprised. I didn't understand it in the beginning. How could that be? I was as dumbfounded as anybody would be. Nobody prepared me to expect such a thing. So if you are on the correct path, that's where you'll end up, because that is what is there. You can't go astray. Everywhere you look, it is there. Absence looks at you from all directions.

There is no place you need to go, nothing you need to do. Just relax and don't resist. Quit the resisting mode and the defensive mode. You don't even need to orient toward anything. Relax and take it easy on all levels. If you just truly take it easy, you'll disappear. This is why people keep themselves busy and tense: in order not to disappear. So people fight and create problems. They work on themselves in a goal-oriented way, they meditate or pray to God day and night to get somewhere, or they find somebody to hate.

One of the good ways not to disappear is to find somebody to hate for a few years. If you have somebody to hate, you know you're not going to disappear those few years at least. A more subtle way to avoid disappearing is to find somebody to love. Hate and love, however, have different relationships to true nature. If you love completely, you will disappear because love taken all the way is pure consciousness.

Disappearing is really wonderful, is beautiful. Everything else within the realm of consciousness is paltry compared to it. Once you experience absolute absence, you know that all the wonderful sublime states of essence, of being, of consciousness and God-realization, are all on one side and the Absolute is on the other side. Regardless of how sublime and wonderful, these states are not one-millionth as wonderful as the state of the Absolute. Consider the highest, deepest experience of consciousness you have had, the most fulfilled and blissful condition. Now imagine a state a million times more satisfying and liberating. That is the Absolute.

STUDENT: So what happens when you stay in that void forever?

ALMAAS: If you stay in the void forever, then, you are the void forever.

STUDENT: If somebody were in that void forever, what would happen to the person sitting next to them?

ALMAAS: It is very dangerous to sit next to somebody who is in the void forever. That person is like a black hole. They will swallow you if you stay there long enough. Anybody who experiences the Absolute a lot will be like a black hole. That person will have a corroding influence on you and your felt sense of existence. You will realize that little by little different parts of you are disappearing. Every time you come into contact with a person like this, you might think you have wonderful experiences, but after a while you realize that you are losing things in the guise of having experiences.

STUDENT: I think that is what I meant by the hatred; it is the resistance to absence. There is so much resistance.

ALMAAS: Yes, that makes sense. All resistance is ultimately resistance against absolute absence. But you have to inquire about the hatred, as it might be about specific things within consciousness. When you really know absence, it is hard to hate. You might hate it before you know it, but in that case, what you hate is your idea of absence. Hating absence does not make sense. What is there to hate? In spite of what we said earlier, in a sense even to say you love absence doesn't make complete sense. Absence is the source of everything; in its realization, love simply overflows.

STUDENT: Usually when I have these types of conversations I get nauseated.

ALMAAS: Hate is a good defense against nausea. Most likely, absence scares you, and you experience this terror as nausea. It is reasonable to fear absence before you know it, because you can sense that it will annihilate something you still treasure.

STUDENT: How much time do you spend in this state?

ALMAAS: Not very much. Sometimes I am in it. I am a novice in this state. I don't know it as well as some other people do.

STUDENT: Why would someone not want to spend all of their time in this state?

ALMAAS: If you could surrender to it completely, of course you'd want to spend all of your time in it. But most of us still have things to understand and work out within the realm of consciousness. The moment you experience absolute absence, you fall in love with it in such a way that you feel that it is all. You immediately recognize that it is the deepest nature of things, the absolute truth of all phenomena and experience. You feel contented and satisfied, peaceful and carefree.

When I recognized the Absolute, I immediately felt that I had found what I had been looking for. There is no more search after that. You don't seek anything else and you know that there is nowhere else to search. Not only is there no longer any search, but there is nobody left to search. The Absolute is you. And even though sometimes I am not it exactly, I know I am it anyway. I might be experiencing one or another manifestation of consciousness instead of directly being the essence of consciousness.

STUDENT: So from this state something we erroneously call "you" forms and we go back to the self?

ALMAAS: Yes.

STUDENT: Is there no individualized sense in that state?

ALMAAS: No, this condition is not a matter of being an individual or not being an individual. There isn't anything there to be individual or not. What I notice when somebody realizes this condition is that their state is either absolute absence or cosmic consciousness. Sometimes they individuate out of cosmic consciousness as a person. But usually, when there is no personal contact, the state is either absence or pure consciousness. It goes back and forth. No one lives in absence all the time, at least not anyone that I have met. Also, various degrees of integration between absence and the conscious presence exist, but I will leave that for another time. I have discussed only the most general case of coemergence between absence and consciousness.

STUDENT: How is this connected with the luminous night?

ALMAAS: The Absolute, characterized by total absence, is the night, and it is the Guest that arrives at night. It is the unity of awareness and absence, presence and emptiness. Another name I have for the Absolute is the Beloved. I myself like the word "ipseity" for it, as I mentioned earlier. I find it the most descriptive. Many teachings talk about self or identity and the Absolute as the ultimate self. Although this is true, the Absolute not only is the self but is the nature of everything. Ipseity includes both of these meanings. The Absolute is the self because you experience it as the ultimate identity, the ultimate truest self. At the same time, you realize the Absolute is also your nature and the nature of everything.

Also, I like the word "ipseity" because people don't know what the word means. They don't attach all sorts of associations to it. Although I prefer "ipseity," I change words every once in a while, depending on my experience and the necessities of the teaching. Sometimes I use the Guest and sometimes I call the Absolute the Mystery or the One Reality. There are different ways of relating to the Absolute, each of which brings up a name that makes more sense for it.

STUDENT: "The Guest" implies something that doesn't sound like what you describe.

ALMAAS: "The Guest" implies a sense of visitation. When your heart is completely empty, you feel a visitation. When your heart is completely poor, completely devoid of everything, you receive a visitation. That is what I call the Guest. But the visitation is not that something goes into the heart. It is more that the heart becomes a window into infinity, becomes completely empty and completely open. You don't experience love or no love. The heart is absolutely empty. When the heart is that empty, we glimpse the luminous night of the Absolute through it. Here, I say that the Guest has arrived. In the beginning it feels like a visitation, but when the Guest actually arrives in the heart, then it is everything. The Guest is how the experience begins. That is how it arises. But I also call the Guest the true owner of the heart. The Guest is the true possessor of the heart. That is why the deepest longing a human being has is for complete disappearance.

STUDENT: Then why are we so afraid of disappearing?

ALMAAS: Because we don't understand it, and also because of how powerfully we want and need it. We feel a subtle, deep pull of longing toward such cessation, like a gravitational force toward it. Although in our mind we don't know what it is, in some deep, intuitive way we sense it is the cessation of the self. Because we still believe in the self, we become terrified of ceasing to exist. We look to other things and think that these are what life is about. Although it is important to have somebody love you, the longing you feel is not for an earthly beloved and cannot be satisfied that way. We search so many places before we look into our own heart, which means first emptying the heart of all of its objects of attachment.

STUDENT: What could be left to work out once you have experienced the Absolute?

ALMAAS: Even after experiencing the Absolute, things remain in the unconscious that are not necessarily clear. When we truly realize the Absolute, the things that remain obscure will arise on their own. You will experience them as some kind of lack of understanding, but not necessarily about the Absolute. The Absolute erases the primary illusion, that is, the illusion of who you are. But the Absolute does not erase attachments. These attachments are habitual and will have to work themselves out. But now the attachments are not supported by the illusion of what reality is and the illusion of who you are. Consciousness is like a spring, uncoiling as obscurations arise and are revealed, and the obscurations simply dissipate. The things that need to be worked out are parts of consciousness that are still somewhat compacted and need to be opened and relaxed.

Also, even though the Absolute is the ultimate natural condition, human beings will want to experience everything that is possible as consciousness unfolds from the Absolute. As our consciousness becomes clarified, all kinds of things will be revealed, such as perceptions of essence, of dimensions of reality, and perceptions of the so-called ordinary world, which are new and unfamiliar to our ordinary mind. Our lack of understanding may be experienced as a kind of opaqueness or obscuration. As an unfamiliar and unexpected state of consciousness arises, you might experience a subtle contraction against it because your mind resists the new experience. The resistance to a new manifestation may get connected to something in your past that reminds you of this new experience. You may see a personal issue about it. Although the personal issue might not be what's most relevant, it still needs to be worked out and made transparent.

Furthermore, there is not a single definitive way of experiencing the Absolute. The experience and re-alization of the Absolute reveals many unexpected mysteries of reality. We will be amazed at how many subtle concepts we have, many of which we take to be ultimate fixtures of reality. These become transpar-ent, transforming the realization of the Absolute to further and deeper realizations.

STUDENT: So is the development of the Pearl, the Personal Essence, prerequisite to someone's individual process? And isn't that moving back into consciousness?

ALMAAS: Let's see if we can understand the relation-ship of the Pearl to the Absolute. Pure consciousness, or conscious presence, manifests in different forms such as love or peace. It can also manifest as a person, a true person, an essential person. We call that the Personal Essence. It is a certain manifestation of pure consciousness or aspect of essence. But as I said earlier, the Absolute, although it is the ultimate reality, is not the complete development. It is true that it is the inner nature of everything and the ultimate experience; it is where we are going and where we came from and where we come from all the time. However, realizing the Absolute is not the entire story of the inner path. In order to complete the story, consciousness as pure presence becomes inseparable from absence. Consciousness can develop, whereas the Absolute does not. So, in a sense, the development in consciousness is the work. Much of this development can happen before the discovery of the Absolute or after it. It depends on the person. Some people don't embark on the development of consciousness until after the recognition of the Absolute. Others do a lot with the development of consciousness before the realization of the Absolute.

The development of consciousness has to do with living in this life from the perspective of the Absolute. The Personal Essence, the Pearl Beyond Price, has to do with being a human being and still being the Absolute. If you're just the Absolute, you are not a human being. But you live in this world, you have a physical body and a mind, you have work and relationships. You need the Personal Essence in order to be able to live personally as a human being and still be the Absolute. So the development of the personal aspect has to do with integrating all of these things that are important for our life into the various levels of consciousness, and then into the Absolute. This is an actual process that has to do with the metabolism of the Absolute into the Personal Essence. Although it is rarely mentioned in spiritual literature, the integration of the person into the Absolute is vital because we live in the world and not in a monastery or cave.

Integrating the person into the Absolute is more difficult than experiencing the Absolute. Integration requires that you deal with and metabolize your unconscious and your personal history. You have to really let all of the unconscious come out, to face all of your specific issues and areas of conflict and ignorance. Many traditions don't care about integration but strive only to reach the Absolute. They don't care about the personal life. The point for them is to know the Absolute and leave. In other traditions, and in our work, the point is to know the Absolute and live in the world as an expression of it. So how can you live a human life from the perspective of absence? That is the realm of development, change, and transformation within consciousness.

STUDENT: What do you mean when you say that consciousness and absence can be together or coemergent?

ALMAAS: I have been emphasizing absence because it is the essence of the Absolute, but the Absolute is the nondifferentiated coemergence and coextensiveness of consciousness and emptiness, of presence and absence. The Absolute is a presence that is at the same time absence. In this condition, you experience everything as usual, both you and the world. You live a normal life, and everything exists in the sense that it feels like the pure presence of consciousness. Simultaneously, you feel and know that nothing exists. So there is both presence and absence at the same time. Consciousness exists, in the sense that it appears in and as experience without its being a construct, but its nature is absence. True nature is both being and nonbeing, both presence and absence, but also not either, because these two facets are not differentiated. Everything has this nature, and everything is constituted by this nature. You realize that even the physical matter in front of you is the Absolute. There is no difference. Such perception implies a further and deeper integration and understanding of the Absolute.

STUDENT: When you said that some schools think that experiencing the Absolute and then leaving is the point, what did you mean by leaving?

ALMAAS: Some people feel that after knowing the Absolute, the next thing is to die and that's it. The point is to finish. Finishing means reaching the Absolute. That is the final rest. Others believe that the point is to leave the world with its cycles of living and dying, and that the way to do that is to realize the Absolute. These systems tend to believe in reincarnation, and here the point is to not reincarnate, to not come back to the world. So the idea of the whole system is oriented toward leaving life and the world once and for all.

STUDENT: Earlier you mentioned the importance of relaxing. Is that the same as surrender?

ALMAAS: Surrender is complete relaxation.

STUDENT: How can you have goals and work toward something if you just surrender?

ALMAAS: You can't. Surrender means you have no goals.

STUDENT: But to get somewhere, you have to have goals.

ALMAAS: It does seem that way. But it depends on where you want to go. If what you want is the Absolute, the depth of true nature, the method is complete surrender, complete relaxation. The Absolute is not something somewhere else; it is you. You do not see it because you are tense. So making an effort to move toward a goal of getting somewhere will take you farther away from what we truly are. The best thing is to take it easy and relax and have a cup of tea. Don't worry about anything. Be assured that you will never die. Ultimately, nothing will ever happen to you. All that will happen is that you will put on different robes, different clothes. Some you will like, some you won't. Clouds will come and go, but the sky always is. As the Absolute, you are like the sky and nothing will happen to you. Nothing can happen to you.

It is important for you to realize what we are doing here. Anyone who is not interested in the work the way I am discussing it is in the wrong place. The longer you stay here, the more corrosive influence you will experience. You will lose everything in time. So, if you are coming here to accumulate and gain things, knowledge, feelings, experiences, whatever, forget it. You have come to the wrong place. If you are not interested in complete annihilation, don't stay here. It is not that the final condition is simply annihilation, but the way to it goes through annihilation. If anything else is more important to you than the truth, you'll find all kinds of reasons not to like what we do. Everything we do is oriented toward the truth. Even when you think I sometimes help you with practical things, with your relationships to your father or mother or lover, with your work, I am actually doing all of these things just to make it possible for you to relax. It is not my intention to make you successful in your life. What is twenty years of success? You have an eternity after that. That is the true perspective. You have all the time there is to relax. If I tell somebody, "Well, I'm going to help you be successful for twenty or thirty years, or help you get a lover who will like you for twenty or thirty years," what's the importance of that? It is insignificant compared to someone guiding you to experience the absolute final nature where you are going to be forever and ever. Really, think of that. I'd be doing you a disservice, shortchanging you, if I tried to give you something less than that. And from the beginning I am not going to pretend that I'm interested in this little thing or that little thing. From the beginning you must know that is our orientation.

STUDENT: What happened to the truth, and the love of truth that you frequently talk about?

ALMAAS: The truth is the way. If you follow the truth, the thread of truth will take you directly to the Absolute, for the Absolute is the Ultimate Truth.

STUDENT: How do you know what the truth is? How do you know it is the truth?

ALMAAS: You know the truth by seeing the lies, by first seeing what is not true.

STUDENT: I don't understand.

ALMAAS: You are asking about the fundamentals of the whole work and the whole process. To find out what is true or not true, and to understand how you stop yourself from seeing the truth, is an enormous undertaking. We begin by seeing a lie as a lie. This is the beginning of seeing the truth. Recognizing the truth is a gradual process of seeing through the lies. The more you see the lies, the illusions, and the conditioning, the more you see what structures your experience and perception, the more truth you can perceive. What the truth is will change. Even what truth means changes. Still, you look for truth. You love truth. You seek truth. Truth is what is really here, what the fact is, what reality is. To begin with, that is truth.

If you follow the truth, you will get to deeper and more objective truth. And if you keep following the truth, you will get to the deepest and the Ultimate Truth, the Absolute. That is why we always emphasize the truth. If you seek anything else, you might not get to the Absolute. If you seek anything that is not truth, you will get the thing you seek. But if you seek truth and you really want the truth, the truth will be revealed to you. So our perspective here is that we work on all kinds of things. We work on personal things, practical things, day-to-day things. Ultimately we work on these things not for their own sake, but to follow the truth to ultimate reality. What will ultimately satisfy you is the truth. You might not believe me in the beginning, but that doesn't matter. You will find out on your own if you truly follow the track of truth.

When I say that our orientation is to follow truth all the way to the Ultimate Truth, I mean that the inner journey transcends life and death. When we talk about the ultimate or absolute truth, we don't mean some kind of mysterious thing someplace. In the beginning it might appear that the truth is some kind of distant, mysterious, unknowable thing, maybe at the depth of your heart or at the center of the universe. But the truth is everywhere and is everything. When you realize the absolute truth, you realize everything is the truth. You cannot see that until you realize the Absolute, its reality and its purity. Then you realize there is nothing else. You forget about spiritual experience. You are not spiritual anymore. You become this-worldly instead of otherworldly. You realize that the world is the Absolute. Everything you see is the spirit, the Absolute. There is nothing else.

The Sufis use some expressions in the Qur'an that contain two words referring to God's sense of unity. One word means oneness and the other word means singleness, but it is usually translated as unity. Oneness means that everything is made of one thing. Since there is no separation between things, it is multiplicity in unity. Everything is connected. You see differentiation, but differentiation in unity. The other, singleness or unity, sometimes called the One, means no differentiation. It means just unity, just one. Both words stand for one. In Arabic they are *wahid,* which means one, and *ahad,* which means one. But the meaning is slightly different. One is unification of all differentiations and One is singlehood. *Ahad,* or the single, is the Absolute. It is considered the deeper aspect. Ultimately, the oneness and the unity are one. There is a unity between the oneness and the unity, between the one and the single, between *wahid* and *ahad.* You realize that the physical universe and all the manifestations are the Absolute itself, without differentiation or separation.

Once you realize the unity of the world and the Absolute, spiritual experience has no further value. You do not need inner experience; actually, inner experience does not exist. There is no inner separate from the outer. What you see is what you get. Walking in the street is the most elevated, spiritual experience. Eating your meal is a fundamental, sublime experience. Cleaning your house is as spiritual, as sublime, as refined an experience as the Supreme. No differentiation endures between inner states and outer manifestation.

In traversing the inner path, we make a full circle. We first leave the practical, in terms of our value system, and go to the complete Absolute; from the Absolute we come back to the practical and see it as the Absolute. When I say our destination is the Absolute, I don't mean a rejection of this world. I mean coming back to the world from a different perspective; coming back to the world as divine, as Absolute, as real. In this realization, matter itself is spiritualized. You realize that matter, the physical universe, the ordinary stuff of your life is the ultimate reality. There is no separation between essence and appearance.

SIX

Beyond Consciousness

Today we will revisit the poem I have called "The Guest Arrives Only at Night."

Annihilate mind in heart,
Divorce heart from all relationships,
And then love,
Love passionately,
Consume yourself with passion
for the secret one.

When you are absolutely poor,
When you are no more,
Then the Guest will appear
And occupy his place,
In the secret chamber,

His abode,
The heart he gave you.

He is the inner of the inner,
He is the secret,
He is the guest,
And he arrives
only at night.

When you are no more, then the Guest will appear, then the absolute truth of reality will reveal itself. What do we mean when we say he arrives only at night? The whole poem is an exposition of the title. To understand this poem, we need to understand what "night" means here. How is night different from day?

Astronomically speaking, the night is first, prior to the day. The night is the fundamental condition of the universe. The day comes and goes, as a periodic interlude in the limitlessness of the night. There is day only when the earth is facing the sun; otherwise, we are facing the immensity and endlessness of the night. Cosmically speaking, we can say that the night is before creation, before there is anything. In theological language, we say that the night is before the Word. Another way of saying it is that the night is before the big bang, before anything was. This emptiness and darkness of night continue, then, as the fundamental ground of the universe, interspersed with blips of light that make day possible.

Experientially speaking, we normally live in the day, the world of light, perception, events, the world of experience. However, even though it is normal to live in the world of the day, there can be no absolute peace and rest there, for peace is the realm of the night. Day means there is light; when there is light we see all kinds of things. There is experience and the consequences of experience, with all of its pleasures and pains. But the night is the place and time of rest, deep peace, and stillness. We are not implying that the day is bad. Day is just one side. Night is the other side. There is night and there is day, and human beings are supposed to go back and forth between night and day. We are not supposed to have night always or day always. We would be very tired if there were only daytime. We'd have no life if it were always nighttime. In the true night of reality, there is nothing; nothing happens.

This metaphor of night and day brings us closer to comprehending the poem. The poem plays with this metaphor to reveal a glimpse of how to penetrate the absolute dimension of reality. The first line of the poem says to annihilate mind in heart, which is the first major step toward the realization of the night, the fundamental source of all light. When I say mind, I do not mean our thoughts. I do not mean what we usually call mind. What we normally call mind is only part of the mind referred to in the poem. We usually think our mind is our thoughts, beliefs, images, knowledge, and all of that. This is partly true, but when we say that is our mind, we do not see the implications inherent in what we are calling mind. If you truly and fully understand your mind, you realize that every single thing you ever experience is your mind. Mind is the realm of the day, the world of experience, the world of light and perception. The whole difficulty in realizing the true night lies in understanding what the mind is and how we can annihilate mind in heart.

When we begin any path of inner work, we question certain assumptions about self and about life and reality. As we continue the work, we question more and more assumptions. If we practice the work diligently, we will have to question all of our assumptions. Questioning all of your assumptions means questioning all that you know, and it also means questioning all that you perceive.

When we first begin to pay attention to ourselves, we become aware of our mental and emotional patterns, our past and the effects of the past on our present experience. We begin to recognize how we were loved or not loved, our need for love, and we may feel unhappy and unwanted. We may become aware of how we don't have real will and how we need to develop real will; how we need to learn to be compassionate toward ourselves and others. We question the aims we have in our life, our goals and dreams, whatever they may be. All of this really is only part of the mind I refer to in the poem. All of this is your personal mind, your small mind. This mind does need to be annihilated to behold the world of the night, but that annihilation is the easy part of the path, even though everyone believes it is the difficult part. Most work schools don't even deal with the personal mind, because they assume you already know how to work with it.

As we continue the inner journey, we learn a little more. We learn about essence and true self. We learn about God and divinity, God's will, and surrender to God's will. As we examine our experience more deeply, we discover that we still adhere to basic assumptions that we have not yet confronted. Do you believe your mother didn't love you and you need to be loved? Do you believe you don't have will and you need to actualize your will? Do you believe you haven't surrendered to God and you need to surrender to God? Do you believe your awareness is either limited or expanded? As you work through these issues, you realize that these beliefs imply basic things that you have learned somewhere, whether from your mother or from school or some other place. These beliefs are not certain, direct perceptions but still assumptions about reality.

Take, for example, the basic assumption that your mother is actually your mother. Who said that your mother is your mother? I do not mean that someone else is your mother, but the belief that she is your mother, or that you even have a mother, implies deep assumptions about who and what you are. We don't question these deep assumptions when we think, "My mother didn't love me, my father didn't support me." Who said your mother is your mother and your father is your father? How do you know you are something that can have a father or mother? When you say, "My mother didn't do this," "I haven't surrendered to God," "I am not successful yet," you are taking how you usually know yourself to be an Ultimate Truth. We live many basic, implicit assumptions, and the world of these assumptions is a world of suffering.

Working to become somewhat free from our history is useful, as is developing the capacity to surrender or to actualize essence. But these very capacities of surrender and actualization will naturally lead us to question much more basic assumptions. As our ordinary identity is affected or even displaced by essential qualities, it will not be so obvious that your mother was your mother or your father was your father, that you are who you think you are or even a person who has an essence or true nature that you need to actualize, that there is a God that demands your surrender. You do not know for certain whether these things are true.

In my perception, these are the bases, the ground, upon which other assumptions and positions are built. You cannot think of being loved or not being loved, being successful or not being successful, whether or not you have essence or have lost it, love God or feel that God doesn't love you, unless you believe that you are the person who you think you are. Historically, you had no choice but to believe the idea that you are the person your mother took you to be. We all think of ourselves the way our mothers thought of us. We think of ourselves as the entity, as the person, that our mother took us to be. We live our lives with this belief that we take to be truth. And all the usual historically based problems we have follow from that basic belief: whether our mother loved that entity or not, whether God loved that entity or not, whether that entity has surrendered or not, whether that entity has an essence or not, whether that entity is successful or not.

The belief in entityhood is so powerfully entrenched in the human mind that if we look at our thoughts, we see that we can't think without that concept in our mind. Without believing the assumption that one is a separate person, it is difficult for a human being to do anything in life. This assumption will be confronted at some point on the path of inner work. As long as we assume that we are that identity, which is a separate entity, there is no way to go to the realm of the night and behold the inner Guest.

The foundation of the belief in entityhood is the conviction that physical reality is the most fundamental reality determining who we are. If you take yourself to be the person you think you are, you are bounded by your body. Your body, more than anything else, defines you as a person. In other words, the most superficial dimension in reality defines the rest of reality. Entityhood always depends on taking physical reality, as we normally experience it, to be the ultimate reality. This is true regardless of how much you experience love, surrender, divinity, essence, expanded awareness, or whatever else. If you believe that you are a separate entity, then you still believe that physical reality is more fundamental than all of these spiritual experiences, and that physical reality is what determines all of these experiences.

We recognize at some point that the idea, and not the actuality, of physical reality determines how we usually experience things. This idea of physical reality determines who and what we experience ourselves to be and how we experience our lives. The assumption of the primary reality of physical reality structures a large part of what we call the mind. The moment we make this assumption, the normal mind is created. If we believe that physical reality is the most important and fundamental dimension of reality, then immediately everything we experience appears as part of that solidity: there is me and there is you; other people; chairs, rooms, earth, trees, stars, galaxies, space; past, present, and future events. Everything comes into being from the assumption of the primacy of physical reality.

The belief in the primacy of the physical actually changes how we experience the physical, so that it appears solid and permanent. In other words, the physical world will appear differently when we do not make such an assumption and will reveal how it is simply a manifestation of something more fundamental.

Of course, for most of us it's true that physical reality is what we see; but this seeing is not complete. We are seeing with only a portion of our awareness. This might be a disturbing idea, but this disturbance is a blessing, an opening to something beyond this world of objects. As long as we are working on ourselves from the assumption that we are going to be an enlightened person, a free or happy person, our work is going to be defeated. There is no such thing as an enlightened person. If you have any belief that one of these days you are going to see God or have a relationship with God, you are going to be defeated.

All of these spiritual ambitions assume that you are the entity you take yourself to be. It is very hard to pierce that assumption, because it feels so real. You have felt it for such a long time, and everyone around you thinks and feels and operates as if we are all entities. We think it would feel very strange not to be the person that we usually think we are. Not being the person that you believe you are does not mean you will be a different kind of person or a different kind of entity. That is not the point. When you realize that entityhood is actually not real, your perception and view of reality alter radically. It is not like today you are the ego person and tomorrow you will be an essential person. You might have those experiences, but they are transitory experiences within the realm of the mind. The experience of being an essential person, even though real, is not ultimately who you are.

This is a very serious matter. Most of us quite naturally insist on adhering to the assumption that things are the way we normally see them: "There's me, there's you, we are two different people, God is something else entirely, and one of these days God will love me and everything will be fine." Or we think we are this person who has a self and one day will be enlightened and become a person with no self. But all this amounts to believing that one of these days you will find a good mommy. You are still being your mommy's good little kid. Your mommy will take care of you and you will live happily ever after. But what if things really aren't like that? You will discover that for years and years you've been barking up the wrong tree. When you perceive reality without assumptions, you realize there actually are no trees, no mommies, no you.

In addition to the basic assumption that we are separate entities, we also believe that we have separate feelings. When we hold the view that we are a separate, autonomously existing entity, we experience what we call differentiated feelings. We begin to feel sad, angry, hurt, afraid, loving, compassionate. These differentiated feelings become a primary way we know ourselves and express ourselves as this entity.

We are now approaching what the poem means by "annihilate mind in heart." We need the belief in the existence of differentiated feelings to know and to express ourselves. To annihilate mind in heart does not advocate having feelings instead of thoughts. Annihilating mind in heart means going beyond differentiated feelings, which are inseparable from the sense of entityhood, which is itself a feeling differentiated and patterned by the idea of an independently existing entity. To move to the dimension of the night, we need to go beyond the experience of ourselves as an entity, which is a mentally determined perception based on the physical. To go into the night requires that we move beyond our normal conceptualizing mind. And without the concepts of this mind, there will be no differentiated feelings. So, to annihilate mind in heart is to go to pure feeling, which is beyond the feelings carved out by the conceptualizing mind.

But what is feeling free from the conceptualizing mind? If we suspend our conceptualizing mind for a moment, we realize that the only thing we know for sure about our inner experience is that sensations arise. If, for a moment, we do not use the mind and do not say that this sensation is anger or hurt or fear, if we just forget about these names for a while, we will have the chance to see what "annihilate mind in heart" means. To see what heart without mind is, we need to be willing to let go of our sense of being an entity. When we do that and simply look at our feelings, what we actually experience is nothing but sensations. The conceptualizing mind singles out certain intense sensations and labels them as various emotions. This is the ordinary way our experience happens, and there is nothing wrong with it. This is how human beings have always operated, what we have always known. However, if we want to meet the Guest, if we want to leave the realm of the day and have a glimpse of the true night, we need to go beyond this normal experience of things. We need to see the mental quality of what we call our feelings and emotions, and allow ourselves to suspend the conceptualizing mind that distinguishes and labels them.

When we are able to go beyond the conceptualizing mind and can experience our heart fully and directly, we go beyond all ordinary feelings. Pure feeling turns out to be something like nondifferentiated sensation, just an ocean of sensations. We can be aware of the differences within this ocean, but if the conceptualizing mind is not operative, we simply experience the waves as inseparable from the ocean. We experience an expanse, a field with no boundaries and no content. We experience the sensation of sensation, the feeling of feeling, the consciousness of the expanse itself as an expanse of feeling or sensation. We are then experiencing pure consciousness, a field of presence that is self-aware. It is awareness of the presence of the field, with this presence being nothing but the ocean of sensation. The awareness of the field is identical to the field, for it is a field of awareness. There is no duality in the awareness or pure consciousness that is an expanse of sensation.

Our ordinary emotions and feelings are nothing but

collections of sensations that we wrap with a concept or idea. When we wrap them with that idea they become a particular feeling. The moment we do that, the mind is born. There is no mind without that conceptualizing. The mind is nothing but taking different sensations, inseparable from what we experience in the heart expanse, and wrapping them in different colors. We call the collection of these sensations feelings. So we see here that there is no mind without conceptualization. There is nothing without conceptualization. The mind constructs everything, all the differentiated and conceptualized experiences, whether inner or outer.

We have lived our lives believing that we see reality. We experience the emotions and feelings, and we see the objects in what we take to be the external environment. We have not been aware of the role our mind plays in this experience. We have not known that we have been experiencing our conceptualizing mind. When we get to the roots of how the mind works, we realize that the things that we think really exist are the things that are in our minds. They are not real in the autonomously self-existing way that we normally believe. This is difficult to understand because of how much we have believed these differentiations and conceptualizations and names. To annihilate mind in heart means to go beyond the conceptualizing mind, to stop this process of labeling and discrimination.

As long as we base reality, what we do, and the meaning of truth on the belief that these labeled phenomena exist absolutely, then our mind will be predisposed toward judgment. The opportunity to judge things as either good or bad arises. Before such conceptualization there is no possibility of judgment. The moment we take ourselves to be separate entities, our feelings too become differentiated as good or bad, pleasurable or painful. And the moment we begin to judge, we begin to attach. We want that which is good and avoid that which is bad.

From this perspective, the whole world has been created by our mind. We are attached to something that doesn't actually exist. Neither what we believe nor what we perceive is the real world. The good that we pursue and the bad that we avoid are made up by our own mind. In reality there isn't anything good or bad. God never creates anything good, neither has he ever created anything bad. Our minds create these distinctions.

The conceptualizing mind is of its very nature conducive to suffering. A world created of good and bad entities encourages comparison, preference, judgment, and attachment. The concept of a separate self is nothing but a collection of these sensations and feelings that have been lumped together and labeled in a certain way. But what if we don't look at things this way? What if we stop labeling things, stop saying this is different from that, and simply experience what is there without concepts? When we perceive without concepts, we realize that there isn't a separate self, an essence, an I, an other. There is only consciousness, the presence of consciousness. All these things are differentiations of the same field of consciousness. When you experience yourself in such a way, you realize there is just one consciousness. There is no body, no mind, no essence, no personality, no love, and no hate. There is simply one consciousness, one cloud with thicker or thinner parts, green or red parts. Consciousness is one unbounded cloud. There isn't anything else. You are not many things: essence, personality, mind, body, this or that feeling. You are one consciousness with different qualities, with various differentiated regions.

Let's do a little experiment. Are you sensing yourself right now? Be aware of your inner sensations and don't assume you know what this or that is. Don't go along with the demarcations and labels that your mind continuously provides. As you do this, the only thing you can know with certainty, without the use of concepts, is that you are perceiving something. There is consciousness, there is perception, there is awareness. That is the most you can know when you become aware of pure consciousness; the most you can say is that there is something there, there is the appearance of existence, something is perceived. That is all you can say when you do not fixate on the specific conceptualized objects of perception: There is some kind of conscious existence, an aware presence.

Different sources refer to this conscious existence differently: some call it God, others call it universal or cosmic consciousness, still others call it boundless presence or Being. We don't have to call it anything. When we do call it something, we are creating the first word to describe the beginning of experience. This word is something like "existence" or "being." It's the beginning of the big bang. We are aware of existence as a boundless ocean of conscious light, a boundless ocean of sensation. Everything else is a product of the mind. Everything else is a differentiation within this cosmic consciousness. The mind does not create these objects completely on its own. The cosmic consciousness is a unitary field that possesses variations and differentiations. Our conceptual mind abstracts these differentiations, labels them, and then believes they exist on their own, instead of recognizing that they are manifestations of one field of existence. Our mind creates the universe we normally view by reifying the already existing differences in the unified field of consciousness.

When we finally become aware of this process of re-ifying, and experience the world independently of our mental concepts, we realize that we are in touch with this pure cosmic consciousness all the time. We are never out of touch with this consciousness. Everything manifests the one consciousness. This pure presence of consciousness creates every sensation we are aware of, all that we see, all that we hear. Pure consciousness is one. There are no entities separate from pure consciousness or separate from each other. So, to dissolve mind in heart means simply to allow the awareness of pure consciousness.

Allowing is not an active doing but is simply desisting from reifying concepts. We cease looking at the world through concepts and we stop indulging this discriminating mentality. In the beginning we will of course rebel against such inner silence and stillness, because for so many years we have assumed the created mental world to be reality. We have believed it so thoroughly that no one can now convince us otherwise. We believe, "I am here, I have my feelings, and I am feeling bad today. I don't care what you say. I have been doing bodywork all these years to learn to feel my feelings and now you tell me I haven't got feelings. All these years of working for nothing! I've been learning to actualize my essence, my true nature, and now you tell me that there isn't any essence. Why did I do the whole thing?" We fear that it has all been a waste. But we need to do all these things to be able to relax enough to see through the beliefs. In a sense, we do need to play around with the concepts, beliefs, and ideas and, for some time, assume that they are true. We get rid of some old ones and create some new ones, all of which allows more openness and more possibility of relaxation. For some time on the path of inner work we need to believe our concepts. We need to go through this process with awareness in order to develop our knowing capacity and to unfold our potential.

Although going beyond the conceptualizing mind is a simple transition, it is not an easy one, because our concepts are so powerfully entrenched. We have taken apart the cloud of consciousness, hardened it by wrapping concepts tightly around it, and held it in place in order to avoid change. We call these reifications tension, or a certain feeling, or an identity, but they are really solidifications of concepts about some manifestation of consciousness. When we actually sense ourselves, and sense whatever tensions we have, we realize they are simply sensations. Whatever feeling of love we have is not love but a sensation. Whatever feeling of anger we have is not anger but a sensation. Before the mind existed, there was simply consciousness, the mere fact of conscious awareness of being. On this dimension there is no difference between essence and ego, between body and essence, between the good and the bad. No difference at all. If we allow pure perception to occur, if we allow ourselves to simply see, everything that we perceive is the substance of one field of consciousness.

The more we allow the pure perception of consciousness to happen, the more all the tensions, difficulties, and hardness begin to soften and dissolve. The different categories merge into each other, melt, lose their separateness. Love merges into hatred, the good merges into the bad, you merge into the other, the rug merges into the air, the air merges into you. The world becomes one big patterned medium, luminous and beautiful. If you allow the various contents of this medium to keep melting into each other, little by little the medium obtains a blissful quality, a deliciousness. It is not a chaotic mass, but a luminous and blissful field of consciousness. You can't say it's physical, mental, or spiritual; it is simply a deliciousness. Visually, it is a luminous field of conscious presence. In terms of feeling, it is like an ocean of sensation, where sensation becomes more and more relaxed. Because sensation is relaxed, it is more blissful. Whether you're feeling your arm or a chair that you're sitting on or the body of your lover, it is all one blissful type of consciousness.

Only when we allow ourselves to be this conscious field of blissful presence, and realize that is all that we are, does it become possible for us to make the transit into the night. To allow pure perception means that we let go of the primary concept of entityhood. As we allow the various differentiations to melt into each other, we see how these differentiations have been functioning. We recognize that one of these differentiations is the idea of self, with the attendant notion that we are separate from others, and we begin to see how the belief in the reality of differentiated concepts functions as a support for this concept of entityhood. When we understand the nature of our assumptions, our boundaries begin to melt.

On this dimension of pure consciousness, there is a sense that consciousness is conscious of itself. Consciousness is the basic quality of life, of the day. The day is characterized by light, and by knowing. When you consume all of the concepts that construct your sense of self and world, you become pure consciousness, merging into God, into divinity, into cosmic being. But to have a glimpse of the Guest, of the secret one, consciousness will have to consume itself too. The consciousness itself will have to burn with the fire of passion. The totality of consciousness, which is the totality of all that you perceive, the whole universe, will have to burn. In other words, God himself will have to burn with passion. You cannot do anything about the secret, about the Guest. The initial step is to go beyond the sense of being a person, to realize that there is only consciousness. What is left after the mind is gone is a sense of consciousness, beingness, presence. But to go to the realm of the night means there will be no consciousness. To go to the night means consciousness itself must be consumed. The sense of presence will have to die; God himself will have to dissolve. The word has to die, even the first word, which is "I Am."

What will be left if consciousness goes? For consciousness to go, beingness and existence also must dissolve. There needs to be absolute nonexistence, absolute darkness, darkness so dark that you don't know it is dark. The moment you know it is dark, consciousness has already arisen, the big bang has started, the word has been uttered. To realize the truest, absolute, utmost nature of who we are, and of all of reality, we have to let go of consciousness.

That is the night. The night never changes. The night never comes, never goes. The night is not born. The night will never die. When we glimpse this truth, we see that however obvious have been the notions that your mother was your mother and your father was your father, thinking through concepts has actually separated you from your truest nature, the nature that was never born. We have to confront many assumptions in the mind before we can really get a taste of the Guest.

The realm of the night is like deep sleep. When you wake up, you are completely refreshed. Creation begins all over again, the whole universe arises. Only when all sensations cease, when there are no more sensations, no more consciousness, do we really know who we are. Then we know the absolute truth. As the night, we perceive the whole of existence, the totality of the daytime realm, as nothing but thoughts that arise in the night.

To really be in the realm of the night, to really know what you ultimately are, what the secret of reality is, means to be not self-conscious. The moment that you are conscious of yourself, you are conscious of the consciousness, you are conscious only of the daytime. You see the light of day but not the darkness of the night that far transcends and contains the day. You see the transitory but not the eternal. You see the manifestation but not the unmanifest ground. You see the front but not the back. Your back, your ground, is the night. When you are the night, you can behold the day, but you see it as your front. Your back is something you cannot see, for it is the seer itself, the primordial eye of awareness.

To be the back means to be completely spontaneous. You are not conscious of yourself; you are aware only of your front, the manifest world. You are then absolutely spontaneous because there is no self-consciousness whatsoever. Your action simply arises on its own, without premeditation, without any prior knowledge. We cannot truly understand spontaneity before then. As long as there is one atom of self-consciousness, there is no spontaneity. Spontaneity means there is no self-consciousness at all. What you say, what you do, comes out without your knowing it is coming out. You don't know where it is coming from. And only from the night can such complete and utter spontaneity emerge.

Our work on the inner path reveals the fundamental beliefs and assumptions of the mind. Our work is a matter of increasing annihilation of what is not true. If we are really honest with ourselves, if we let ourselves live in our aloneness, away from the influences of all that we've learned and been told, all the beliefs about the good and the bad, if we really delve into the matter, we see that the world is not what we think and that we are not what we think. For sure, your mother was wrong about who you are and never really saw you. How could she see you? She couldn't go into the night; she barely lived in the day. What your mother didn't see is your true nature, the unmanifest ground from which you and the world emerge.

Whoever goes into the night will be eaten up, consumed in an instant, incinerated in a second. The night does not love you, does not do good things for you, does not have mercy on you, and does not make your life easy. The only thing the night can do is incinerate you. This is its only effect: absolute annihilation. This sounds scary, but when you see the falsehood of your entityhood and recognize the pure consciousness, you will be consumed with the passion to annihilate what is false. The longing for cessation is the ultimate desire that we have. It is the ultimate death wish, not the usual physical death wish. To die in total and complete annihilation means not knowing that you ever were or that you ever will be. It is absolute darkness, absolute peace. The Sufis refer to this as *fana fi al-dhat*, the death into the Divine Essence. Christian mystics refer to it as disappearing into the divine darkness. The Buddhists refer to it as the cessation leading to nirvana, or the *dharmakaya* of the bardo. All genuine inner teachings speak of this death and consider it the most definitive experience on the path.

So, to love the truth means that you want to annihilate the false. If you go into the matter deeply, you realize that everything you perceive will in time be revealed as false. Everything to which you can give a name does not really exist as you see it. This includes even what we think of as God. Simple religious people think that God is merciful and good and will give us blessings and rewards. Why would God do anything like that for you? You don't truly exist anyway, so why would God give you blessings? God is not deluded like you are. You are the one who thinks that you are an individual person who needs this or that. God doesn't think that way. For God there is only God. If you think that you need blessing, God will say, "Who do you think you are? Do you think you are separate from me?" So, to think of blessings or of God's grace is fine, but it betrays a limited understanding of reality. Although it begins to understand the divine realm, if you really see what God is, the only thing you want to do is forget that you exist. Letting God be there is loving God. Loving God doesn't mean wanting to be with God. To love God means that you want only God to be. Anything else is not love of God, but love of yourself, love of your belief in a separate entityhood. Ultimately, what you think of as loving God actually is loving a part of your mind.

Regardless of where we are in our inner work, despite whatever we are working to realize, at some point on the path we are going to have to let go of it. Whatever it is that you feel you're attaining you will have to drop. Whatever it is that you're accomplishing you will realize is false. What is true shifts. In one sense, truth is what you experience to be real in the moment. But when you really understand any particular experience, you realize it is not truth, it is falsehood. Then you discover a new dimension and realize that as the truth. You stay with it for a while until you realize it too is false. Even when you get to objective truth, you realize it is not ultimately true. So what we refer to as the various dimensions of truth are in a fundamental way only levels of conceptualization. The dimensions of truth are identical to the levels of falsehood. From one side they appear true, but from the other side they appear false. If you look from beneath, it is truth, and if you look from above, it is false, until you discover something that you can't look at from above or below.

Our method here in this work is to understand the truth. We want to understand the truth because it is what we love. Today I am talking about an ultimate sense of truth. Understanding the truth is fundamentally a love affair. If you really seek truth and nothing else, you're bound to get to the truth. But if you seek anything else—happiness, love, immortality, God, anything that is not the truth—you'll get only those things. You find them because you assume they exist, because you construct a world out of these concepts. However, truth means what is, not what you believe. Truth is the actual state of affairs, not what your mind thinks, not what society believes, not what someone said five thousand years ago. Investigating the truth means not only working on your emotions but also confronting your assumptions about reality.

So let's have questions now.

STUDENT: What does any of this have to do with our lives? What does the absolute truth, the night, have to do with my life?

ALMAAS: Many of us will ask this question. We have to get up in the morning, brush our teeth, drive cars, go to work; we have troubles, taxes, and all of that. However, when you actually experience and understand what the realm of the night is, when you allow the annihilation to happen, this question simply does not arise. The only thing that your consciousness will be concerned with is an appreciation of the beauty, majesty, and reality of the night. Who cares what happens! You are so bedazzled by the beauty that your heart is completely upside down, your mind is evaporated.

So from this perspective, such a question simply doesn't arise. Daily concerns and activities will be there, but as various differentiations in your consciousness, nothing else. That totality of the consciousness with all of its differentiations, which is the whole universe and all universes, is simply the clothes that you are wearing. It is the manifestation of your mind, the appearance of your cosmic body. So while you are brushing your teeth, who is brushing your teeth? You are not brushing your teeth, driving your car, paying any taxes. Nobody is paying taxes to anybody. There is only one, you see. Nobody has a hard time. Nobody is happy. There are no separate entities. There is simply a witnessing, an observation of all these things happening.

On the level of the differentiated person, on the level of entityhood, this sounds meaningless and even terrifying. But our feelings will change when we realize we are not that entity. The entity can only look from the perspective of entityhood. If you are identified with being a separate entity, some people are going to give you a hard time, some people are going to give you a good time, you are going to be happy or miserable. There is no other way of experiencing reality if you think of yourself as an entity. You stop thinking this way when you go beyond the realm of entityhood. Then you realize one consciousness everywhere. You understand that you and the rocks over there are made of one blissful consciousness, one luminous light. Everything you see is made of the most scintillating, the most delicious and cozy intimacy.

STUDENT: So are you saying there is only one consciousness, that you are not many things but one consciousness with different qualities?

ALMAAS: Yes, experience is in actuality unitary, and everything we experience is consciousness. Whatever you feel, sense, and experience is really nothing but consciousness; you can only be aware of consciousness and nothing else. Now, usually you don't perceive pure consciousness, because you focus on the details of the forms that arise, giving them different names and believing they are autonomous self-existing entities. For instance, in terms of inner sensations, you call it sadness, or essential experience, or an insight, or a thought. But if you go beyond the labels, you find out that you are only in touch with consciousness, with a quality of pervasive sensitivity. If you eliminate the concepts, setting aside the conceptual distinctions between the various manifestations, you will see that what they all have in common is consciousness.

STUDENT: What does consciousness itself feel like?

ALMAAS: In normal experience it feels like everything that you feel. Everything you see and feel is consciousness. But when you focus on the field that underlies everything instead of on the particular manifestations, then the feeling is pure blissfulness.

STUDENT: What is meant, then, by altered states of consciousness?

ALMAAS: These days the term is used specifically to refer to states different from our normal experience. We are focusing today on how pure conscious awareness underlies all of the various discriminations of consciousness. Whether ordinary, altered, or unusual, all states of consciousness have a sense of sensation and knowingness.

STUDENT: Is the night beyond mind or consciousness?

ALMAAS: The night means no mind and no consciousness. The mind rests on consciousness and diversifies it into myriad things. But the night is beyond consciousness, beyond mind. The night is absolute annihilation, which is our truest nature. How can it be that all this splendor arises out of absolute annihilation, total nonbeing? It's like a magic trick. You see, this nature that is our Ultimate Truth is a strange kind of Guest. This Guest will not come unless you are a perfect host. A perfect host keeps the house absolutely empty and clean. The house is clarified and purified to be fit only for the Guest. You realize that your heart, which is the feeling of the consciousness from which everything arises, is really the house of the Guest. The Guest ultimately resides in the heart. The heart exists only to serve as the abode for the Guest. The Guest is very jealous and will not show up if there is the slightest other thing in the heart, if there is the slightest movement toward anything else. The heart is completely clarified when there is absolute detachment, when it is completely empty, totally divested of its other occupants. Then the Guest arrives.

STUDENT: Do you mean our physical heart or the emotional heart?

ALMAAS: What we call heart is not exactly what we usually think of as the heart. More precisely, our usual understanding of heart is a very limited way of knowing the real heart. At the beginning of our inner work, we experience our heart as emotions and feelings. At deeper levels, we experience our heart as the essential heart with love, compassion, joy, and all of the qualities of essence. The essential heart leads to the aspect of truth, the solid gold of truth, which is the source of the essential heart. Beyond the aspect of truth is the heart of nonattachment, which does not distinguish between heart and mind. Knowing and feeling coincide as pure sensitivity.

STUDENT: Is the experience of the Guest the end of the path? Will it last forever?

ALMAAS: No, not necessarily forever. Many established habits and patterns of thinking persist and take time to dissolve. The grooves in our mind have become very deep because of how much we have used them. So even though we realize that everything is differentiations of one consciousness, and that pure consciousness arises from the ground of the night, our habits of assumption will not just evaporate in a second. So our ignorance will be gone, but our attachments endure longer. Furthermore, just because the night is the source and ground of all awareness and experience, realization does not necessarily mean identifying with it forever. The night can become a station, something finally realized, but realization may continue to reveal other parts of our potential.

STUDENT: What kind of sitting meditation do you recommend for the realization of the night?

ALMAAS: The collaboration and, ultimately, the synthesis of two kinds of practices—the stabilizing meditation and the analytic practice—are useful here. During the stabilizing meditation, you contemplate your being, not trying to understand but simply being the consciousness with no differentiation. During the analytic practice, you use your discriminating intelligence to understand reality in all of its differentiations. This is our central practice of inquiry into experience. You need to do both back and forth. Each one helps the other. Ultimately, the analytic meditation is a play of consciousness, revealing the underlying truth of pure consciousness. The objective of the stabilizing meditation is to simply *be,* without observing the differentiations that arise. You not only are not analyzing, you also are not observing. Putting it another way, you are observing without discrimination, without labeling. You notice something but you don't call it this or that. You simply feel it, the actual sensations, the actual being, the actual consciousness. You do not follow the experience or hold on to it or do anything to it.

The stabilizing meditation is actually a form of concentration. In time this practice relaxes and dissolves the various habits and contractions of the mind. But we don't really know what it means to do the stabilizing meditation until we understand what it means for there to be no concepts. So we have to go far into the practice of inquiry, far enough to experience the oneness of pure consciousness, before we can begin to meditate without conceptualizing. Before that, all we can do is discriminate. Before that, we don't know how to meditate, not in the way necessary for the realization of the night.

We each require different lengths of time to dissolve the habit of assumption and the belief in concepts. Some concepts are easier to abandon than others. But the fundamental idea we have to see through is concept of being a separate entity. Once that go everything else becomes easier. You realize little little that you don't experience yourself as a separate person. Although you behave as a person and you do things as a person, you don't feel that way. The transition from pure consciousness to the absolute truth is a spontaneous process. You just let yourself be. Then the darkness encroaches upon you little by little and you get eaten up. That's probably why people have so many fears about being eaten up and swallowed whole. Ultimately, we will be consumed.

From this perspective, the many things that people say about giving, loving, serving, and sacrificing mean seeing through the entity and all of its attachments. What you surrender is your mind. Being a giving person means not holding on to an entity. Surrender means losing the belief that you are an entity. Service means that being an entity is not the end. All of these are conceptual ways to approach the reality. But, in a sense, the reality cannot be approached, because the moment you approach it, you are already dealing in concepts. You are already taking yourself to be something approaching something else.

Reality doesn't really work that way. The reality infiltrates you, your mind, your soul. The reality acts on you from within and without, like a corrosive acid that eats more and more, dissolving you gradually and completely. You have many kinds of experiences and realizations as the reality feasts on you inside and out. You think you are gaining something, but you are actually being thoroughly consumed. You wake up one day not knowing what's happened. You thought you were going to be happy and realized, but now you see that you're gone. The ordinary mind cannot fathom the reality, cannot know what to do and how to get there. The mind that is a prisoner of concepts will never know the night.

STUDENT: What do you mean by consciousness?

ALMAAS: One way to understand consciousness is as the experience of pure existence, which is the beginning of your mind, the seed of all experience, the root of all concepts. Such existence is actually a presence, a conscious presence. When we experience it fully, we recognize it as pure consciousness, a field of awareness that includes our capacities of perception and experience. And furthermore, we recognize consciousness as the underlying ground of everything. Everything turns out to be a manifestation of and within this field. We find out that this consciousness is the ground of mind too, of all concepts and knowing. Although pure consciousness is nonconceptual, it is the ground of all concepts and all kinds of knowing, both the ordinary and the gnostic.

We also experience consciousness as presence and being, as the realm of the day. To move to the realm of the night, the absolute dimension of our true nature, consciousness needs to dissolve, needs to thin out till there is no existence at all. For consciousness to consume itself means that consciousness realizes that its existence isn't really ultimate. For consciousness to consume itself means that consciousness realizes its own nonexistence.

A deep longing for annihilation tends to arise in this process. We may experience this longing as passionate love. Essential passionate love is absolutely annihilating. The deeper the longing, the more intensely the passion burns. The sense of being consumed with passion feels like the night encroaching upon you and annihilating your being and consciousness. This passionate love is nothing but the Guest touching the consciousness. We can experience it either as the Guest passionately loving the consciousness or as the consciousness passionately loving the Absolute. In reality it is neither: We are simply realizing the inseparability of the consciousness and the ground. The consciousness is completely annihilated in this impassioned embrace. The mystical images of sexual union with God likely come from such experiences.

Unlike other kinds of love, real passionate love is self-consuming. Passionate love feels annihilating rather than giving and sweet. The more you are passionate, the more you disappear. You burn up from within, as if with black fire. You feel as if all your atoms are passionately in love. You don't know at the beginning what it is that you love. You just feel consumed with passion and longing. You feel you just want to not be, until you finally disappear. And you want to disappear, out of passionate love. When passion completely dissolves the consciousness, then the Guest arrives. The intensity of the contact with the nearness of the Guest, like a hydrogen bomb, incinerates your every atom with passion. The consciousness burns like a raging fire until nothing is left.

The outcome is the absolute presence of absence. You are present as absence, absolutely. You cannot comprehend this with the mind. The mind does not know what it means to be present as absence. What it means is that there are no sensations, no consciousness, no thoughts. Like the most delicious and deepest sleep, being present as absence is being the Absolute completely; it is being the awareness contemplating its absolute emptiness. There is no perception of anything. True emptiness is total absence, the ultimate ground of consciousness and of everything. True emptiness is the nonbeing of being, inseparable from being and from all the manifestations of being.

After this initial experience of cessation, it is possible to be the absolute reality and to have pure consciousness arise without ceasing to be the absolute reality. Consciousness arises inseparably from the emptiness. This happens when there is awareness of manifestations, of the forms arising within the consciousness. Thoughts arise, and you see the whole world as a bubble and everything as images reflected in the walls of the bubble. Some teachings refer to this perception as the great sphere, the totality that contains the whole universe. This also leads some traditions to say that this world is a dream. The world appears ephemeral, like a hologram. But this is not because the world is not real, but because we are seeing the world inseparably from its absolute ground, the nonbeing of consciousness.

We can arrive at this true perception of reality through many routes. If we arrive through the heart, we are burned with passion. If we arrive through the mind, we are eviscerated with clarity. We feel absolutely clean, so clean that we don't recognize ourselves. We are so pure, so crystal clear, that there is no sense of it at all. This is what living in annihilation means.

The moment consciousness arises in absence, there is perception and thought. If we get caught in the concepts of these thoughts, then duality arises. The Absolute is the nonduality of absence and pure consciousness, nonbeing and presence, the unity of emptiness and awareness. The absolute is aware in one direction only because it is not self-reflective. There is nothing to reflect back to, for its inner self is absence, nonbeing, emptiness. The Absolute only sees what is in front. It is like the back of the universe. Sometimes the back becomes what is in the front; the nonbeing and the being become one. If you look to the back, there is nothing to perceive. It is not that you feel *nothing* or see *nothing*, but there is simply no perception. At the edge of this no-perception there is a sense of absolute clarity and purity. However, the Absolute in its absoluteness, apart from manifest phenomena, is unfathomable. You cannot know it because the consciousness cannot go there without being totally annihilated.

Pure consciousness feels like deep presence. Sometimes the experience is that conscious presence thins out little by little as you abide in it. After a while only a few atoms of consciousness remain here and there. You begin to realize the absence in the place between these atoms, the place they are manifesting, the place where there is absolutely nothing. These atoms feel like islands of consciousness, awareness, and sensation in the ocean of absence surrounding them. At some point even these few atoms of conscious presence disappear, and consciousness totally ceases. There is a gap in your experience. At some point you perceive again, awareness returns, and with it the whole manifest world.

What we're seeing here is that self-realization is ultimately self-annihilation. We don't gain anything. Rather, we are going to lose everything. We lose the concepts of our mind, one after another, one category after another: people, objects, values. When all the concepts and categories are gone, only the nonconceptual awareness, which is a field of pure consciousness, remains. This spontaneously dissolves into its under-lying ground, absolute nonbeing, total absence of being. This nonbeing, when we recognize it as the ground and inner secret of all of reality, is the night of reality, the inner of the inner. This is the Guest.

SEVEN

Here's Looking at You

I thought I'd start this talk with one of the classical sayings of the Prophet Muhammad: Whosoever knoweth himself knoweth the Lord. Then, on second thought, I noticed it didn't exactly express the spirit of the times. So I modified it: Whosoever knoweth himself or herself, knoweth the truth. That is more what we do here, expressed in the spirit of the times. But still I wasn't satisfied. It sounds a bit too sanctimonious. That is not exactly how I look at our work.

Guidance finally intervened and gave me the title for this talk: a modern saying that goes, "Here's looking at you, kid." That better expresses the spirit of what we do here.

So how does this expression reveal our work? It describes precisely where we start. We start looking here and now. You are looking at me, and as you are looking toward here, you have in your mind that I am sitting here. I am an individual sitting here in a chair looking at you and talking. I don't necessarily experience my-self as someone who is sitting here looking at you. I might not be experiencing myself as someone who is sitting in a chair. I might not be the one who is talking. I might experience a sixty-headed being sitting in this room, each face looking at another face. So this gives us an entry into what we want to talk about today.

Our approach to inner work is not oriented toward solving problems or relieving emotional issues, al-though that is partly what has to happen just to get to the point of what we do want to do. I'm not interested in turning toward some spiritual or transcendental re-ality to pray to or to worship. Our interest here is to find out what the present situation is. What is it that is actually here? What is it that is actually now? You can explore what's really here, instead of starting from a place of assuming you already know what you want to happen, whether it's to divorce your husband, or to get a different job, or to see God, or to dissolve in the void. All of these things are fine to do in your life. Why not? But how about really finding out what is actually here? Is there such a thing as a husband? Is there God? Is there a void? If these things do exist, what are they?

We investigate reality with the attitude of "Here's looking at you, kid." We explore with an attitude of affection, appreciation, and celebration. We inquire openly into what's here, with love and tenderness. So we begin by examining the situation in which we find ourselves. There are people sitting here. Everyone is looking and listening. Someone is talking. We see tables and chairs and lights. But these are notions we bring with us. This is a table because that is what your mother taught you. Your mother told you it was a table, and you heard it repeated many times by many people. You have believed that there are tables. You realize that there are many things: tables, houses, people, emotions, God, this and that. All of these things that you were told actually exist became your universe. And then you have lived your life from that learned perspective.

The work we do questions all that we have learned. Is there such a thing as a table? Is it true that sometimes I am sad or hurt or angry? What does it mean to get married? Who are we? What the hell is here? What is this world? What is reality? What is life? And once I know what I am, what this world is, what reality is, what humanity is, I want to find out how I am supposed to live. What is life and how do I go about living it?

When people begin any path of work, they carry with them their ton of cabbage. This refers to all of their ideas about the world and their expectations that the path will teach them how to be happy in the world they know. They want to be given recipes for preparing tastier cabbage. But real work schools try to get rid of your ton of cabbage altogether, all your ideas and your beliefs about who you are and what reality is. You drop not only your ton of cabbage, but also you drop your clothes, shed your skin, and lose your mind. So the ton of cabbage includes the one who carries it.

As I see it, we do not engage the inner work in order to be enlightened and live a happy life. That is not the meaning of realization. Realization means finding out what is really here now. When you find out what is really here, it becomes obvious what to do and how to live. And then, if you do it, if you are courageous enough, lionhearted enough, to venture into the unknown, which means nothing but letting go of what you know, then you realize that the world you live in is a world of mystery, a world of wonder, a world of

beauty. The world is magic. If we allow ourselves to
see the world without our ton of cabbage, what we see
is full of wonder and mystery all the time. It's beautiful, colorful, magical, transforming each moment.

When you see reality as it is, your mind dissolves.
Instantly. Your mind cannot know what reality is. Are
there human beings here? Are there individuals here?
That is what we believe. That is one of the ways of
seeing reality. But is that the only way of seeing and
experiencing what is here? Am I really an individual,
a man of such and such an age, who was born to my
father and mother, had my brother and sisters, went
to school, had my problems? And here I am now sitting talking to you. That is the common way of seeing
it, from the perspective of what our mothers taught
us. But as I see it, the person who was born many
years ago is forever gone. And the person who lived
yesterday is also gone. And the person who said the
last sentence is now gone. I am not saying these things
because I am somebody who lost his ego. This is a fact
for everybody all the time. All of reality is mysterious
and new from moment to moment.

You saw somebody yesterday and you see them
again now, so you think they are the same person.
How can that be? How can something that existed
yesterday—and yesterday is no more—exist now? You
came through the door. You sat here. You think that
the person who came through the door is the one who
is sitting now. But the person who came through the
door doesn't exist anymore. That moment in time and
space, that existence of somebody going through that
door, is gone. That person exists only in your memory. The person who is here is the person who is sitting now. This person isn't the person who entered
through the door. The person who is sitting now is a

person who is appearing in front of my eyes right now. Everyone here is appearing spontaneously, in this instant and place. This is what I mean when I say the world is full of magic when we allow ourselves to see without our usual ideas and beliefs of who we are and what the world is.

As it appears to me, the world is amazing. Human beings are especially amazing. The body that we have is a sensory organ, an organ of perception that is an eye through which the universe can experience itself. There is the universe—the stars and the galaxies, empty space, earth, ocean, rocks, and all the physical manifestation. Every once in a while there is a soft spot in this universe. This soft spot has become so soft that it perceives its environment. That is what a human being is. Why not look at the world this way? Why look at it as if you are a human being who is born one day, only to die another day, with problems and spouses and taxes in between? Why not look at it as if you were an organ of perception for the universe? There is no other way for the universe to know itself. Whether you choose to call it God or the cosmic being or the universe, there is no way for that existence to perceive, to experience, to live, except through living beings.

Being human is being a magical, amazing kind of eye or sensory organ that can experience and live all kinds of things. We can know the universe and the nature of reality in all of its levels and dimensions and manifestations, in all of its aspects and richness, beauty and wonder. To engage the work is to participate in this world, in this magical universe. We don't work to solve emotional problems. We don't work to have religious experiences. We work to participate in the real world. The world as it really exists, not the world that we have been conditioned to see. It is mind-blowing to realize the nature and extent of our conditioned beliefs about the world. If you look at the universe objectively, it lives, pulses, and breathes. Everything is alive. The world is one living, huge, infinite, eternal kind of beingness.

To lose this teeming aliveness in order to experience ourselves as little things walking around in the street, driving cars, having our emotional problems, is itself an amazing occurrence. It begs investigation. That is what is meant by "whosoever knoweth himself."

To know yourself, to know who you are, is to find out what the hell you are. What is it that is you? Are you still what you were knowing yourself to be when you were thirteen years old? Most of us have been told we were born. And then one day, around age three or so, we said, "Oh, that's me. My name is Hameed. Hi, Mommy. Hi, Daddy. Good to see you." We started living our life as if what we were told was true. Everybody addressed you as a certain kind of entity. They called you to them, they told you to go away, they punished you and rewarded you, and after a while you believed that you were the person to whom all that was happening. You are someone sitting here, walking around, eating things. That is who you are. That is what reality is. You take it for granted. Then you have to go through the whole big mess of therapy and go to a spiritual school to find out that is not who you are or what the world is.

Our mother and father, our teachers and society, taught us that there is this entity, this individual that parks the car, walks through the door, and now sits here listening. I don't perceive it that way. What I perceive is that being pops into existence in different places. Now it pops up here. You would see it that way if we eliminated the concept of time. Your mother told you that you were born on such and such a date. That doesn't mean anything to a kid. But after years of hearing it, by the time you're seven or eight, you figure out that there is something called time. What is time? You never saw it, but they tell you it exists, so after a while you believe them.

And we spend the rest of our lives trying to make the world, ourselves, our reality, conform to an idea, to a world that we created when we were very young. That activity consumes a tremendous amount of energy. You try to create an entire universe that doesn't exist. All the time, each one of us expends an enormous amount of energy, effort, and attention trying to create a reality that doesn't actually exist. Day and night we fight to keep reality in place. Even when we sleep, the struggle continues in our dreams. Molding reality to fit an image in your head creates vast human suffering.

Eventually, one day you begin to wonder why you are suffering. Maybe because the one you fell in love with loves somebody else? If he just loved you, everything would be fine. You feel rejected and worthless, go to a therapist, work on your history, notice something about how your mother didn't want you. But what if the problem is not that the man didn't love you but that things are just not like that? There is no man and no you in the way you think of it. Men and women do exist, but not necessarily in the way we think of them. Maybe they exist as fingers of the hand. I sometimes call people God-fingers. Have you heard that expression? Imagine you are a finger that belongs to the hand that belongs to the body. Now, if the finger believes and behaves as if it exists on its own, as an individual with its own self and will and volition, it will create a lot of trouble for itself and for the rest of the body. Imagine the havoc.

Now imagine this finger going to another finger for therapy. "I have this problem. This finger doesn't love me, it loves this other finger." The therapist might think, "Yes, I can see that this finger doesn't love you. We have to find you one that does." But if the finger is wise, it realizes that it is not really a finger, but that it belongs to a hand. You are not an isolated finger. You don't walk around by yourself. You belong to a larger thing. And if you realize that you participate in a larger thing, you realize that the connecting fabric, the connecting substance that unites everything, is love. From this perspective, what does it mean that that person doesn't love me?

We are all made of love anyway. Fingers are made of love. The hand is love. So we notice that the way we normally look at emotional problems stems from a fundamentally wrong perspective about ourselves, about reality, and about life. Correcting that perspective is what resolves emotional suffering. It's not easy, because for years and years we have believed that we are separate fingers. To realize the perspective that we are God-fingers is to participate in the mystery of existence.

Existence is far more vast than you think. By believing we know what it is, we stop it. We make it stand still, static, and we fit it into a certain mold. We make reality old and stale. It is no longer new, no longer fresh. We deprive it of wonder and mystery. That's why we engage this work—to understand the fixation of that specific, rigid, frozen way of experiencing and seeing the world. True understanding allows reality and ourselves to unfold, to change, to manifest all of the richness and variety of being. The entryway to this world of wonder, magic, and beauty is who we are. So if you know yourself, that human person is the opening, the door into that mystery. Being human, in fact, is the expression of that mystery. The most perfect expression of the mystery that exists is the human being. The human being has the potential not only to perceive and experience and see the totality of existence, but to *be* existence and to live existence.

We start knowing ourselves in childhood as individuals who grow and develop, mostly thinking of ourselves as the body. But we can more thoroughly know what we are by truthfully and affectionately investigating our experience. We may discover that a significant dimension of living is the illumination of its particulars and its nature. We realize that the finger that becomes the hand that becomes the body is only the beginning. The body is the totality of the universe. The universe isn't inanimate. It lives and breathes. The world is made of consciousness, of beingness, of love. The way to know the world is to look not at rocks but at ourselves. When I say to look inward, I don't mean inside your body but into your nature, into your subjectivity. Looking inward means investigating the nature of what you happen to be at any moment.

Whosoever knoweth himself knoweth the truth. When you know yourself, you will know the truth in the totality of its various manifestations. The world we see, this physical universe, is the surface expression of a multifaceted reality. Those black volcanic rocks look pink inside, and within the pink there is bright yellow, and inside the yellow is this living, roaring purple, and within the living, roaring purple are mysterious lights. Usually you can't see that by looking at the rocks. You have to look at the sensory organ itself, the human being.

To see, participate, and live in reality is our inheritance as human beings. So how do we go about doing that? The method of the Diamond Approach is to know yourself, to know precisely the nature of what you are. The more exactly you know who you are, the further you delve into the mystery of existence. You see things you've never seen or imagined. Things that your mother never mentioned, that your father never conceived. And the further you go, the more things keep emerging. After a while you realize that your body is very light. At the beginning everyone says that their body is heavy. When you begin to experience essential states, you seem to be delicate and soft, while the body seems sort of thick. In time you realize your body is very light.

What you are is much more substantial and real than the body. The relationship between what you are and the body is like the relationship between a rock and a feather. You are a rock and the body is a feather. Your beingness is more real, more substantial, more there, more indestructible, than the body, which we usually regard as the ultimate and most substantial reality. Inner work does not lead you to subtler things in the sense of less substantial things. Although the body becomes less substantial in some sense, the experience of consciousness and being becomes more substantial. The body as we usually know it is ultimately an idea, a thought created by that immense beingness.

So I'm giving you examples here and there of what I mean by mystery and wonder. Imagine living your life like this. Imagine living your life in the wonder of not knowing what will happen next. I don't mean not knowing whether someone will reject you or love you. I mean not knowing as you walk through a doorway whether you will exist on the other side of it, not knowing whether you will exist as a two-legged being or a ball of light or a flying diamond. You don't have the vaguest idea what is going to happen next. And if you walk through the door thinking you'll be a two-legged being, a ball of light, or a flying diamond, by the time you cross the threshold you realize that you are a rolling planet. What actually arises is amazing.

What is consciousness? What is the nature of the human being, the human soul? Many systems, disciplines, and practices want to correct the universe, want to correct our life from the smallness of one limited perspective. Such activity is not only endless, but ultimately it is fruitless. Many systems devise a treatment for the entire body of the universe based on the examination of a single unhealthy toe. No matter how healthy the toe gets, the remedy is not useful for the rest of the body. Single-minded adherence to any one perspective misses the magic of existence. Romantic relationships, fame, and success are paltry compared with the wonder of the world. They are not the true mature pleasures and delights of the human being. I'm not saying they are unimportant. They need to happen. Everyone needs to find love in his or her life; each of us must be able to work to support ourselves. These things sustain the physical and emotional parts of us so that we can rest and be quiet and allow ourselves to be, allow the wonders of the world to bubble up. And finally they become direct expressions of the mystery of reality, different venues for this truth to reveal further mysteries.

How do we go about knowing ourselves? What are you? What is the self? What is the soul? What is essence? What the self is depends on the level or dimension from which your mind operates. The answer changes according to your capacity to perceive, according to how sensitive you are. The sensitivity of the human organ of perception transubstantiates and

matures. Perception becomes more nuanced and refined. One of the main contributions of modern Western
psychology is that it explores the realm of emotions.
The movement of awareness from the physical level
to the emotional level is, in most cases, a refinement
in perception. It is important to experience and operate from the perspective of emotions. The capacity
for a genuine and loving relationship with openness,
pleasure, and mutual respect is an expansion of being
human. Feeling the value of work and creativity and
friendship refines the soul.

Other dimensions manifest when we realize the
perspective of human emotions. As we become established in our feelings, whole new realms open to perception. The self or soul relaxes and settles whenever
it actualizes a certain dimension. That settledness and
contentment invite new and more refined perception.
To become established in the various dimensions of
existence is to become human. If you allow your mind
to be open without enshrining your experience as final, your perception of reality becomes more discern-
ing and complete. You can appreciate and enjoy where
you are while remaining open to change.

You might be lying in bed with your lover after making love, feeling relaxed and good, and as you look at
your lover, you might see a ring of pearls around her
head. A crown of pearls and diamonds that makes her
look like a queen. She might notice that she feels like a
queen. And you feel a sense of majesty, as if you were
a king. You realize you're wearing purple robes and a
crown with gold and silver. By being relaxed and contented in that moment, your beingness has manifested
as a new dimension, a new facet of knowing who you
are. You didn't know and weren't looking for it.

If you were looking for it, you probably wouldn't find it. As the satisfaction, the contentment, and the settledness relax the tensions in your mind and in your being, your perception becomes more clear and intelligent. You perceive the surface of things in an entirely new way. Everything that you perceive is a surprise. The world wears a new skin. And you experience yourself in a way that you've never known. You see that we are of royal descent. There are stories that say that human beings are royal born. You realize that the royalty is essence itself, being itself, the nature of the soul. The true self has a pure blood, a royal quality whose preciousness bears a quality of gold, silver, diamonds, and pearls. You might experience yourself as a prince or princess, a king or queen. That is the human dimension, what I call the personal dimension, of essence emerging. Some traditions refer to the personal dimension as the realm of power or the realm of individual source.

As the restricted self—what we call the ego—lets go, its very substance unfolds like a flower. The ego doesn't die, it transforms. The ego is nothing but the perspective of the surface of the soul, which is the true being. Many spiritual traditions go on about slaying the ego. But you can't kill the ego. There is no separate thing that is ego. The ego is action, simply an activity that fastens your being, your soul, your psyche, and your self in a particular way. The ego becomes rigid, fixated, and forms a dry plaster on your gut that restricts the movement of your soul. As the ego dissolves, you experience essence and being more directly. You might be sitting in a café when suddenly you experience yourself as an infinite, boundless emerald-green light. You can't help but see the pain and hurt of whoever passes in front of you, and your heart swells with kindness. You want to do whatever you can to alleviate their suffering. That is the emergence of the aspect of compassion.

But as you see, reality is quite a mystery, quite an amazing thing. You were this royal person wearing a crown and now you are a subtle, intelligent green light. Then someone looks at you, and you become self-conscious and remember your mommy, who told you not to look at her when she was in the bathroom. You put on your clothes again, the green light disappears, and you become a sulking little kid. And you think it's terrible that your ego has come back. But nothing has gone wrong. One reality has simply transformed into another reality. Imagine that this radiant, limit-less light suddenly becomes this little kid, sitting there sulking and afraid of his mommy. Isn't that amazing? How can that be?

That is what I mean when I say, "Here's looking at you, kid." No matter where you find yourself, there is wonder and change. But most of us refuse to believe that's how things are. We cling to the self with two legs, two arms, and two eyes who sometimes has an experi-ence of light. It's like Chuang-tzu wondering, "Am I a butterfly dreaming that I am Chuang-tzu, or am I Chuang-tzu dreaming that I am a butterfly?" You can find out only by examining where you are. If at the mo-ment you are light, then you are light. Now you dis-cover you are a body, so you are a body. But habitually you return to being the person your mother and father and everyone you've known for the last thirty years say you are. You revert to what is familiar. Otherwise, who will do what needs to be done? That is the fear. If you are this wonderful light or this jeweled queen, then who is going to clean the house tomorrow?

This fear arises when a person has not completely established the aspect of the emerald compassion, which has to do with trusting reality. When it comes time to clean, you will become a person with a broom, walking around sweeping the dust. It will happen. It never fails. It's not necessary to believe every second that you are a person who can hold a broom for you to be able to use a broom tomorrow. You will be able to use a broom tomorrow even if right now you are the universe. Even if right now you are a rolling, thundering planet.

Working with basic trust involves exploring your relationship with your parents during early childhood to see how you stopped trusting reality and trusting who you are because you couldn't trust your environment. Basic trust is the perspective that the human being has all the capacities to take care of various situations. What's the worst that could happen? You could die? So you die. What's the big deal? If you die, you become something else instead of someone who walks around with two legs. God knows what you will be. Brilliant light or an infinite universe or decaying matter or whatever your religion happens to believe. There is no experience that has to be looked at as a bad thing that should be avoided. The usual way we think of ourselves has a beginning and an end. It is only a small part of our human potential.

Do you ever think about it? Every once in a while I sit in bed at night before I fall asleep and think: If I die, what does that mean? One of these days I'll be gone. I wonder how that will be. What does it mean that one day I just stop walking, stop thinking, stop talking to people, stop going for the groceries? Something else is going to happen. Something entirely unknown. Contemplating that in a serious way can allow us to start contemplating who we are. To really answer the question of what death is, you have to answer the question of what life is. What is it that is you living this life? If you think of yourself as this body, this biological, physical organism that breathes oxygen and eats stuff, then it is understandable to think that you will die and the atoms will go back to the earth.

But if you think further, you realize that there are things that are not explained by thinking of yourself merely as a physical organism. How can this body, this physical thing, have dreams at night? When you are dreaming at night and you are walking in your dream and talking to people, it seems real. You feel things. You sense things. Everything is as real as it is now. How does that happen? Something in your mind can create a reality out of nothing. You are in bed. You are doing nothing. But in your experience there is a whole universe you've created that is exactly like this universe. But when you wake up, you say, "Oh, that was just a dream. This is the real thing." How do you know? If we have the capacity to create a dream and live in a dream in which everything feels real, then we have the capacity to create what we are doing right now. Maybe we are creating sitting here together just as we create our dreams in sleep. One of the perceptions that a person has at deeper levels of consciousness is the realization that all of reality is a manifestation of the mind. It is amazing to contemplate that this whole universe is actually created from the very stuff of your consciousness.

So there is a mystery of existence. There is a participation in the mystery of existence. The way to participate in the mystery of existence is to know who you are. And to know who you are is to start from where you are and to be open and relaxed and curious about what you might be. That allows the unfoldment, the emergence, of your being in its various facets and dimensions. But saying that is still a little vague. As we know, it is not that easy.

I want to talk a little bit about the actual work we do. What are its basic qualities and attitudes? This is where Bogart comes in: "Here's looking at you, kid." First, we look and investigate. But it is not the usual scientific way of looking at things. It is objective in the sense that you really want to know what you are looking at. You really want to experience and know it as accurately as possible. But you are going about it with the eyes of the lover. Bogart, as Rick in *Casablanca*, wasn't carrying around a microscope examining things. He was being really appreciative, lovingly looking at Ilsa's face and seeing its beauty. He was celebrating that communion, that experience of being with a being that he loves. So that is one of the basic attitudes of this work. The attitude of appreciation, of love, of tenderness and affection. So when you look at yourself, it is important to do it with love and appreciation. If you are looking at your ego in order to get rid of it, it is going to hide. The ego experiences itself as a little kid. If you are looking to slay it, what is the kid going to do? It is not going to reveal itself. It will say, "God, this guy is going to kill me; where is the best place I can hide?"

So you want to know yourself, not because you want something out of it, not because you want to solve your problems, not because you want to get rid of certain parts of yourself, but because you are really interested. When you are with a lover, you want to know who he is because you are curious about what you love, not because you want to decide whether to marry him or not. If you are on a date firing off one question after another in order to determine whether the two of you will make a good match, that is not an attitude of appreciation. "How old are you? How many kids have you had?" That's not love, you see. It is a cold and scientific way of trying to know. You want to know with affection, with tenderness, with compassion, with true appreciation and value of the being you are confronting. Whatever you call it, ego or soul or self or body, it doesn't matter.

The basic attitude in the Diamond Approach is to go about knowing where you are in terms of loving the truth for its own sake. You want to find out the truth about who you are, not because you want something out of it. Not because you want to be enlightened. Not because you want to be happier in your life. Not because you want to be more successful. But because you really love the truth. When you are really interested in a person or an activity or a place, you love finding out about it; you lose yourself in some sense. You are not self-centered. You go about it with love and appreciation and curiosity. That attitude is of paramount importance in terms of exploring ourselves. Otherwise, the beingness will not unfold. If we go about it from a purely therapeutic perspective, or from a purely scientific perspective, the unfoldment will not happen. The parts will just rearrange themselves in some different way.

But for the unfoldment to happen, the essence child within us, that part of us that is vulnerable, delicate, pure, and innocent, but also scared, must let itself be there. The wonder of reality appears when we look with the attitude of lovingness, tenderness, and sweetness. Of course, a lot of times we don't have it. A person might come to a private teaching session and say, "I hate myself. Will you help me?" And I say, "What do you mean, help you?" The person says, "I want to get rid of this trouble." My job then is to sort of turn the person around to being a little softer about themselves, a little more compassionate or loving. The attitude of "I hate myself, my life is terrible, I want to change it" only generates more hatred and suffering. The investigation of the truth of yourself and reality is a heart concern. It shouldn't come from the mind. Your heart has to be engaged and interested out of true consideration, true love, true appreciation.

To know who you are, you have to be curious about the truth in addition to having a loving attitude about yourself. You have to develop the sense of lighthearted curiosity. That is another wing of the approach. Not just appreciating reality, but being curious about it. You are not only looking at it lovingly, but you want to find out about it. You don't look at the face of your lover and say, "You are pretty, I love you, you are wonderful," and stop there. You want to find out more. You want to undress the lover, touch here, investigate there. You are not investigating because you want to get something out of it. You are investigating because you are really curious. "What makes you tick? How come your shoulders are different from my shoulders?" You can spend half an hour examining shoulders. It is a love affair that has not only love but also an openness of heart in terms of curiosity. You want to delve into it and find out what is really there. I am using the analogy of love and the lover because knowing the truth is basically like making love. Neither is about just having your discharge. Both are ways of knowing yourself and another being in an intimate way, with some kind of contact that is exquisite and unique and constantly changing.

The childlike quality of the heart manifests as curiosity. Children want to know about everything. What is this and why is that? That attitude has to be there when you want to know what is here. You don't want to leave any stone unturned. You want to know not from the goal-oriented scientific mind of trying to figure something out, but from the joy and wonder in every moment of discovery. If you really get into knowing what is here, each moment feels like the first time—just like a child who repeats something over and over again without losing any delight or interest. When you explore what is here and now, everything is always for the first time. Who we are is such an infinite richness. If we allow ourselves to go through that investigation, that loving and curious investigation, that then becomes life. Life is nothing but the unfoldment of who we are. Life is not about going to school, getting a job, getting married, having kids, going through a midlife crisis, getting old, getting sick. That is not life. Life is the unfoldment of the richness that is a human being. But if at the age of twenty-two or whenever you graduate, you say, "This is who I am. Now I am going to get this job and marry that person," and you want who you take yourself to be to carry you through life, then you are already dead. You have already stopped. So, as you see, investigating who you are, doing the work, is nothing but authentic living. What you discover, what you experience, what you feel, is limitless.

There will come a time when you realize that the inner experiences you have disappear when you're at the grocery store. Why is that? It is strange; you sit and meditate and dissolve in bliss; you wake up full of wonder. But then you go to the grocery store or the movies and you're the same clunky old guy. What happened? How come when I am walking through the grocery store I don't experience myself as a rolling planet? I am always a two-legged being. It took me three years to investigate that phenomenon. Then I realized that there is something, an aspect of being, a way of experiencing oneself, that I never thought about. I didn't see that I am not only a body that walks around, I am not only a beingness, I am not only a loving consciousness, but also I am an organism of consciousness. I am not only a body that is inhabited by some kind of impersonal consciousness, I am actually a living organism, a living presence that moves, that does, that feels, that thinks. And the body, the way I see it, is the external sheath, the external manifestation of that organism. For that organism to really function, to go through the grocery store and pick out the oranges and radishes, that organism will have to be understood and integrated and realized. Then I can function in this world, in this physical universe, not only as a body, but as a body of consciousness. And that body of consciousness is the subtle reality that underlies what we call ego or personality.

That body of consciousness needs all the various realizations of essence and being and consciousness and emptiness in order to operate. With those elements, you realize that you can truly think for the first time. Thinking is not a haphazard passing of thoughts. You can actually think with focus, with direction, with smoothness and flow. Your mind is completely clear, completely void, completely absent. In that absence and absolute void, thinking occurs for the first time. Thoughts are real for the first time, rather than habitual modes of cogitating. Not only can you think, you can actually feel. You realize that your usual feelings were reactions from the past, pseudo-feelings. But now this human organism of consciousness can actually feel for the first time. You can be a loving organism, a loving human being. Not only can you exist as love, but love is integrated into the human being in the sense that your very substance flows as love. You can feel sad, you can feel concerned, but the feeling has to do with what is here and now.

Feeling sad is the complete response to what is happening now from who you are in this very moment, not from your past history. And then you realize that you can act, you can move. You can really move your hand. Before, your hand moved mechanically. If you really move your hand slowly, you realize that it jerks as messages go from the hand to the brain. That experience is the body of consciousness actually moving for the first time. And that body of consciousness that moves can go to the store. But if you don't go about knowing what you are in an open, curious, and loving way, you won't perceive the human organism of consciousness that does, feels, and thinks for the first time.

As you see, every problem that arises is an indication of something that we still don't know. This is one of the premises of the Diamond Approach. Every personal problem signals something about yourself and reality that you don't understand and that you have not integrated. Difficulties are invitations to investigate with curiosity and find out what is actually here. When you begin to investigate a problem, you realize that some part of you is not there. You encounter a hole in your beingness and consciousness that feels as if something were missing. If you go about investigating what is missing with sincerity and truthfulness and curiosity, you will start to find out about it. Your love affair with knowing what you are will deepen. What you find out will not necessarily be a solution to your problem, but a realization of who you are. And the problem fades away in some way.

Loving the truth for its own sake means you love the truth because you want to know it, not because you want something out of it. That is why I don't like it when somebody says they're going to pray to God so God will forgive them and save them. For me, that is not a true attitude. If you ask anything from God, you should say, "God, do whatever you want to do and let me find out what it is. I just want to see what you do, God. Whatever you want to do with me is fine; I just know that I am really interested in participating." That is a true religious attitude. But to pray, saying, "How miserable I am, and my wife left me, and I need some money too, why don't you enlighten me, send me an angel?"—all that stuff is making a business deal with God. That is not a love affair. The way to the truth is more like a love affair.

Of course, there is a place for a scientific approach in the sense that truth is precise, exact, and definite. If you really love the truth, you want to know it exactly as it is. And if you want to know it as it is, you have to cut away the bullshit. You have to be exact and precise.

So right now, what am I experiencing in myself? Do I know exactly? Well, I'm sort of feeling depressed today. That is not enough. It doesn't do it. If you are really curious, what does depressed mean? Heavy? Sad? Is there a temperature? Where do I feel it? What does it make me see? How does it make me look at my life? You have to go about finding out the truth with exactness and precision as well as tenderness and appreciation. Real scientists go about their work with equal measures of rigor and love.

To know the truth, you have to be both a scientist and an artist. To really go about doing the work from the perspective of truth, you have to unify the two sides of the brain. You have to be rational and intuitive at the same time. Loving truth for its own sake creates some kind of sincerity, some kind of humility and honesty about who and what we are. Am I angry but pretending

to love? Do I want something from you while pretending to give you something? You have to be ruthlessly
honest here, out of loving the truth and loving who you
are and who the other is. Your will engages with exact
and utmost precision. You want to see exactly why you
are doing this and what it's about. So as you see, knowing the truth is a precise, scientific way of looking at
what's here now. You don't just open yourself to grace
and sit there waiting for something to happen. Although
that's part of what is necessary, our interest and participation have to be more wholehearted. You want to
put something into it. You want to put into it care,
commitment, effort—whatever it takes. You want to
really grapple with it, whatever it is, whether it feels
painful or good.

One of the biggest blocks in working with oneself,
and in life in general, is that when things hurt, we want
not to feel them or deal with them. We only want to get
rid of the pain. As for pleasure, we want to enjoy it and
have good times with it, but we don't necessarily want
to investigate it. Loving truth for its own sake means
you don't have either of those attitudes. Whether you
hurt or feel good, you still want to know what it's about.
What does it mean? What is it a sign of? Where is it
going to lead me? What does it mean about who I am?
What does it mean about this universe? People complain a lot that this world is full of suffering that no one
seems to be able to alleviate. That certainly is how it
looks. But what are you going to do? Are you going to
feel helpless or messianic? How about finding out what
it means? When I say that the world is full of suffering,
what does that mean? Is it really full of suffering? What
kind of suffering? What is the suffering about?

So, to completely engage in knowing who and what
you are, you need the attitude of "Here's looking at

you, kid." Knowing the truth is a love affair. We go about it with true sincerity, which is appreciating the truth, and all of the lively, playful curiosity that will allow our minds to open. Curiosity already indicates that you accept that there is something you don't know. If you are investigating something, you have to go about it with ignorance. If you don't allow your mind to be open, you can't be truly curious. So you have to start from a place of not knowing, which is not easy for us to do. Most of the time, we assume we know something. What if you feel or experience something and you approach it like a little kid? You haven't seen this before; what could it be?

Not knowing, forgetting all that you think you know, opens the centers in the head. The centers of perception and understanding are blocked by the belief that you know something when you don't actually know. It's that simple. If you believe that you see things as they are, or that you know things as they are, the centers of perception and understanding are blocked because you are taking an illusion to be reality. You are looking at your mind instead of at reality. So the way to do it is to always be ignorant. Why do you need to know anyway? Why do you need to feel that you already know all the time? What's so wonderful about that? The transition from not knowing to knowing is far more wonderful than the feeling of "I know," because the feeling of "I know" is not a discovery.

You might know God because God comes in front of you and says, "Here I am, look at me." You say, "Good, that is God, how exciting." And tomorrow you say, "I know what God is." Three days later, God is an old memory, old stuff, no good. God loses its power, its beauty. The discovery that God is sitting there is joyous; remembering it three days later is stale. True joy is seeing what's new and different, the freshness of who we are, what other people are, what reality is, what truth is here and now. True happiness perceives the changing, never-ceasing process of emerging, of happening, of appearing and manifesting. That is a happy life.

Knowing the truth of who and what we are is painful in the beginning because what arises is our personal unconscious, which contains our memories of hurt and pain and fear. But being willing to go through the swamps is the price we pay for a few years. What helps us get through it is our loving curiosity about the truth. And as you see, the curiosity that is based on truth requires an openness in the mind, a sense of presence and thereness without needing to believe that you already know. As your curiosity is engaged, you realize that you need some kind of strength to keep going toward the truth, because sometimes things are difficult. You might feel weak and hopeless. But if you are really curious, you will wonder what the feeling of weakness is about. You don't try to block it; you will allow it to be there just as it is. What does this weakness feel like? You notice that your right side feels shriveled up. You see images of yourself as small and helpless. You let it happen and wonder why you feel weak, because you're not a little kid now. Asking that question indicates that the aspect of intelligence is functioning in your brain. These are intelligent questions to ask.

To stay with your experience without manipulating it means you have to be objective about what's here. Objectivity doesn't mean being cold. Objectivity means not laying your trips on what's actually here. True objectivity does not mean that you are unfeeling but that you are full of love for the truth. To be objective means that you don't burden what's actually here with your preconceptions and ideas from the past. You simply let it be as it is. In examining your weakness, you see that you have to eliminate your associations, reactions, and beliefs about it. You have to find out what this weakness is right now. If you really go about it that way, the hole of weakness emerges, which is the opening for the aspect of strength. And suddenly strength arises and you are this raging fire. You have the courage and excitement, the openness and curiosity, to go on finding out who you are and what the world is.

Different things arise as you investigate who and what you are. You have some experience of openness, love, curiosity, and strength. For example, maybe one day as you walk down the street, you realize that your knee hurts. You go to the chiropractor. The next week your other knee goes out. The chiropractor fixes it. In a few days your sacrum is not right. Going to the chiropractor again won't work, so you go to an acupuncturist. The acupuncturist balances your meridians. You feel great for a whole week. On the eighth day, your hip goes out. If you are intelligent, you might start to wonder what's going on. First this, then that. What is this? Am I getting old? I'm only thirty-five. If you investigate and really sense yourself, you realize at some point that you exist only from the waist up. You have no legs. No wonder your legs are going out; you've been walking on something that you actually don't feel. Realizing that your lower body, your support, is gone is one of the ways of experiencing the lack of will.

After a while it feels as if you can't go on. You haven't got what it takes to continue. The will to persist has disappeared along with the lower half of your body. It's as if your bones got mushy or leathery, cartilage-like, wobbly. These are ways in which people experience the absence of the actual sense of will. You might get curious at this point and wonder what it means that your legs feel like cartilage. You have bones, but they feel soft. You feel as if you can't walk right. It's fine to go to a chiropractor if you are hurting, but to know the truth, you have to be interested in finding out about this phenomenon.

If you are curious about the truth, you follow where your experience leads. You have no legs, no will, you feel castrated, you can't really move. You notice that some armor around your pelvis and legs that used to support your sense of identity is softening. As your investigation into who you are changes that sense of identity, the old support is no longer adequate. If you stay there without resisting and gently, compassionately, and lovingly investigate what's happening, your strength and courage are engaged. After a while you realize that a certain aspect emerges. You see a shift to a more fundamental sense of support. Suddenly your legs are solid, like mountains. Nothing can stop them. One of the ways the aspect of will manifests is as a solidity, an immensity of support for the process of being.

It's true that your kidney meridian affects your legs. But to correct the kidney meridian is a temporary measure. The will aspect of being is what allows you to move solidly from an essential level. When true support is absent, in time not only the kidney meridian but all kinds of meridians will go. This is not to say that there is no use for the chiropractor or the acupuncturist. They have their area of usefulness, but there are other areas where you personally are responsible. Your inner practice is what develops will, strength, joy, compassion, and openness of mind.

As you go about exploring who and what you are, experiencing various qualities of essence, one day you realize that you are not a person at all. You have been walking around like an automaton, unable to make personal contact with anybody. Everyone seems like an object to you. You can even feel loving and compassionate without feeling like a real human being. Experiencing inner states does not necessarily make you a real human being who interacts with others and who has a human life. Not feeling like a person, you might feel ashamed, terrified of being found out. It's the last thing you would show anybody. You feel that you're missing something very basic, that you lack something fundamental. Everyone feels this lack because it is the basic quality of ego, but no one wants to tell anyone else.

When you have not realized your being, it is true that you haven't got it, that there is something that you are not in touch with. If you allow that sense of lack, that sense of the incapacity to make personal contact with others, in time the personal essence will emerge in the heart center, which is vital to being a human being and living a real human life that is fulfilled in a genuine way. A large part of the fulfillment is what you are. You are the fulfillment. The process of discovering and exploring who you are is filled with joy, like the rejoicing of a little child who discovers something completely new. True living is full of joy, full of appreciation. You are discovering who you are. You are becoming intrinsically who you are.

In another sense, true living is the beginning of the unknown world. The world becomes full of richness and color. Most people experience the wonder of the world once in a while, but it's not a dominant way of life. When you are a real human being, the wonder of the world dominates. The usual personal mode of emotions and habits doesn't disappear, but recedes and dims. Other aspects of you create and participate in your life. When you leave yourself open, new things emerge. That is the natural way. The more you close your mind and think you are finished, the more you establish ego. When you are open to change, things flow easily and smoothly from one event to another.

In time you realize that you are not bound by the body. Sometimes I experience myself sitting in my own lap. What does that mean? What does the finger feel sitting in the hand? Is it like sitting in a chair? If you really investigate that, you might get interested in studying mathematical topology and multidimensional spaces. You might wonder how things fold into each other from different dimensions, how the dimension of consciousness melds into the physical dimension. You might buy a fancy, hand-blown Klein bottle or start playing with a Möbius strip. You realize that you are a four-dimensional being. The fourth dimension is more like consciousness and being. Not only are you a four-dimensional being, but you expand more and more, and come to realize that you are one with humanity. And that humanity is one beingness, one living being. At the core of who you are—at the center or heart of the soul—your experience is intimately connected with all humanity. The connection is not through your mind, but actually the way a finger is connected to another finger.

And if you go further, you realize that you are connected with and in fact *are* everything. That's what we call universal consciousness. You are the universe. The whole universe is the Logos, the Word. The universe is a beautiful harmony of everything as one being in constant transformation, one being in a constant state of resurrection. Even further, you realize that you are the mystery from which all of that comes. You can perceive the whole show, not just your personal show but the whole cosmic show, as something emerging and happening now. Not only do you emerge and transform, but the whole universe emerges and transforms. That state of transformation and change includes life and death and everything in between. All of this wonder is revealed through knowing who you are.

So, in my perception, things work better and are more enjoyable, more real and festive, if you go about the work from a perspective of love rather than a perspective of having a problem that needs to be solved. Starting from a problem-solving orientation gives you a fixed point of view. There is the world of problems and there is the world of mystery. The world of mystery contains the world of problems and a thousand things more. Better to discover those thousand things with the eyes of a lover, with the attitude of "Here's looking at you."

I don't like to look at the work we do as some kind of spiritual therapy, or a path to enlightenment, or any of those things that give people strange ideas about what's supposed to be happening. We are not trying to live according to someone's ideal. I like to look at what we do as finding out who we are and what this world we are living in is. Who are we? What is this world? How do we live? We find out simply by examining what is here now. From that perspective, there is no end to knowing the truth. Who you are changes, flows, and transforms from moment to moment. Your body changes. Your environment changes. Everything changes at each moment. What we see is the changing surface. When we perceive only the changes on the skin of Being, we are not yet looking at the totality of Being. When we realize Being and see its totality rather than just the outermost layer, we realize that Being is change all the way down.

So now we will have questions.

STUDENT: Does the realization of Being require years of working on oneself in various ways, or can it happen spontaneously?

ALMAAS: I think it always happens spontaneously, except most of us miss it. We miss its manifestation because we want to hold on to some other perspective. Being can't help but manifest all of the time, but we miss it because our mind is focused elsewhere. And we feel threatened if we don't focus on our usual concerns. So some people get to notice that being is happening spontaneously. Other people work on themselves, with or without a teacher or a school. Guidance is there to show you what is happening, and you learn to trust it in time. But really there is no other way for being to happen but spontaneously. The whole universe is a spontaneous happening.

STUDENT: Would you say something about the role of other people—teachers, students, family—in the process of development that you described?

ALMAAS: That is a whole subject in itself. You develop with or without a teacher, with or without family. If you have a family and a job, that becomes part of the process. You can't separate anything. You realize that you have to investigate your family and your life and your work. Then your life becomes enriched with new discoveries about yourself, about the truth. You can't separate your life from your process. Sometimes this creates problems for people. By investigating yourself, you might realize that you've held a certain job for your whole life just to please your father, but that your heart is not really in it. You might not want the job or might feel bored with it; you might want something else. Or you might be angry with your dad. You will feel separation and grief until you start doing something that is more in accord with who you are. Other times, people find that their lives transform with the new discoveries, become filled with being. So it really depends on the person.

We do the work here in the context of our lives. People don't have to separate from their lives or isolate themselves, taking a period of a few years to go to some special place. We do this work as a part of our living. So we have our meetings regularly, every other week or so, and your life and your mind are part of what we investigate. We do the work as a part of life because ultimately the actual process of the work becomes your life.

STUDENT: I guess there's still something I'm looking at. I can't move one finger over here without this other finger coming along. I'm wondering about change and reactions against it.

ALMAAS: That will happen, yes. If someone begins to change, people around them will respond or react to those changes. People could feel positively affected by change or feel threatened by it. But it is not true that you can't move the finger away from the other fingers. Things are more organic and mysterious than we think. Two fingers might go together, or they might go their separate ways. Things happen normally, just as they do in regular life, but they can be seen a different way. For me, to participate in the real world does not mean anything unusual. I live a normal life, drive a car, have family and work and interests such as movies.

Living a normal life is an important cornerstone of our work because it tends to ground the work in our life instead of making it some kind of mystical, spiritual, otherworldly thing that exists apart from our daily experiences. This *is* the other world. This table, as you see it, is God's back. In the beginning, you might have all kinds of far-out experiences that separate the face from the back, the depth from the surface. In time you realize that the very world we live in, what we see, everything around us that looks like stone or rock, is really the love that we feel in our heart. The world lives in harmony and luminosity. And the more you see that, the more your need for love from other people relaxes. You pine after love, and one day you open your eyes and see that the rock is made of love. People see love manifesting all around them all the time, and yet they still want this one person to love them. Who cares about all this other love! But in time the love and the true beingness touch your consciousness. Your sense of ego dissolves a little and you relax. You become more reasonable and less of a brat.

The consciousness refines as you realize that things are what they are. Things change and transform. And if you want things to be a certain way instead of the way they are, you will suffer. That's one of the natural laws of the universe. But desire isn't simply a matter of being stubborn or acquisitive. It's more the idea that if you let go of that love affair, or the possibility of having just the right thing, or the right situation, or the right job, you are going to lose part of yourself, to expose another thing that you didn't know. So the moment you let go of the need for that person to love you,

you start feeling shaky inside yourself. You wanted to love so that you would feel supported, because you see yourself as a little infant that needs Mommy to hold you in her arms. And you see the deep identification that made you feel that you need someone to love you in order to feel support. When you see that and you feel vulnerable and empty, you expose another hole, which will take you further into the mystery of who you are. It does not mean you won't have somebody who loves you or somebody you love, but love becomes an expression of true being, not only a need of a separate individual.

The way I see it, the mystery is always being revealed. The transformation is always happening. What you perceive is a matter of the lens through which you look at reality. Some lenses disclose just a slice of reality, while others expose several slices, and there are those lenses that see telescopically, revealing reality all the way through. So it depends on which lens you look with. It's not that the world we see, the physical world, doesn't exist. The world exists, but as one dimension of how we see things. The world is far too wonderful and rich to be just one thing.

STUDENT: If we live in what's happening now, what happens to memory?

ALMAAS: I've recently been noticing that I forget a lot. There seem to be gaps, more than what is usual, when I'm talking about something that happened last year. I think this is a transitional state in the process of integration. Certain states, such as emptiness in the mind, interfere with personal memory. As you stabilize in the new state, memory becomes more normal. You remember, but you don't exactly control what you remember. You spontaneously remember what is needed.

If I try to remember something, I might not be able to, but if the need arises, I remember. So memory becomes more organic.

There is the need for a tremendous kind of trust, knowing that you are in good hands. We realize that our memory, our thought processes, our minds, begin to function in ways different from what we know and expect. Usually we use our memory and mind to define who we are and what the world is. We live in the past instead of being in the now. We use old ideas to constrain what is fresh and new. The tendency of memory to freeze our experience relaxes as we live in the now. Sometimes you might experience lapses of memory, but then you realize that the now has nothing to do with time. The now contains all time, and memory is a small part of your mind.

Memory is useful if you have to go somewhere and you need to remember how to get there. The mind helps you figure out how to make a meal, what things you need and how much, which recipe to use, where to buy the ingredients. If your mind is doing what it is supposed to do, things are fine. But the moment the mind reflects on who you are and what you are doing, problems arise. You might feel depressed or angry about having to cook and wish your mommy could do it for you. All sorts of issues come up around functioning in the world. But when you are actually thinking, what you need arises efficiently and completely in the moment. There is neither lack nor excess of what is needed. Memory is no longer reconstituting the past but is aiding the present.

STUDENT: Do you see any value or difficulties in using chemicals or drugs to reach various states of awareness?

ALMAAS: I'm not an authority on drugs. I've had some experience years ago, and I do read the literature here and there. I will say that drugs might help some people glimpse a certain reality. Drugs are useful insofar as they reveal that there is more to reality than you usually think. But I don't know. The research is still not conclusive about the harmful effects that drugs might have. In my experience, the states that arise naturally from the unfoldment of reality have a sense of groundedness and realness that doesn't exist in the drug experience.

The drug experience can also have various side effects, psychological and otherwise. Drugs might undermine your will, making you feel that your experience depends on drug use. Feeling that you need a drug to experience your being is similar to feeling that you need a lover to experience love. After a while, that need becomes a restriction. Some people can use drugs without having these things arise, but the human mind is complex and intricate. You might think you know yourself and can manage the effects of using drugs. But that is how most people feel before they get hooked on heroin or painkillers. There's no way to know how drugs will affect you. If someone tells me they want to do drugs, I don't forbid it. It's up to you. But I don't recommend it either. So, who knows? Maybe in time there will be enough research and knowledge so that we can know for sure.

STUDENT: You talk on the one hand about suspending judgment and not knowing, and on the other hand about making decisions and discriminating. How can these two things go together?

ALMAAS: The meaning of curiosity and discrimination changes as our investigation into who and what

: are proceeds. At the beginning, our inquiry is full of ego. In time you question whether the egoic perspective and its accompanying effort are needed in order to remain steadfast in inquiry. The curiosity that fuels your investigation becomes more spontaneous and free. Your questions elicit increasingly subtle responses.

Everything I've talked about manifests on different levels of subtlety and refinement. Loving the truth, openness of mind, courage to be where you are, joy of discovery, and steadfastness of will introduce us to the essential dimension. You first have to see how your ego, your personality, your fixed point of view engage with these qualities. As you explore further, the balance keeps changing. That balance that keeps changing is what we call going through the various levels and dimensions. As each level dissolves a certain idea, a certain way of looking at things and doing things, who you are and what the world is become more real and defined and refined.

STUDENT: Groups doing this work often go on long retreats, and you also talk about the value of living in the world. Could you say more about these two perspectives?

ALMAAS: I think long retreats can be useful as we investigate who and what we are. Once in a while the work might include a period of retreat, but it is not a way of life for this work. Sometimes we go on retreat or we go into seclusion in order to be away from all influences. But I don't advocate living a monastic life, or wearing certain robes, or adhering to a specific diet. Why not just wear trousers and have the latest haircut and still be real? Why not have friends and drink café au lait in the morning? What matters is detachment, not what you are doing. What matters is your attitude toward what is happening. If you value the state of detachment and mystical poverty, then what happens in external life doesn't much matter.

So, for instance, some people are monogamous in intimate relationships, and some people have six or seven lovers each year. I don't know which one is better. Some people will go to retreats every year. Some people never go to a retreat. Who knows? Maybe it is different for different folks. But I think that everyone should try to investigate, try to find out. That is one of the principles of some Sufi schools—that you, the student, have a lot of responsibility at the beginning, before joining any work, to investigate on your own as much as possible. To find out as much as you can. To do whatever you can do on your own. To explore, to educate, and to inform yourself. Everything that you can do, you should do first, rather than go into some discipline and immediately take on the whole system. That is not necessarily a good way of doing it. It is good to investigate and to trust yourself some, to rely on your own intelligence some. And if people tell you things, it is good to not take them at face value but to investigate.

I go hear people talk and I read books. My attitude is not to declare them wrong or right but to find out what they mean. It doesn't matter who is saying it. It doesn't matter if it is Buddha or Bob Dylan. Who knows who is right and who is wrong? The truth is not written in the sky. And maybe what was right in the time of the Buddha is wrong now. Maybe Dylan is more correct now than the Buddha. Maybe the universe changed. The world constantly transforms, after all. Maybe in the time of the Buddha there was no self, and now there is a self. Maybe after five thousand years a true human self developed. That's why I say to find out what is here rather than to accept anything as given. You don't have to dismiss anything outright; take any notion as a working hypothesis.

So perhaps someone tells you go sit there and experience *shunyata*. You could say, "Maybe you are right. You seem to be a nice person. Maybe I'll trust you and I'll sit." But you don't go about it absolutely assuming that there is something called *shunyata* and that you will experience it by sitting there. Because you don't know. If you go about it as if you knew, you will block your practice. So the attitude of openness involves being open to the truth, to reality, to what is actually happening. You are not open to a person or to a teaching. You might read or hear certain things that seem to correspond to your experience, giving you some sort of support and validation for your experience. That's fine. In time, though, you have to go beyond those validations.

True states of realization occur when you throw away all the teachings. All of the teachings, absolutely. Everything. Then you are investigation itself finding out what you are. You realize that many people have said many things along the way. Somebody said you are an eternal soul, you have to be saved, and you have to believe in Christ. Somebody else said you just need to realize that there is no self. Another person said the true self is the Brahman. Somebody talked about God. And if you really believe that those people are not lying, you start wondering what they're talking about. Who is right? You need intense sincerity and ruthless courage to discover the turth for yourself. "This person says this and that person says that. I believe that they mean what they say, but how can I say one of them is right and one of them is wrong? And who knows what they mean by what they say anyway?"

That is one of the things I discovered when I realized the state of no-self. The state was different from what I thought. I realized that many people go around talking about Buddhist no-self, and they haven't got the vaguest idea of what it means. What they think is no-self is not what Buddha talked about. When Buddha said there is no self, he also meant there is no table and no house. He didn't mean that you walk around without a self, but that everything is conceptual. The self is ultimately a concept. This thing or that thing is a concept. But people don't think that way. They read about no-self and think that after sitting around for a while they will be this person sitting in lotus position with no self. There isn't anything like that. No-self means you realize that you are not sitting in that lotus position. So we don't really know what those people meant. At some point you have to achieve an independence of mind, which is the state of aloneness. You have to know intrinsic aloneness, allowing yourself to be free from all influence, independent from anybody, from anywhere, even from your own experience.

Yesterday you might have experienced God, but right now you are sitting. You don't take yesterday to be the truth. Right now maybe God has lost to the devil. You don't know. If you are honest with yourself right now, you don't know what's happened. What was real a moment ago might not be real in the moment now. And after a while, you realize that you have to investigate all of the time. You detach from needing to have reality be one way. Ultimately, detachment means you are not only detached from your husband or wife, from your money or body, but you are also detached from what reality is. You don't have to have reality be one way.

This is the position of no-position. You don't have a position. Somebody says, "You're wrong, there is a self." You say, "Okay, good, there is a self." Somebody says, "No, no, you have to believe in God." You say, "Yes, good, believe in God." What difference does it make? Needing to fix reality in a certain way supports your sense of identity or self, which is the activity of the ego. Any fixed system of belief props the ego. The whole system, the whole teaching, reinforces the sense of identity. But true realization happens when you let go of that support, let go of that identity, and deal with what is. Then you realize that you can't ultimately say anything fixed about reality.

You do work within a system for a time. The teaching carries you a long way, but there comes a time when you have to be completely alone. You might be sitting with your teacher, but you are alone. The teacher has his ideas and experiences, but you must experience reality firsthand. That is how you know a genuine teacher. A genuine teacher helps you to be alone and independent. A genuine teacher wants you to get to the place where you know for yourself. The only way to be certain is to know directly.

EIGHT

Living a True Life

Our intention in doing this work is not to make our lives comfortable. Having a comfortable, idyllic life is possible, but we don't need the work for it. The work we do is for individuals who want to see their true nature, who want to see the intrinsic value of their life.

If you want to be real and to live a life that has value of its own, that has significance independent of society or external pressures, then the work is for you. Neither this path nor any other spiritual work aims to provide students with a nice life. There's nothing wrong with having a nice life, but it's not the purpose of the work.

If you want the truth, if you want to be real, if you want to live a real life, then the work can speak to you. Being real and having a real life might not feel comfortable and ideal a lot of the time. But then you need to make your choice. What do you want, truth or comfort?

Although the truth is not intrinsically contrary to feeling good or being comfortable, sometimes, because of our personal history, the truth comes with pain and difficulty.

The work is for someone who wants to live a life that's not vacuous, that's not part of the common tide. We don't do the work to be special or better than other people, but because we want to be genuine, because we want to be real, because we feel a deep longing for living a genuine life. If we are truly pulled toward living a real life, then even if we suffer and feel miserable for a long time, we wouldn't want to exchange our life for an easier one, because what we value most is the truth. To live a genuine life, we have to dedicate ourselves to the truth.

Being real is not easy; it comes at a price. We cannot live a real life without taking risks, suffering difficulties, and making the necessary sacrifices. There's no easy way. We call our path "the work" because we often have to do things that are difficult. Although sometimes our work might feel like play, and playful exploration is fundamental to it, more frequently it feels challenging. The inner journey is difficult because we have to deal with issues that we'd rather not deal with, issues that we've avoided for a long time. To be real, to live a truthful life, we have to be ruthlessly honest with ourselves. We can't say, "I want to be real," yet continue to run away from ourselves and from our lives. Being real is the result of confronting ourselves, the result of being honest about who and what we are.

The help we get from our teachers is secondary to our own honesty and sincerity, is secondary to our own committed practice. We are transformed by our own risk, our own sacrifice. If we want to be real human beings, we have to live like real human beings, regardless of how difficult that may be. Nobody can give you the gift of being a real human being. If you want a real life, a life with truth and integrity, a life with true meaning and significance, you're going to have to live that way. A real life is not the result of the work—it *is* the work. We have to take the risks, make the sacrifices, and confront our demons.

If we devote our life to security, pleasure, and satisfaction, we won't be real adult human beings. We will continue being little kids. If we don't confront the difficulties in our life and our reality, we're not going to live a real life. It's as simple as that. We're not going to become real by having certain experiences. The experiences might give us some direction and guidance, a taste of what is real, but true transformation happens when we learn to live according to the truth.

We've explored in much detail loving truth for its own sake, sincerity, and functioning in the world. These aren't just nice stories we tell or interesting questions to explore. Our work is not for our entertainment. This work is practice for us to be real in as many areas of our life as possible. Real human beings make themselves real human beings. A real human life is something you create. A real human life is beyond pleasure, enjoyment, and security. A real human life is beyond success. None of these things are contradictory to real life, but true satisfaction is something else entirely.

To live according to the truth, we need to be able to allow the truth. We need to have the integrity and the self-respect to confront ourselves. We must be willing to see things about ourselves that are problematic, selfish, or reactive. We need to acknowledge and confront difficulties and delusions, and learn to deal with them instead of doing everything to run away from them. We need to learn to confront not only the beautiful truth of essential states, but also our fears and vulnerabilities and inadequacies. That's how we become real. We don't become real by running away from difficulties; we become real by understanding them. Fulfillment, love, and satisfaction happen as a side effect, a by-product of being real. To be real, we have to bring forth what is real in us. We have to start doing it, being it, acting according to it, expressing it, saying it, and living it.

We each have our difficult places. They're called our demons, or our shadows, right? We might feel hateful or terrified or inadequate or immature. Most of the work is about confronting those identities and learning to accept them, understand them, and harmonize with them. We're not going to become grown-ups if we run away from our difficulties. We cannot take a detour around the difficulties and get to the good stuff. We might succeed temporarily, but we'll wind up in an even worse situation.

We're going to have to start living the truth we know and the understanding we have gained. It's not enough to have insights and experiences. When we talk about doing, we mean really doing, despite the difficulties. When we talk about loving truth for its own sake, we mean really loving truth for its own sake, despite the consequences.

Our life is not a movie we go to every once in a while. If we think the truth is like a movie that we go to every other week, we're never going to be real human beings. We're going to live on the fringes of reality. If that's how you choose to live, that's fine. It's nobody's business to push you to be anything, but if you want to live a life of truth, you're going to have to do something about it. No teacher, no school, no teaching can do it for you. The teachings simply indicate the way. For instance, studying engineering at school is not enough to make you an engineer. You've got to actually go out and be an engineer. You don't become an engineer by having experiences in school. Likewise, you can't become a human being by having experiences. You've got to actually integrate what you learn into your life.

Living according to the truth requires courage, boldness, and a willingness to sacrifice. We're sacrificing what is false in us. In the beginning, it will appear as if we were sacrificing our security, safety, and comfort, sacrificing the possibilities of pleasure and love. But these seem small sacrifices once we have a taste of what it's like to be real, once we have a taste of the satisfaction and freedom of really living as a human being.

Our usual ego perspective is that satisfaction comes from having what we believe we should have. In my experience, it doesn't work that way. I could have the whole world, but if I am not the person I can be, it doesn't mean anything. Comfort or pleasure, a home, a mate, work: these are external ornaments for a real human being. They are not life itself, not the stuff of life. They are the husk of life, the package, at best the manifest expression of life.

The real substance of life is who and what we are. We tend to get lost in the container, in the packaging, in the things our eyes can see. We forget that if we live from that perspective, we are bound to be husks or shells ourselves. We are imprisoned in a fake world. When we take the packaging to be what is real, we're going to be like the packaging. If we want our life to be real, to have true substance, we have to be a human being of substance. We have to put ourselves on the line. We have to live with courage, boldness, integrity, and self-respect. These qualities depend on our being honest and sincere.

Being honest and sincere means confronting our inner experience and our outer life in a truthful way. Being sincere means not lying to ourselves, not rationalizing, not comforting, not postponing, not bandaging difficulties. Being sincere means grappling with our life and coming to terms with it with a sense of integrity and self-respect. Over time we gain self-respect by grappling with our deficiencies, by learning that we can do that. If we run away from the difficult parts, we'll feel like a coward. If we feel like a coward, we won't respect ourselves. And we can't lie to ourselves about what we're actually doing; on a deep level, we know the truth. So we have to grapple with the difficulties in a courageous way. That's how we gain respect and value. If we run away from things, there's no way we can value ourselves. To have a sense of integrity, we have to prove to ourselves that we're worthy of it. I don't mean we have to prove something to our superego. I mean we have to bring forth what we are, bring forth all our resources to confront the difficulties that we have in our life.

As far as I know, we can't become real, can't become truthful embodiments of reality, unless we take the risks to live that way. We must make the necessary sacrifices to be and to live that reality. It's not likely to happen that you sit there meditating, have wonderful experiences, and then suddenly you're a real human being. Living according to the truth requires sacrifices and risks. The work is a self-confrontation, an attempt to be more and more truthful and sincere with yourself. We gain integrity and value by living according to the truth. The work is not separate from being real, from living our life. The work simply guides us about how to go about living life in a real way. For me, it's sometimes much more satisfying to say one real word to somebody than to go on a vacation and have fun. Pleasure and re-laxation are necessary and important, but it's much more valuable to me if I can confront a situation squarely, and be what I can be in that moment.

If we don't bring to bear in our life our true quali-ties—our strength, our will, our intelligence, our com-passion—we won't recognize the preciousness, integrity, and beauty of being human. We won't respect ourselves if we don't act in a self-respectful way. We won't value ourselves if we don't conduct our life in a way that rec-ognizes the value of our true essential nature. We won't have confidence in ourselves if we don't grapple with difficulties. Conducting our life with confidence, value, and respect is connected to loving truth for its own sake. What is truth, ultimately, but the nature of the human being? Truth is essentially what we are, who we are, what we are capable of, our very substance, our nature, our reality. So to love truth for its own sake is not sepa-rate from valuing what you are as a human being.

We cannot become real human beings if our top-most concern is safety, comfort, or security. These things simply don't exist in the way we tend to think about them. Ultimately, security is certainty about who you are. There's no other security in the world. We could lose our money at any time, our house could burn down, our spouse could die. At any moment we could lose any of the things that make us feel secure. The only refuge is in the truth of what we are, what we can be, and what we can do. That's the only home, the only rest.

If we don't learn the work of living as a real human being, we're just not going to become a real human being. If we don't make the truth of the work our per-sonal concern, we will remain part of the world of lies, part of the empty world. If we don't make the work an intimate love affair, something of utmost concern within our heart and our mind, we're not going to grow up. The principles of the work, living a true life, have to become a deep, personal concern. The work has to become so important to us that everything else, by comparison, fades in significance.

We could try, like most people do, to make our lives safe. We could try to remain small so we'll have security and comfort, so that people will like us and not reject us. But when the time of your death comes, will you be satisfied with that life? What's the use of living as an empty person, without respect, without real value, running away from your life, from yourself, kissing people's asses, pretending to be one way or another, avoiding failure? That's how most people live, and we could easily live like that. Is that the kind of life you want to live? Sixty to eighty years of that?

It seems to me that five years of real living is worth eighty years, a thousand years, of a fake life. What's the point of that fake life? Feeling scared and running for security or comfort, wanting somebody to pat us on the back, trying to get society to think we're wonderful—what's that all about? You might answer, "Well, I'm scared. I can't do it. I'm weak." Would you rather live like a scared little mouse so that somebody doesn't reject you or you don't lose a job? Is it really worth living even one hour without self-respect? Is it worth letting people attack you and not speaking up because you're afraid you're going to end up alone? Is that the kind of person you want to be? Is it really better for people to love you if inside you feel fake? Or is it better that people don't love you but you are content with your own actions? Which one is more important? Which one is more valuable?

If we're going to find out our true worth, the true value of life, we have to be willing to live according to those principles. How often do we run away from the truth because we're afraid someone's not going to like us? How often do we indulge those childish insecurities?

To be real, we need to put ourselves on the line, to take the necessary risks. We need to decide that we're going to be real even if it means everyone we know will abandon us. We're going to be real even if it means we won't eat for days. We're going to be real even if it means we're going to get sick. If we don't take that kind of risk, we're just not going to be real. How else could it be? If we don't feel that our truth and our integrity are valuable, then we won't take that risk. We will remain a shell, a hypocrite pretending to seek the truth. How will we find rest if we know we're a coward who prefers a little bit of comfort to the integrity of who we are? We can't lie to ourselves about these things.

Human beings who really live the true life have to put themselves on the line. That's how our true resources come forth. Our true nature comes forth when we value truth above all else, when we live it. We cannot cheat our soul, our essence. We have to be sincere with ourselves. We can't decide to postpone reality for ten years because we're afraid of taking risks. We can't decide to kiss people's asses for a while to make ends meet and stay comfortable. If we spend ten years doing that, we'd lose all self-respect, all confidence, all value.

We have to gain our own respect, our own value, and our own love. At each moment, we have to exert utmost attention to be real. We have to do that every minute. We have to put ourselves on the line every second. The moment we're not doing that, we're failing ourselves, we're failing our potential. Can you really respect yourself, love yourself, or value yourself if you're scared to tell the truth because you're afraid somebody's not going to like it? You might lose some money or experience some discomfort, but if you fail to tell the truth, you're sacrificing something precious for something temporary.

We only feel fulfillment if we are genuine, if we deal with things in a genuine way, if we don't run away from our difficulties. And even with pleasures and successes, we tend to like ourselves more when we deal with them in a mature rather than in an indulgent way. Forget about superego judgment and what other people think. We're talking about you in your own heart, your own inherent sense of value, how you feel about yourself and your life. The morality of the superego developed from this core, from the way that human beings actually work. The sense of gaining value through right conduct has a true origin. If we are who we are and do what we are capable of doing, we tend to like ourselves, appreciate ourselves, and respect ourselves.

So we're not courageous to earn the approval of the superego—our own or anybody else's. That won't affect our real sense of value. We're courageous because we know the value of knowing and living according to the truth. Acting courageously often is scary and painful. But by allowing that fear, that pain, something happens in us. There is a transformation that makes us feel satisfied, even though we might have had a difficult time.

As you can see, this satisfaction is personal. It's not something between you and other people; it's between you and you. Between you and your own integrity. Between you and your own sense of truth. Loving the truth for its own sake means preferring to be sincere with yourself, preferring to be honest with yourself. Loving the truth means not lying to yourself, not being hypocritical. It means having the courage to penetrate your experience. It means having the courage to see your deficiencies and fears, your lies and delusions. The love of truth for its own sake can be expressed even with mundane issues. Every minute, we interact. Every minute, we conduct ourselves in some way. And we can notice whether the love of truth is present in these moments.

Now, it's also true that we are ignorant. We often don't know what's happening or what's driving us or how to find out the truth. The teaching provides the means for paying attention and seeing what's real. But we're the ones who need to do it. We're the ones who need to practice, to grapple with our life.

If you take a minute to consider your life in an intimate way, what's important, ultimately? That people like you or that you like yourself? If a million people like you, can that substitute for liking yourself? What's more important, the image you present to other people or the image you have of yourself? Or is it the actuality of your experience that's important? When you're really intimate with yourself, when you really confront yourself, when Judgment Day comes, what is important to you?

How much we suffer, how lonely we are, how scared we are, doesn't matter as much if we know we are being honest with ourselves. We have self-respect when we know we are doing the most we can do to be honest. Regardless of how much pleasure or security we have, we can't be fulfilled if we know we are hypocrites. If we're not honest with ourselves, we're not going to value ourselves. Most likely we'll hate ourselves.

We're looking at the difference between a life lived with sincerity and a life lived with hypocrisy. Although sincerity and hypocrisy begin with being truthful or dishonest with ourselves, they manifest also in our dealings with other people and the world. You cannot be sincere with yourself if you are insincere with others, and if you are insincere with yourself, you can't help but be insincere with others.

As I've said before, the work of living a real life is not kid's play. People sometimes tell me we should have more fun, more pleasure. Fun and pleasure are little things, by-products when compared with being real and living a true life. Sometimes I have a good time; sometimes I have a bad time. Sometimes I'm heavy; sometimes I'm light. Sometimes I'm joyful; sometimes I'm sad. So what's the big deal? What matters ultimately is that I'm honest with myself, that I am sincere. When I'm sincere, I am satisfied within myself. All the other things are ornaments. It doesn't matter a bit if people think of you as wonderful or horrible. It doesn't matter a bit if they think you are the most realized human being or think you are a creep. What matters is whether you are honest with yourself, whether you know the truth and are living it. This is integrity in relation to yourself.

So the joy in the work is a celebration of the truth. It's not a celebration of something superficial or transitory or fake. When I'm working with someone, I don't necessarily feel joy about their successes in life. Joy comes when I see the person being truthful, being sincere with himself. Joy comes when I see the person turning toward the truth, regardless of how painful it is, regardless of how much he is suffering. Seeing the person suffering makes me feel compassion, but what brings me joy is when I see the person confronting the truth and wanting to live according to it. That's what I enjoy seeing in people. That's what I enjoy seeing in myself.

So what we're exploring here is sincerity as it functions in our lives. Sincerity means actually being who we are, doing whatever we can to be genuine in our feelings and actions. Sincerity means actually living the principles that are true. We can know many wonderful principles, teachings, and philosophies, but if our lives are still an indulgence, what's the point? We don't want to be armchair philosophers or zafu buddhas, real only when we are sitting or doing spiritual exercises, but little kids when it comes to living. We don't want to be sincere when we're meditating or meeting in this group, but hypocrites the moment we step out into the world.

Sincerity is an attitude or a capacity of the heart that orients us toward recognizing the truth and loving the truth for its own sake. But loving the truth for its own sake does not simply mean feeling love for the truth. Although that is part of it, feeling love for the truth will not actualize a real life. To love the truth for its own sake means also to live according to the truth. If we really love the truth, we gladly live according to the truth regardless of how difficult the situation might get. We actively choose truth as our priority, not in terms of what we experience but in terms of what we do. Our love of the truth determines how we interact with people, how we run our life, how we conduct ourselves, how we maintain our living environment.

So doing the work is a serious matter. It's not for tourists who want small tastes of everything, who want to learn a little something here, a little something there, and then go off and get married and have kids and forget about the work. If that's what you want, the work will make your life miserable. If you come to the work because you're looking for a wife, you're in the wrong place. If you come to the work because you want a better job, you're in for trouble. The work is not contrary to those things, but it will make our life satisfying only if we value the truth above those things, only if we value the principles of the work.

Although it is important to experience and to understand various truths, the genuine work starts when we live according to those truths, and when we value not only having experiences of love but also acting in a loving way. Your heart could be full of love every night, but it doesn't mean anything if in the next moment you go and hurt someone. Every week you could have wonderful, sublime experiences, but if you live your life as a neurotic, then all these experiences will be used as food for your neuroses. These experiences will only increase the neuroses and, in time, you'll suffer more. To live the work means to do our best to actualize the life of the truth.

So to support our realization, to support our heart in terms of loving truth for its own sake, we need to actualize the life of the truth. We need to start living according to the truth that we know. We need to live according to what we have experienced and what we have understood. We need not only to love with sincerity but to act with sincerity. Otherwise, not only will we waste our time, but we will also create trouble for ourselves.

Often, if we experience deep realizations without working to actualize them in our life, without trying to live according to them, we will create a profound split inside ourselves. We'll drive ourselves crazier. If our life doesn't embody our experience, doesn't reflect our sessions, our work in the group, our personal inquiry, then we're being psychotic. We will experience a profound schism between the wonderful things we know and the neurotic way we live our lives. This gulf between what we know and how we live will make us miserable.

It is important to examine how seriously we are doing this work. Do you really want to live according to what you're learning? Or are you learning these things in order to support how you're already living your life? If you've experienced yourself as strength, then what does it mean to continue living your life as a wimp? What good is your realization if you discount it? Of what value is your nature if you forget it?

The experience of strength is complete only when you begin to live your life from that perspective. If you've realized your essential strength, why do you pretend that you are weak? What happened to the strength you experienced in your session yesterday? Even if it's gone today, why don't you remember that you felt that way? Do you reserve the truth only for your sessions? Only one hour of truth a week or a month? Do you hope the rest of your life will just magically transform? Most people in this work secretly dream that they will go to the group and their sessions, will listen to the talks, meditate, have ecstatic experiences, and then their life will automatically become wonderful.

But the insight of the work will have to penetrate our lives in a very genuine way if we want to live according to the truth. We actually have to go about creating our life by acting according to the knowledge of who we are and what reality is. Living according to the truth means taking care of yourself. If you recognize that you are precious, then you have to treat yourself as somebody who is precious. If you realize that human beings are precious, you have to treat everybody as if they're precious. If what the world is and who you are

are preciousness, then you can't walk into your closet and put on a dirty shirt because there are no clean ones. If you're precious and you haven't got a clean shirt, you go wash one right then. You let your knowledge and experience live through your actions.

It's possible to examine the extent to which our lives reflect the truth we know. What kinds of foods do we eat? Do we exercise? How do we manage our schedules? Do we find out what we enjoy doing and then set about doing it? Do we allow ourselves the rest and the aloneness that we need in order to experience the preciousness of reality? Or do we spend day after day being lazy, procrastinating, living routines that make us miserable? What do we do in terms of our relationships? Do we try to live those relationships according to the truth that we know? Do we apply the experiences we've had of ourselves and others and the world, or do we reserve our insights for special occasions? Do we create the kind of environment that supports the actualization of the truth? Or do we believe that it's sufficient to experience ourselves as precious, and then expect the angels to come and clean our room every day?

We're talking about very practical matters here. We're talking about applying what we know and what we learn, making the effort, expending the energy to live with sincerity. We do the work, we practice the teaching, every minute of our lives, not only when we meditate or go to a session or a meeting. For example, if we know that we are more in touch with ourselves when we are relaxed, do we try to pay attention so that we're as relaxed as possible all the time? Do we organize our time and our life so that we minimize confusion and unnecessary activity?

So we see that there are practical sides to loving the

truth for its own sake. To love the truth for its own sake, which has to do with the heart, we have to involve the belly. Our belly center—known by names such as *kath* in Arabic or *hara* in Japanese—supports the heart's love of the truth. The heart cannot survive on its own, cannot survive without the support of our actions, which are centered in the belly. Sincerely loving the truth is ultimately useless if we don't sincerely live the truth.

When we gather together to do our work, we create a teaching situation that provides the conditions in which we can perceive the truth of reality. But, in order to actually learn the truth we perceive, we need to learn how to behave in the world, what kind of life to live, how much activity to have, what interests to pursue, what relationships to maintain.

If we're genuine about being real, about discovering who we are and what reality is, we need to dedicate time to studying the matter, finding the means, developing our capacities. How can we best use our teachers? How can we take advantage of these teaching situations? How can we develop the capacities needed to live a more truthful life? We'll find out, for instance, that sometimes we have to exert ourselves and other times we have to rest. What is a good amount of activity? And where and how and with whom do we spend our time? These are relevant questions that we need to consider to live a life of truth.

So, for example, instead of spending months worrying about our taxes, we can spend two weeks looking them over, gathering the figures, and doing the calculations. We can know exactly what the situation is and not spend the rest of the year worrying. Instead of waiting until the last moment, spending all that time worrying, we could actually do something about the situation. We can do practical things to deal with the issues in our life so we don't have to think about them during our meditations.

Many people complain that their mind runs amok during meditations. We think about things that are not yet finished. It would be much simpler to spend the time figuring things out, finishing with them, emptying our minds of them. If there's something you want to say to someone, if it's important for you to say it, why don't you go ahead and say it? Instead of spending six months thinking it over during your meditations and then complaining that your meditations are not still, you could simply deal with the issue at hand at whatever level of truth you know.

We may wonder why it is that when we start to feel somewhat empty, instead of taking a few minutes to explore the emptiness, we choose instead to go shopping. We go to the store and buy this shirt and those shoes, and then we call our friend and have a forty-minute conversation. Rather than spending three minutes feeling emptiness, we spend an entire day and a lot of money avoiding it.

To want to do the work, to take the perspective of truth, means paying attention all the time. Loving the truth means trying to live according to the truth that you already know, instead of having to learn it all over again each time. For instance, if you experience oneness and loss of boundaries, that one experience should be enough for you to start living from that perspective. What does it matter if next week you don't experience oneness? You already know it. You start living your life from the perspective you know. Why wait for the next experience, and then for the one after that, and then for the final one? Often, even after three thousand experiences of oneness, nothing changes because we don't live the truths we know.

We each know different things and perceive different depths and understand different truths. When I suggest living according to the truth, I don't mean the Ultimate Truth. I mean whatever truth you know, whatever truth you have actually understood and experienced.

I'm giving you some examples of what it means to live according to the truth so that you can reflect and see if you are living what you know. Are you applying yourself or are you kidding yourself? Do you believe you're doing the work because you attend the meetings and go to your sessions? Are you really living it?

One major obstacle we face in living according to the truth is our identification with being inadequate, small, weak, and impotent. We believe that the true life is for big people, for people who are serious and capable. We sit around and wait for the deficient kid to disappear before we start living our life. Usually we're not even aware of what is in our way. We cover up our core deficiency with all kinds of ideas: I'm not interested; it's not the right time; it's not the right situation; the other person is not letting me; I still need to have more experiences of this and that. All of these responses obscure our deep sense that we can't hack it. Simple as that. We're not up to it; we haven't got what it takes. And we're not truthful enough with ourselves to see that we're just chicken.

To live according to the truth, we need to confront our core sense of deficiency. We need to admit that we're chicken. Not acting is not a matter of not knowing; we have all the information we need. We've been talking, learning, experiencing, and understanding for years. We have a thousand times more information than we need. We simply haven't got the heart to live according to what we know. We haven't got the guts.

Instead of disguising our deficiency with excuses about money and time, we need to confront the truth of our fear. We feel small and inadequate; we're chicken and refuse to act. What if we live with that truth for a while instead of believing we're enlightened but other people are not allowing us to live in an enlightened way? This deep identification with inadequacy is covered up by all kinds of excuses. We think we have to resolve that inadequacy, get rid of it somehow, before we can act in the world. Otherwise, life feels too overwhelming, too big. Most of us put off living according to the truth we know until we feel big enough, strong enough, and adequate enough to act in a more grown up way.

But there is only one way that deficiency will dissolve and be resolved. It will not happen by having more experiences. It will not happen by having more insights. None of that will make it go away. The only way to loosen that knot is to live according to the truth. The resolution is the exact opposite of what everybody expects. If we refuse to live the truth until we resolve that deficiency, we're in for a long wait—forever in fact. But if we start acting according to the truth that we know right now, the deficiency will dissolve on its own.

So, if you know that you are strong, what is the feeling of weakness? It's a lie. If you experience yourself as solid will, what does impotence mean? It's an emotional state. If you continue living your life as if you're deficient, you're living according to what is false, and your life supports the falsehood. Your actions support your false identity. But if you start living according to the truth, however limited it may be, you're starting to support what is real in you. What is real in you is simply not deficient.

So what does it mean to live according to the truth? We have talked before about truth in terms of different levels of understanding. To live according to the truth means to live according to the level of your understanding, to live your deepest experience. In the beginning, the truth might be insights about yourself, about your personality, about your self-image. So to live according to that truth means to actually apply your will, to put your attention into living according to what you have already seen.

Ultimately, the truth is you. So to live according to the truth means to live according to who you are. Otherwise, you won't have a truthful life. Living means the living of who you are, the actual flow of your true nature. So if you're not living according to the truth, you're not living. If you're not living according to the truth, then what is living is the false, the shell, the empty image. You're living according to the self that is the ego, which is empty, deficient, and small because ultimately the ego is not real. The ego doesn't exist. How can something that doesn't exist be anything but inadequate when it comes to living? The life of the ego is an unreal life: mechanical, superficial, and external. If we live the unreal life of the ego, we support an identity that is by nature deficient. If we live according to the identity of ego, then we are supporting and actualizing what is false.

So to live according to the truth ultimately will mean the life of essence, the life of who we are. To support our realization, we have to start living according to that realization. Otherwise, we're actualizing something that not only is not our true nature but that perpetuates the feeling of inadequacy and deficiency.

If we start living according to what we know, the ego might interfere and make things difficult, but we can persist in the truth we have already experienced and understood.

We can learn to live according to our immediate experience rather than according to the habits we've acquired. So, for example, we learn in school that the bright spots we see in the sky at night are stars that are huge fireballs of nuclear fusion. Our teachers and books tell us so, and we believe them to the point that we argue with anyone who says otherwise. We've never experienced the stars as fireballs; somebody told us that's what they are. Now today you directly experience yourself as essence, as existing completely: "I am an indestructible sense of Being." If someone talks to you tomorrow about this experience of essence, would you speak about it with as much certainty as you discuss stars? Why not? You had the actual life experience of essence, with direct evidence from your intelligence. But you more readily believe that stars are fireballs than that you are an indestructible essence.

One of the main reasons we believe what we read in books more than our immediate experience has to do with the sense of the collective. Most of society believes that stars are big fireballs, while the experience of essence is usually private. We don't typically believe ourselves as much as we believe the collective. But that's not the whole story. We don't trust our direct experience, because we're already convinced that we're the ego. We are little and deficient. Regardless of how many essential experiences we have, we're still going to act from the deficient perspective of the ego.

Although we experience and understand that we're not deficient, fundamentally we still identify with that little kid who is the child of our mother. When we experience ourselves as Essence, or as awareness, we realize we're not the child of our mother. We're the child of the universe. We're the child of God. Maintaining this deep belief that you're the child of your mother means continuing to be the little kid who is vulnerable and inadequate, who needs Mommy to take care of him. All of these beliefs about deficiency are based on the conviction that you are the child of your mother.

Living according to the truth means we're going to have to grow up and be mature in our behavior and in our life. One of the main barriers against living according to the truth is the fear that we're going to lose Mommy. We're terrified that if we become clear and present in our actions, then we are going to be all alone. We might feel the loss of comfort. We might feel naked and unsupported in this world. We might begin to feel insecure, afraid of losing our house, our money, our job, our girlfriend, our husband. The fear of loss of mother takes many forms. Fundamentally, the fear arises from taking yourself to be that little thing that needs Mommy. The moment we realize that we're not a little baby who needs our mommy, we start wanting to live according to what we really know. We realize that growing up means not losing Mommy, but gaining the universe. What you lose are the ideas in your head. I've never seen anybody lose anything else.

So in doing inner work, we become aware of that little kid, the ego identity that believes it is something from the past. We explore that sense of deficiency and experience countless resolutions, but that alone is not enough to actualize the real life. We're going to have to start to behave from those experiences if we want to live a real life. Because we're habitually identified with it, the ego identity will not simply dissolve by dint of awareness. We have to actively disidentify from the ego.

Our mind will have to think of things from the new perspective, our heart will have to feel from the new perspective, and our body will have to act from the new perspective.

Practically speaking, we need to learn to act according to the truth we know. In our work together in this group, we use Sunday afternoons to put our sincere love of the truth into practice. During our work periods on Sundays—what we refer to as life practice—we apply what we're learning in a context that is still part of the teaching but also similar to our daily life. We're not sitting listening to someone in a meeting or lying on a mat doing a breathing exercise; those are unusual situations. In our life, it would be much more likely that we'd be mowing the grass or doing laundry or paying bills. So we practice activities that we are more likely to encounter in our daily lives, and we perform these actions with awareness and understanding.

If every human being were real, we wouldn't have these meetings, we wouldn't need to learn breathing practices. We would simply live our life, mow our grass, clean our room, and cook our food. These are the real things of life. We create this artificial teaching situation because people don't yet know how to live a real life, how to live a sincere life. The work we do on these afternoons is the transition from our experience of the work to the work itself. We create a training ground in which to practice the work and develop our capacity to live according to the truth.

First of all, it's important that we sense our arms and legs, and look and listen as deeply as possible while we do our tasks. This is our practice of presence. We do our tasks with as much presence as possible. Since we don't need to consider time, we do our tasks as slowly as is needed to remain present. So the task isn't done as if you were working for someone and on a deadline. Part of the task is you, not just the external task. You're learning how to live, how to actualize your living. You're training your essence, your very substance, to be there, present, doing, involved in the task at hand. So you need to be sensing yourself, to be present as much as you can. And if your attention wavers, you exert whatever effort, whatever knowledge, is necessary to become present in your task. The practice is to actualize a sense of presence, to pay intense attention to the here and now.

Whatever task you're doing is like an immediate experiment in how your life can be. If you're washing a window, how can you wash a window and be living? Living is not only when you're in bed with your husband or when you're seeing a movie. Living continues when you're washing a window. How can washing a window be intrinsically valuable? That has to do with the quality of your attention. If you don't see that you are the preciousness, that your very presence and the quality of care you give the task are what makes it valuable, then the rest of your life will be equally meaningless. Without that sense of precious attention creating your life, most of your activities will be boring and unfulfilling.

You can learn to wash a window and be present, to give it the attention and the care that come from knowing the preciousness of who you are. You can learn to wash a window with the understanding that you are essence, that you are goodness, that you are love, that you are the source of strength and beauty and clarity and intelligence. Even though you might not feel that way at the time, you could go about your task from that perspective. You could devote the effort, energy, and time to having the attention necessary to do a good job.

Our Sunday afternoon work periods train us to pay attention not only to ourselves but also to the environment. We learn to pay attention to our body, to rest when we need to, to return to the task with renewed energy and vigor. We learn to apply what we know in terms of our relationship with the people we are working with. Are you aware of the people around you, the environment around you? Are you working so that you don't hurt them? How do you relate to people when you have to talk to them? Are you direct and genuine? Are you apologetic or angry? So even though you know that your nature is good and loving, you might feel hateful as you're clearing a trail with a group of people. Do you bark at someone to hand you a rake? Or do you feel your hatefulness and still manage to appropriately ask for what you need?

During the afternoon work periods, we do tasks that do not serve our own needs. The deficient ego identity, in contrast, acts only for its own benefit. From the perspective of essence, we clean someone else's window with the same care and love as we clean our own. Living according to the truth requires surrender of the separate self, letting go of that sense of boundary. What do love and compassion and understanding mean if not that you grant the same energy and the same care for someone else as you do for yourself? The work actualizes the true self, which is, by its nature, selfless.

So at the beginning, and maybe for a long time, we might find that doing tasks that are not simply for our own benefit is difficult because of the boundaries and the self-centeredness of the ego. Even though we might not see the value of selflessness, we will need to sacrifice some of our time and energy, trusting that our actions will reveal the truth. What you give, what is of real value, is yourself, your sincerity, your time, your energy, your action.

Living the truth is what actualizes it. If you don't approach the work with an attitude of surrendering for the sake of the truth, for the sake of learning, then nothing is going to happen. You're simply going to protect the ego shell and harden your boundaries. Sometimes you'll be asked to engage some process or task that you are not immediately going to understand. You might not be able to discern how it's useful for you. It might even not be useful for you. You might not know why your teacher asks you to do certain things. But if you always have to know why your teacher is suggesting a certain practice, that means you always have to be completely in control of your experience. And if you're always completely in control of your experience, how will you get beyond the boundary of the ego?

The ego controls how you feel. If you don't let yourself surrender to the situation or to the teaching, how are you going to learn to be selfless? How are you going to learn to let go of your boundaries? How are you going to learn to trust reality if you can't trust your teacher when she asks you to do some simple task? You might not know why, but you trust that it is going to be good for you. Most of the time in our work it is obvious why we do certain practices. But sometimes it might not be obvious, and you won't understand what's useful about the activity until several years of practice. We don't know the value of selflessness until we see selflessness. We don't know the value of boundlessness until we experience boundlessness. We don't know the value of surrender until we experience surrender.

If you want to learn from the teaching situation, you need to let your teacher teach you. That's part of the price you pay. But if you always have to do things according to your own choice, that is an assertion of the ego. And since your teacher knows that, she might ask you to do things that are silly, that don't make any sense, so that you do something without calculating your self-interest. Some teachers ask students to do things for years that have nothing to do with the work simply so that the student can develop the capacity to act without being self-centered.

If you feel that you always have to know what's happening in the teaching in every moment, if you feel you have to do only what you choose, if you feel you have to be always in control, then this work is not for you. Part of the work we're doing is to understand the ego's need for control and choice. Of course, we also need to apply our intelligence and ensure that we're not being exploited or hurt in some way.

Working with a group of people who are all making that effort provides tremendous support for everyone. Practicing presence together makes it easier to pay attention to our immediate experience. It's much more difficult to cultivate our attention in an environment where everyone else is scattered and not being present. Paying attention to the truth is possible in those times as well, but at first we have to practice in situations where it is easier to pay attention to ourselves.

So the sense of being present, the focused attention, the caring for the task, and the caring for the interaction with the people around you, are all fundamental to living according to the truth. Otherwise, we're just cleaning windows in a room full of people. Without the attention to the truth there's no value in the action; we're not getting anything and we're not giving anything. But if we do our tasks in a genuine way, we will feel that we're getting something and giving something

at the same time. And that real thing that is both getting and giving is the actual living itself, the actual living presence in that situation. The living presence is
where the value is, where the true taste of life is.

The work we do here involves both realizing the
truth of reality and living according to that truth. The
time we spend learning to function with presence fine-
tunes our consciousness. We learn the value of our
realization by living the life of our realization, and in
time our actions will embody our awake attention. It
is our way of stabilizing and establishing our realization. We can live our lives with a clear and strong sense
of presence. We learn to strengthen our spine not only
by understanding what is true but also by acting in a
genuine way. We perform our tasks even though we
are aware of feeling inadequate and lonely. We practice attention in presence while we work, focusing our
attention primarily on the tasks. Even though we are
aware of our emotions and issues, we don't waste our
energy analyzing them. If we are aware of our inner
state without blocking it in any way, our presence will
continue transforming.

When a group actually functions together with the
sincere intention to be present and real, and to treat
people and our tasks well, then something is created
that is not possible in any other place. This is the only
time that the true heart unfolds. The true heart unfolds
when each person in concert is living according to the
truth. If one person withholds their attention from the
work of the group, it will interfere with the overall energy. When we're here together doing this work, it's
important that we each participate as best we can.
Without that intention, it is better not to come. You
don't have to be in the work.

The work we do here affects not only ourselves but

everyone else too. This is not simply an individual work; the totality of the group is working together. If we all come to the work we're doing with the same sincere heart, with the same awake attention, we could create something that is very rare. We could create some kind of community. When we work together, when we make one body, we can create a community of truth.

NINE

The Basic Fault and the Resurrection

All the various spiritual teachings address some vesion of our fundamental separation from reality. The understanding of this separation connects to a concept in psychology about a universal, painful disconnection in the infant soul, which the theorist W. R. Bion called the Basic Fault. Today we will use the phrase "Basic Fault" to speak of every person's fundamental separation from Being, acknowledging how it relates to the psychological concept. True transformation happens only through the perception and understanding of this Basic Fault. Our realizations, insights, and experiences are necessary and, at times, painful or beautiful. But if they are to transform who we are and what the world is, these realizations must expose and reveal the Basic Fault.

We have been exploring the perspective of being mature and complete human beings, functioning in the world as real humans and living a normal human life that is fulfilled. Today I'd like to examine the Basic Fault from this perspective of our work. Some students here already feel the effects of experiencing the Basic Fault because of what we have been doing on functioning. The dissatisfaction and resistance that people feel to this work are reactions against the practical perspective, which emphasizes doing and being in the world. The resistance is against functioning, against being a grown-up, against doing things correctly and efficiently and responsibly, in the right way and at the right time.

The resistance to the practical perspective manifests in two distinct but related ways, depending on what end of a particular relationship you find yourself. When you try to actualize that state or perspective of practicality in your life by starting to take care of yourself and your life in a mature way, you might feel some kind of resistance or distraction. "I don't want to do it that way," you say to yourself. The resistance might appear as a rebelliousness or stubbornness or deficiency. You might feel as if something were missing. "I want to have fun. Where's the fun? If I'm just being responsible, taking care of things, being grown-up, I'm not going to be happy." We feel that grown-ups don't get goodies. To be grown up means not to have fun. Taking care of things does not promote satisfaction or fulfillment.

So one side of it is that when you try to actualize the perspective of being a mature, full, responsible human being in the world, the soul child or the libidinal soul—the primary early structures of our individual consciousness—responds by saying, "What about me? I want to have fun and play." The soul child considers the responsibility, efficiency, and realness of the mature adult antithetical to having fun, enjoying things, and just hanging out.

The other side of feeling resistant or dissatisfied with the perspective of practical functioning is that you might look at the school or the teacher as lacking something, as not providing an appropriate model. They are not the way you want them to be. You might feel disappointment: "I'm not getting it anymore. I'm not getting what I need anymore. I want something, but the teacher is telling me that I have to grow up."

So you might start experiencing the teacher or the school or the work as not coming through, as not providing the sustenance that you need. "Where are the nice things we're going to be given? Where is the essence and joy and fullness? What's all this talk about doing and functioning? I want to have nectar in my heart. I want to see an angel over my head. I don't want just to go and rearrange my furniture." This other response to the deficient perspective involved in the Basic Fault might appear as dissatisfaction with the work or the teacher or the school for no longer delivering what you need.

Both reactions point to what I mean by Basic Fault. These manifestations will arise because they are part of the issues that everyone will have to deal with in actualizing the practical perspective of being and doing in the world. The perspective of functioning as a mature human being exposes the underlying basis of those two modes of dissatisfaction and resistance. Actualizing the practical perspective reveals a certain psychic structure, called the central object relation, that we habitually operate from but do not recognize.

Today we are going to discuss in some detail this

.ic object relation, this basic way of relating that re-
ains a big resistance against actualizing the true life
of the human being. We have talked about and worked
on two object relations so far: the rejecting object relation and the frustrating object relation. The rejecting
object relation fixes you in a place of feeling afraid in
the world. This fear makes it difficult for you to function as a mature human being. The frustrating object
relation puts you in a position of being a hungry and
desirous little kid who wants something he can't have
but always seeks. So you're either paranoid or a seeker.
We've talked about how these object relations interfere
with dealing with yourself and your life in a mature
way because in these two object relations you're functioning with an infant identity.

The rejecting and frustrating object relations have
something else in common. You always experience
them as bad. They're negative object relations. One
involves enormous fear and hatred, and the other involves lots of frustrated longing and need and desire.
When we experience either of these object relations,
we always have a sense that something has gone terribly wrong. Both the rejecting object relation and the
libidinal, frustrating object relation are usually repressed or split off—parts of the ego that are hidden
and need to be seen, understood, and integrated.

But there is another object relation, the positive object relation, that is not repressed or split off but is actually identified with and acted out all the time as the
normal object relation that operates as you relate to
the world. This object relation doesn't feel particularly
conflicted or oppositional. To see the Basic Fault, we'll
have to see this positive object relation more clearly.
In fact, the perspective we are working with will expose that particular basic object relation. This is the

central, basic position of the ego: so I call it the central object relation.

I will explain what I mean by central object relation. We have seen the two negative object relations expressed in relationship to the father, to the mother—and, ultimately, to the breast—either as the bad, rejecting breast or the wonderful breast that is not available, either as the rejecting, hostile parent or the desired parent who is not available. These are the conflicted, painful object relations that remain mostly unconscious because it is unpleasant for us to be aware of them. They rise to consciousness in the course of our work here.

The good relationship that you had with your parents also constitutes an object relation. Each of us had moments of relating with one or both parents—and, at the deepest level, with the breast—that were not so conflicted. Without this fulfilling object relation, you wouldn't be here. You wouldn't have survived physically and emotionally. And, of course, this central positive object relation is hardest to see, although it is there and you are enacting it all of the time. Usually we can't see or pinpoint the central object relation for what it is until we deal, to some extent, with the other, more painful object relations. The central object relation is typically not painful. In fact, we usually experience it as normal and nonconflicted, or even as good and fulfilling.

So the central object relation integrates all of the good experiences you've had. You feel supported, loved, nourished, and wanted. It is the most basic object relation, the one you've engaged all of your life. We would be psychotic if we didn't have those feelings of support and love. Things would be too painful, chaotic, and scary without that feeling of good and secure connection that nourishes and comforts us, that makes life tolerable.

In our school, the student unconsciously enacts that central object relation with the school, with the work, or with a particular teacher. As long as that relationship is not pinpointed, it cannot be understood and transformed. Without confronting it, you will remain a student forever—not a frustrated student who isn't getting what you want, not a scared student who is being rejected, but a satisfied student who is being taken care of, acknowledged, and supported. You are satisfied with getting what is available, what is being fed to you. The approach I'm introducing will challenge this satisfaction, will make you feel as if you are losing some basic support and nourishment.

So let's further explore this central object relation. The central object relation is a relationship between the central ego—the core or the central part of the soul—and what is called the ideal object or the ideal other. The object here is ideal in the sense that the object—the parent or the teacher or the teaching or the school or the breast, whatever it may be—is comforting, satisfying, fulfilling, nourishing, supporting, and giving. The ideal object is not absolutely idealized. We need not think the ideal object is perfect. The ideal object is simply good, in a normal, everyday kind of way.

For a long time, the student relates to the teaching, the school, or the teacher as the ideal object. He or she relates to that ideal object through the central object relation. That object relation will have to be exposed because it is not reality. You are still living through an internalized object relation. You are still living through a mental structure. You are still living through images, through a projection. You are still imagining reality as something that is not the way it actually is.

Because you are living your life from a false perspective, there will never be true realization. Realization will not take hold. Transformation will not be effected in a fundamental way. Any experience you have will be a part of that object relation, which will make you forever dependent on that object relation.

The more you experience your teacher or the school as giving you what you want, nourishing you, telling you what you need to know, the more you get into that dependent position. The more the teacher doesn't push you to be independent, the more you identify with that positive object relation. That's why the perspective that I'm presenting now, of being grown-up, mature, and independent, will challenge that object relation. You might feel, "Do I really have to go out and do it all myself? Why not just be taken care of? Why not just get all the understanding, the nourishment, and the blessing that's available and things will be okay?"

The central object relation can be enacted with any ideal object. The ideal object could be your teacher, the school, the work; it could be Essence, God, the truth; it could be your husband, your wife, your child, your job. Any of these can become the ideal object that gives you a sense of support, nourishment, inner ease, and comfort. Any of these could make you feel secure in the world. No true realization happens until you throw away that safety and feel insecure. That security will have to be shaken until you feel complete insecurity.

Overthrowing the central object relation, sometimes referred to as the secure attachment relationship, brings about the dark night of the soul, which we discussed earlier, the terror of the moment, the true situation. But even the dark night of the soul is an indication that the understanding of the Basic Fault is not complete. With complete understanding of the Basic Fault, you realize that eliminating false security does not mean you have to feel perpetual terror.

The central object relation is basic in the sense that it dominates our experience of the world. When something disrupts the central object relation, you resort to the rejecting or frustrating object relations. When things are fine, you come back to the central object relation, which is the basic condition of humanity. There is nothing unusual about the central object relation, nothing pathological about it. It's what we call normal. It is normal. Normal and average and ordinary, but ultimately not real. If you want realization, you have to understand the central object relation.

You develop the central object relation in relation to your parents and enact it with every ideal object, whatever you feel is a source of connection, support, nourishment, love, truth, understanding, security, and comfort. Whatever you relate to as an ideal object, you don't see as it is. If you're relating to your teacher that way, you're not seeing your teacher as he is. If you're relating to the work that way, you're not seeing the work as it is. If you're relating to God that way, you're not seeing God as God is. Anything you relate to in that way, you see as your object, actually as nothing but the good breast.

Ultimately, at the core of the idealization is a satisfying relationship with the breast, the good mother, the good parent, the good provider. In the central object relation, the good breast is not the exciting and unavailable breast of the frustrating object relation. The good breast here is the giving breast, the full and nourishing breast, the motherly breast. In the frustrating object relation, the child is hungry for and excited about the breast, which looks wonderful and yummy. "I want, I want, give it to me." That's how you feel when you're hungry. When you're starving just before dinner, the food always looks so delicious. But in the middle of the meal, the plates of food don't look so enticing. When you're being satisfied and fulfilled, the meal loses that yumminess. The food is good and satisfying, you're contented, but the meal no longer fires you up with excitement. When an object fulfills you, your relationship to that object changes. You don't have the same passionate desire for it. You are more relaxed and settled.

The central object relation mimics the relationship with the breast when you have been nursing for some time—your belly is getting full and feeling relaxed, your cheek is against the warm breast, and you begin to doze. That ravenous fire of passion is gone. What remains is security and contentment. Everything's just fine. The breast does not necessarily look all wonderful. It's just a nice, normal breast. The breast is not idealized through the frustration. The lack of satisfaction is what makes you idealize the object. The exciting breast before you consume it is idealized, but the real breast as it nourishes you loses that shine. Although it's not all that yummy, it's not bad either. It has milk and is soft and warm. That nourishing breast is called the ideal object because it's the good mommy that comforts and takes care of you, it's the good daddy that supports and listens to you, it's the friend, the teacher, or the God that sees and understands you.

Ultimately, the student reenacts the central object relation with the good teacher or the good work. So for a long time the student is satisfied sitting there with mouth open to receive the teaching. When the teacher says, "Get to work," the student responds, "Where's the breast? If I go, I can't eat any more. I have to go and get my own food? That's terrible. I'm abandoned and alone." You experience the disruption of that object relation as the loss of that comforting and nourishing other.

Another way we hold on to the central object relation is to reenact it by identifying with either side of it. On one side of it, you're the little kid, relaxed and happy, with Daddy and Mommy around, your teacher or God taking care of you, essence pouring into you, and you're feeling content. The loss of that object relation will be like the loss of the breast. On the other side, you could be the giving, nourishing breast, and see other people as needing to be taken care of and nourished and supported. Understanding this perspective means also the loss of that position. To be a real human being, mature and down to business, means that you can't only be that nourishing, giving breast, doing everything for the other person. You could lose the central object relation from either end. In both cases, the loss of the object relation means the loss of the comfort, the connection, the security, the support, the nourishment, the fulfillment, and the love that is the chief effect of the central object relation.

So for a long time we don't consider or even want to know that such an object relation exists. We are so identified with this basic position that it is the most obvious thing, so obvious that we fail to perceive it. It's one of those things that is there all the time, as the central background of our relating with the world. But despite its centrality and ubiquity, the central object relation is not real. Whether you're relating to a student or a teacher, to a husband or a wife, to God or the truth, to pure awareness or true nature, whatever it may be, if you are the breast or the mouth that is being fed, you are enacting an object relation, because reality is not like that.

So the Basic Fault is thinking that reality is a collection of breasts and open mouths searching one for the other. The Basic Fault assumes the central object relation to be the truth, to be how things actually work. So when reality starts to assert itself, when you start to grow up, this whole perspective is challenged. When the central object relation is challenged, you experience various kinds of loss.

Usually you become aware of the ego identity that participates in that object relation. Often you feel sort of small and vulnerable, somewhat helpless, scared, and deficient. But at the same time, you feel innocent and young. So when you truly experience the central object relation, it's not overwhelmingly painful and terrible. You are recognizing the truth of the human situation, that as a human being you are vulnerable, you are in some sense helpless, you are in some sense alone. Although it is scary, the vulnerability does not have to be a big, intense, terrifying vulnerability. The helplessness does not have to send you into terror. If you really let it happen, there is a gentleness and delicacy to the revelation.

Working with the central object relation brings up some kind of aloneness. But the aloneness is not so terrible because it is not complete. Because of the Basic Fault, the basic separation from reality, the central object relation is usually not lost totally. The object relation changes from being the fulfilling object relation to being the empty object relation. Suddenly the breast, instead of being full of milk and nourishment, shrivels up and becomes empty.

So you're not entirely alone, but you're left relating to an empty breast. The breast does not disappear. The other person does not disappear. The work does not disappear. Rather, these things continue to exist but on't give you what you want. They don't defer satisfaction like the frustrating object or refuse satisfaction like the rejecting object. It's more like the teacher or the teaching or the school or the husband suddenly hasn't got it anymore. The breast is dried up. Nothing comes through. God is not delivering the goods. And they're not delivering the goods not because they're bad, but because there's nothing there, they're all out.

So you could get angry, but you realize that the other person is not bad. They simply haven't got it anymore. That's the feeling. And you're not terrified and scared, because the basic situation remains. The breast is still there, the mother is there, the teacher is there, but they're not as fulfilling, as satisfying, or as exciting as you thought. The ideal object becomes the emptied-out object, the shrunken object. So you feel disappointed with the teacher or the friend or the wife or the school or God. They don't do it for you anymore.

You might think, "Since this isn't doing it for me, I'll just leave. I'll go do something else. Maybe I'll find another ideal object." But if you do that, you're avoiding the situation. Feeling disappointed with the ideal object is good because you're starting to feel reality. That ideal object that was nourishing you is an image you were projecting. Because that image is not real, it will necessarily feel empty when you see it as it is. As long as you're enacting the central object relation, you don't see God or the teacher or the teaching as they are. You see only your own image, your projection of that ideal object. When you realize that it's an ideal object, you see that it is empty because any image is empty.

You could experience the loss of the fulfilling object relation as feeling disappointed in essence or true nature, "Essence doesn't do it for me anymore. God is, I don't know, fine I guess, but it's not that exciting.

My teacher is okay, but she doesn't have it anymore." Nothing works, nothing does it anymore. The food you eat doesn't have the taste it used to have. Your Big Mac is tasteless and bland. You have sex with your lover and it's okay, but something about it is lackluster. There's no pizzazz or passion or spice. You go skiing and it's no good. "Eh, white snow, nice sun. I used to like it. Somehow it doesn't do it." You can't quite tell what's missing, but everything is flat. You can't tell what's wrong because nothing's wrong exactly. Everything is the same as it has always been, but some spark is gone.

When the fulfilling object relation is disrupted or exposed for what it is, the feeling is that nothing satisfies you. It's not as if you're not getting something or someone is rejecting you, but that the stuff you're getting and the relationships you have no longer fulfill you. The good things that have delivered in the past don't do it anymore. That's an uncomfortable and perplexing situation because you don't know what to do now. You can't simply find something else, because nothing does the trick.

Sometimes you jack up your hopes a little bit and try something new, "Maybe my taste has evolved. Instead of a Big Mac, tonight I'll eat Duck à l'Orange." You remember loving the taste of it. So you go to just the right restaurant, you order it, you're all excited. As you're eating, you realize that it's a little better than a Big Mac, but something is missing. Maybe they've changed the sauce or there's not enough Grand Marnier in it. Everything is flat. The duck's bland.

The things you used to enjoy appear old and out of date. Things are no longer fresh, no longer full of promise. Even when you speak to God and he replies, your attitude is, "Oh, well, I guess I'll listen." But you don't feel all of that old excitement of "Wow, God talks to me!" Instead it's "What's the big deal?" You might get angry, but you can't really get behind your anger. You're getting just what you've always gotten, but somehow it's not enough. You're not really that angry. You're not really that scared. Instead you feel alone and deflated.

The usual reaction to the loss of the fulfilling object is depression. The promise is gone. You wake up in the morning feeling, "I don't know what to do. Maybe I should die." But you can't even get excited about killing yourself. You're not despondent but just a little depressed. You go about your day as usual. Somehow you feel that passion and excitement are things of the past. Nothing jazzes you up. You're mildly but persistently unhappy.

If you really look at it, you realize that all the excitement and fulfillment you used to experience was not completely real. That sense of bountiful nourishment was necessary to get you to this point. Depending on your early relationship with your mother, or your relationship with the breast, your reaction to the loss of the ideal object could be more severe or less severe.

If there was lots of fulfillment in your relationship with the breast and Mommy was present to some extent, your reaction will be more moderate. You'll feel a little depressed, a little scared, and a little anxious. You'll feel vulnerable because the support and the nourishment are not there, but you won't be that scared because you won't experience the loss as Mommy punishing you; rather, you experience the loss as the passing away of something, as some kind of growing up. Now, if your relationship with the breast was not that fulfilling, you might react with extreme fear, anxiety, deficiency, and helplessness. The loss of the ideal object will feel like a threat to your existence.

Whether you're slightly or severely afraid, the basic situation remains. The ideal object exists but no longer fulfills you. You don't experience the loss as someone willfully frustrating or rejecting you but as the failure of secure attachment. You have to look at something more basic because it's not true to say that your teacher doesn't love you. He does. You might try to prove that he's wrong and that he doesn't love you, but it isn't true. The teacher hasn't changed. Neither has your husband, who for all these years was yummy and good in bed, who now seems a bore. It's all you can bear to talk to him for a few minutes and have sex now and then. You're not rejecting him and don't feel rejected by him. There's just not that extra oomph there. The romance has paled. What used to satisfy and nourish you no longer does.

So what's going on? What's the problem? The love is there, the teaching is there, the pleasure is there, but it doesn't satisfy you. The problem is fundamental, built into the very structure of the situation. The problem is your perspective, your point of view about yourself and about the world. That's what I mean by Basic Fault. Fault in the sense of a break or a fracture from objective reality, from how things actually are. You will see the basic problem if you let go of the object relation completely. You let go not only of the fulfilling breast, but also of the deflated breast, the empty breast. Then it is possible to see what the Basic Fault is. The problem here is the way we look at things, the way we understand things, the way we perceive the situation, what we take ourselves to be, what we take the world to be, what we take others to be. The problem is an entire worldview, propped up by a certain metaphysics and philosophy that rule your daily life.

The most important part of that metaphysics, of that worldview, is that you relate to others and exist in the world from the perspective of internalized object relations. No matter what the object relation is, whether frustrating or rejecting or fulfilling, you relate to the world as a separate entity, a separate individual. The world exists for you as various sorts of objects. Whether the object happens to be the teaching, your teacher, your wife, your husband, essence, God, the truth, your mother, or the breast, it is always something other than what you are. And you merely relate to it in a positive or a negative way. The central object relation rests on the perspective of not looking at the universe as a whole, not looking at the truth as a whole. We see that the fault is as basic as that. We look at the truth and at the reality of who and what we are as a separate entity, a separate something, a separate existence that relates to other separate existences.

This is how it was for us at the beginning with the breast. You had an empty stomach, you were at the breast, and nutrients came from the breast into you. So it's understandable that we end up believing the world functions in that way. For the first year of life, that was our basic experience. There's a breast, a mommy, a you, and a stomach. The breast is either good or bad, either full or empty, and the stomach is either being fed or not being fed. Those sensations of hunger that are relieved by a breast feeding what eventually feels like your stomach are at the core of the object relations we enact in our life.

So your deepest identification is that you're a stomach. Your earliest relationship with your mother is as an embryo attached through the umbilical cord and later as an infant suckling at the breast. Usually, the experience of that identity feels empty and vulnerable. You feel cut off and in search of connection. You might feel as though some kind of umbilical cord is missing. When you experience this embryonic identity, which is earlier than the symbiotic stage, you want that umbilical connection to the mother. But even that is an object relation. You believe the resolution will be connection to the secure other that is the source. But by that very definition, you're empty. Whatever you seek, you haven't got. When you were in the womb, when you were suckling at your mother's breast, you didn't have it. You were helpless and vulnerable. You didn't have anything. Everything came from outside.

The Basic Fault is looking at reality through the lens of the physical world, relying on the experience of your body to define who you are and what the world is. The central object relation is founded on the identification with the body and its relationship to the body of the mother, whether as the stomach relating to the breast or as the embryo relating to the placenta. Many people, when they regress very deeply, think that the teacher is a placenta. When people pray to God, they pray as if to a placenta. "Give me grace. Give me some oxygen. Give me fulfillment." Who are they praying to? The mother's breast and, more deeply, the placenta. I call it placenta longing. People do strange things with their mind. They think they have a relationship with God when they're really fantasizing their relationship to the placenta. I'm not kidding. That actually happens. Sounds funny, but at a very deep level, it's what we do.

As a matter of course, you operate as an entity, as an individual that is separate related to something else that is separate. As you follow the thread back, you experience the suckling relationship of the symbiotic stage. Then you might experience the umbilical connection in the womb. You notice that you rely on that relationship in order to stay connected to somebody else and to the world. Sometimes people will say, "I feel there's a real umbilical cord between us." I see what they mean, but that's a fantasy.

When we look closely, we notice that the focus on the physical world is what creates the fantasy. We take physical reality to be all of reality. We take the three-dimensional world and the passage of linear time to be the basis of our point of view of the world and of reality. From the physical perspective, you were a little embryo connected by an umbilical cord to a placenta. You were a little infant suckling at the breast. You were a little kid relating to Mommy and Daddy. But only from the perspective of the body. And as long as we stay with the perspective that reality is ultimately determined by the physical world as it appears, we will never resolve the situation.

You have to see that reality is more than three-dimensional. There's more to us, there's more to me, there's more to you, there's more to this world, there's more to this school than the physical things we see. We have to look beyond the dimension of objects. The perspective of the physical world and positivist science that posits only what is visible as true is limited. We have to see the world as it is. The world that we see, the world of objects, is not the complete world.

The Basic Fault does not resolve until you get to the stage of the fall on ice. Do you know about the fall on ice? It's when you're out in the cold, in reality and not in your mind. You have to see reality apart from the perspective that you are this separate self relating to a separate object. The Basic Fault can be seen as functioning through object relations, can be seen as taking yourself to be an entity, can be seen as taking reality to be the three-dimensional physical reality, can be seen as seeing the world as a world of discrete objects in space. Only if we allow ourselves to let go of all object relations, not just the negative ones but also the positive ones, can we see the world as it is. We have to be willing to do that. We have to be able to take that risk at some point, to risk being out in the cold, to risk falling on ice.

One of the main things that arise around this perspective is the fear that you're going to be alone. All alone in a world you don't know. The world you know is a world of discrete objects with relationships between them. To leave that world can feel like the whole world is going to go. You feel as if you're going to lose the world. But if you feel you're going to lose the world, you're still holding on to some idea of a self separate from the world. We must go beyond that dualism in order to see clearly. If you really allow the feeling of aloneness, you realize that nothing is disconnected from anything else. I am not somebody giving something, nor am I somebody getting something. There is no separation. If you have to be separate in order to connect, the relationship is not real.

Discrete objects with various kinds and levels of connectedness are the perspective of physical reality. But when we see the truth of the whole perception, see things as they are, we realize that everything and everybody is a manifestation of one thing—waves of one ocean. There's no such thing as one wave. Can there be a single wave without an ocean? You can visualize it, you can draw it, but in reality there's no such thing. Neither you nor God is separate from anything else.

But that doesn't mean everything is connected to everything else through umbilical cords. There are no umbilical cords, because there are no boundaries. What is a boundary? Boundaries assume that our usual perception of physical objects determines reality. The physical world appears like reality separated into bounded objects. But if we perceive more than three dimensions—if we perceive the fourth dimension of Being—we realize that everything is made of one thing. One substance. One living fullness. One reality. One truth.

So the Basic Fault is seeing things from the perspective of object relations, as discrete entities with fixed boundaries. The perception that there isn't separateness, that there isn't discreteness in the way we usually think of it, corrects the Basic Fault. Although discreteness exists, it is a paradox. Difference exists by virtue of being, not through willed effort. There is no separate soul ultimately, although you could experience yourself as a separate soul. As long as you experience yourself as a separate soul, you will feel empty and needy. The true perspective is of oneness, of unity, of no division, no separateness, no duality. We don't usually see or believe or trust the true perspective of reality. We rely instead on the usual perspective of discrete objects. We trust the usual perspective of object relations and continue to live our life from the perspective of separateness.

Now, it's not enough simply to have the perception or experience of oneness or unity. You have to think that way. You have to feel that way. You have to act that way. All of your centers must realize and live from the perspective that reality is one unity. You perceive discreteness, but the discreteness is more apparent than real. Discreteness lies on the surface of things. Discreteness exists as an apparency, and we consider it useful for practical functioning. Ultimately, though, reality can't be but one.

The Basic Fault is the perspective of separateness, and the resolution in all spiritual traditions is oneness and union. There is nothing new in that. The theistic traditions talk about union with God. Buddhists talk about it in terms of dissolution of the self. Other teachings call it nonduality. It all amounts to the same thing. The resolution of the Basic Fault is that separateness does not exist. This belief in separateness is the most basic dilemma, the central spiritual problem. If the notion of separate existence does not dissolve, spiritual transformation has not truly happened.

Now, I'm not saying that if you work with the Basic Fault you will suddenly realize oneness. Perceiving the truth of reality is a long, arduous practice. I haven't talked about the fears and vulnerabilities involved, the challenges to everyday behavior, the shifts of mind required. "Shift of mind" is a euphemism for the actual collapse of mind that happens when you realize the oneness of reality. The mind that always looks from the inside out collapses and looks from the outside in. This is a radical change of mind.

You don't simply have an experience of separateness, you have a conviction of separateness. You literally have a crystallized conviction that reality is ultimately determined by the physical world. The deepest belief of the ego is that reality is how things look physically. So even your experience of presence or truth or God is within the framework of that perspective. You still want to see reality as if you are a discrete object living in a world of discrete objects. To be spiritual means being a happy, discrete object. But the reality is that you are completely connected from all directions, from four dimensions, from everywhere.

So it doesn't matter how many experiences of true nature you have, as long as you consider them fulfillment.

In doing the work, people treat insights, realizations, grace, and essence like food. You eat to fill that emptiness. That food provides you a sense of value, existence, and identity. If you sacrifice your experience to feed the Basic Fault, the basic rupture from reality, then the situation remains unresolved. Whatever spiritual experience you have won't transform you. It's like you eat food, you digest it, and the next day you need more. You feel perpetually hungry. So you focus on gaining more experiences. Every week you go to your teacher and want to experience a new essential aspect or dimension. And you might, but after three days you start feeling hungry again. So you return to your teacher for another helping of enlightenment. If the teacher doesn't deliver, you get mad and you see her as a frustrating or rejecting object.

But in time, you realize that the problem is not that you're not getting goodies from your teacher. The problem is that you don't have the correct perspective. Regardless of what you get from your teacher, it won't work if you don't correct your perspective. Both getting and not getting from your teacher will expose the Basic Fault. You need to go to tremendous depth and sincerity to see that perspective actually and practically, in your very cells. It won't suffice to hear about it. The whole work directs you toward that edge of things, that edge of the world.

Some people won't like this way. They will be disappointed or angry. That's fine, but it does not change the truth. The truth is not how you want it to be. The truth is how it is. If this is not how you want things to be, you can go through your emotional gyrations for a few years. The truth accommodates that. The truth is a grinding stone where emotions gyrate until they dissolve. The only way out is through. You can't simply set aside your feelings. Your feelings are portals to the truth. You must feel the hurt, the disappointment, the fear, the anger, the aloneness. Finally, you realize that you're empty. And all this time you've been trying to fill this emptiness with your husband or wife, with sex, cigarettes, drugs, with essence, God, the Absolute. But you never get filled.

You never get filled because it's not true that you're an empty stomach. How can you fill an image? You can spend eternity piling in grace and love. You might feel full momentarily, but the next day you crave something else. After a while, you might be disturbed by this cycle, "I'm dependent on my teacher. I'm dependent on the school. I should be independent. I should be autonomous." These are the intimations that you are beginning to see the Basic Fault. But if you take independence to mean that you're a discrete entity that is going to go somewhere else for fulfillment, you will simply resume the meal at a different table.

Real freedom is not independence from this or that ideal object but independence from object relations altogether. Trading one situation for another is not true independence. Trading husbands won't do it. It might relieve things momentarily, but the Basic Fault remains intact. You might think bigger and change religions: "I believed in God all these years, but I'll be a Buddhist from now on." That won't do it either. The Basic Fault travels with you wherever you go. In the depths of your being you believe you're an entity, a separate entity among objects. Unless you experience that and understand it completely, there will always be strife and struggle in your life.

When you see through the Basic Fault, I refer to it as basic enlightenment. It is the original experience of enlightenment. This realization does not mean that you'll be able to live in accordance with it. A lot of work needs to happen for your mind to fully open to the truth of reality. You have to unlearn lots of things, and see through many conventional perspectives. This requires exposure to the extra dimension over and over and over again, because you will tend to go back to believing and functioning in the usual way. It is a gradual process. The separateness becomes less and less. Your sense of oneness is more frequent, richer, and more profound.

When you realize the enlightened perspective, the objective reality of no separateness between anything— no separateness between the physical world and the Absolute, no separateness between the Absolute and God, no separateness between God and Colorado, no separateness between Colorado and North Korea, no separateness between North Korea and you—everything is connected. Whatever you can conceive, whatever you can experience, whatever you can imagine is one.

If you can divide that one in half, then it's not oneness, it's twoness. That means, again, you've brought in separation and the Basic Fault. So if you believe that the presence of true nature comes to you from outside, if you believe God is separate from you, if you believe that enlightenment is someplace to get to, you're still operating from the perspective of the Basic Fault. That's not to say that you may not experience things that way. You can see God sitting on a throne, you can see angels, but these are intermediate experiences. You still carry the central perspective of object relations.

All of the work you've done around your relationship with your parents and the conflicts in your relationships now—the anger and the hatred and the hurt and the disappointment—is to simplify the situation until you see it in terms of very few object relations.

You have to work through all that stuff before you can fully confront the fact of objectness. Before that, you're full of emotions that you have to go through and understand. You can't see things simply. But the more you allow the experience to unfold, the simpler things become.

As you see things more simply, you are more able to directly confront the situation and see it phenomenologically. You see not only that your mother didn't love you or that your father rejected you but, more important, that you still believe you are your mother's and father's child. That's the more fundamental problem. You're not your mother's child. You're not your father's child. Not in the real sense. Physiologically it's true, but not fundamentally. Your mother and father and you are objectively one thing. Thinking yourself separate brings up issues of "Do I love them? Do I hate them? How do they feel about me?" The problems that we encounter are a consequence of separateness.

So the resolution is to be objective about the world, meaning not to be influenced by your historical subjective experience and learning. The objective perspective nourishes your soul, nourishes your Personal Essence, nourishes that precious Pearl in you, so that in time you become an objective person, a person truly being in the world and fundamentally grounded in the perception that everything is one. Unlike other nourishment, the objective perspective does not nourish you, as if you are an empty, hungry stomach. The objective perspective nourishes you by being your true nature; it nourishes you as the ocean nourishes the wave.

We're talking about something so subtle and profound that most of us can't even imagine things being this way. You think, "If everything is one, how do I go out on the street and cross traffic? I might die." Dying doesn't change anything. Still you are one—beforehand and afterward. When you see through separateness, you realize that the visible world casts a dark, ugly pall that makes things appear separate. But as the truth penetrates that drab cloak of universal ego, you realize that everything is translucence, everything is preciousness, everything is absolute clarity. The world appears clear, pure, transparent, translucent, with the freshness of an iceberg. That makes your heart warm.

Reality is so beautiful, so breathtaking, when we see that there is no separateness. When you see the deeper dimension, when you penetrate that dimension, you see that this world is the expression of oneness, the expression of one love and harmony and beauty. And that person who is identical with the oneness of the world is the resurrection. The whole world is resurrected. Everything appears and is seen in its true reality.

So the more profound spiritual realization is not the death and resurrection of who you are but the death and resurrection of the world. Not the death and resurrection of the separate individual entity, but the death and resurrection of the entire universe. The whole world as we usually see it is a dead world. Only with the resurrection does the world live. Everything lives. Even the rocks live.

As I said, this is a very subtle and profound transformation that takes a tremendous amount of work and sincerity and dedication. If we're lucky, we glimpse the resurrected world once in a while. When you perceive the oneness, the true unity, the world as it is, you can no longer be happy without it. You know now what you are. The moment that perception fades, the separation from oneness brings longing. What do you long for? To end the separation. You can say you long for God or you long for truth, but fundamentally you long to end that separateness.

Ultimately, we experience longing and sadness and unhappiness because we experience ourselves as separate objects. Then we try to connect to other separate objects through love or sex or spiritual work. But we have to see the basic truth that we're not separate beings. We don't need to do anything to be connected. There is no disconnection. Disconnection is an illusion. In fact, it is a delusion, a psychotic delusion.

This perspective is not new. For thousands of years, the oneness of reality has been the central insight in various spiritual traditions and teachings. Today we examined it from the perspective of object relations because that's the way we've been working with it here. The central object relation, which is the mechanism through which the ego relates to reality, completes the picture. Our work today might already have brought up feelings of vulnerability, helplessness, fear, and depression. I'm giving you this teaching so you don't lose heart. So you don't only believe the feelings that arise. Keep looking. Keep understanding. It is true that the breast is empty. But that's not the Ultimate Truth. The Ultimate Truth is that there is no breast. So you might feel depressed over the loss and then you might see through the breast and realize there isn't a need for depression. You know your heart is absolute freshness and lightness. You know the world is absolute clarity and aliveness.

So let's have comments and questions.

STUDENT: When I get one of these glimpses of reality that you talk about, along with the joy and everything else that comes with it, I realize that really is the truth. But you also said that from the practical point of view we still operate in a three-dimensional world of separate objects. I think what happens is that I revert back to the practical nonreality of operating in this three-dimensional world of separate objects, which is reinforced by how things seem to be and also by my past. I fall back asleep and lose the glimpse of reality.

ALMAAS: That's what happens to everyone. It's not merely because the practical perspective reinforces it from the outside, but because someplace in you there is a crystallized conviction that the physical world is the real world. Even though you glimpse the true reality, your steadfast faith in physical reality has not been completely shaken. The fake crystal will have to crack at a vital place. It requires a lot of deep work. You have to uncover and examine your belief in the physical world. You're convinced, your mind is crystallized around the belief that the physical world is reality, that you are what your mother thinks you are. You believe your mother. That belief is then supported by what people do, what society demands, and how things appear. The more you experience oneness, the more that whole perspective will be exposed.

STUDENT: When I do this work, after a certain while, I feel like I'm giving everything away. "Hey, this is a little ridiculous. You're giving everything away. You're not going to be able to take care of things." It's the same conflict I got into with my mother when I was three or four years old. I repeat that same conflict over and over again.

ALMAAS: So this brings up some object relations that you can see through. There are a lot of things you have to explore: the perception of oneness, the realization of oneness, the realization of many essential states. Ultimately, you have to see the ideal object as the breast.

You will have to see what the breast represents for you. You have to see what the self is. You have to see the self as the soul patterned by concepts and impressions from the past. The soul will have to develop, which is what we are working on.

All of these things support that sense of unity. You will see that even when you have that sense of unity, you still use your mind to fill an emptiness. You'll have to see that the true support in this world comes from somewhere else, from the fourth dimension. So your trust of what supports you will have to shift.

It is true that for some individuals it is a sudden realization, but that is very rare. And even in sudden realization there is a great deal of work and inquiry needed to be able to live such realization, and not have it only as an inner experience.

It's a long process and there's a lot in it. Don't be disheartened if you see that you revert back to the world of discrete objects. Persist in working. Don't completely believe that the physical world is what reality is. Remind yourself, "Reality seems that way, but I know that is a delusion."

STUDENT: So you accept it as a sort of duality?

ALMAAS: You accept it. Sometimes I experience things like they're discrete objects, but I know in my mind that I am deluded, that it's not true.

STUDENT: So the thing to do is to accept the duality and realize that you're going to operate according to the duality quite a bit, and that it is bullshit?

ALMAAS: Yeah, ultimately it's bullshit, but you can't do anything about it. The more you see it and allow it and don't fight it, the more the duality will dissolve. Fighting with it will not get rid of it. Best to accept it, relax, and understand things. To let the fourth dimension penetrate you and affect you, transform you so that the whole world appears in its reality. Accepting it does not mean resigning to it; rather it means not fighting with it.

STUDENT: I get so involved in this three-dimensional world, I get so distracted by it that I don't stay open to let the fourth dimension penetrate.

ALMAAS: Part of being open to the fourth dimension is understanding your being. Sometimes that means you're involved and distracted. You could understand something about why and how that happens. That state I was talking about, of being vulnerable and innocent, is the state of your being. It's true. Being is human, normal, ordinary. To let yourself accept that is by itself a big step because it requires that you go through that other dimension.

STUDENT: If all things are one, then what is a human being? When I experience the unity you've been talking about, I still feel that being human and vulnerable separates me from other things.

ALMAAS: A human being is not a disconnected entity. You feel differentiated from the rest, but not separate. But if you're feeling yourself as a human being who is a separate entity and vulnerable, you're still looking at it from the perspective of the body. You're looking at the soul from a physical perspective. So the soul is limited to the experience of the body. If you allow the soul to be there as it is, without limitation, the soul will naturally fill up and expand and become everything without changing the quality that is the soul. It becomes what is called the universal soul. That's one way of experiencing the fourth dimension.

So when you say, "What is a human being?" it is the same thing as saying, "What is love? What is a house?" You could talk about that. All these exist. I'm not denying the existence of any of these things. I'm saying that there's no separation between them. That doesn't mean there are no houses. There are houses, but there are no houses. There are human beings, but there are no human beings. They exist, but not in the way you think.

STUDENT: I can understand the perspective of differentiation without separation and have some experience of it. Usually, though, I know it in my mind. Could you say something about how the heart figures here?

ALMAAS: The heart, obviously, is very important here, but we need to free the heart. Most of the time the heart is dominated by the perspective of object relations. We experience various feelings and emotions according to our psychodynamic history. Actually, the heart is nothing but the mind filled with love. The heart gives fullness to the concepts of the mind. So the mind and the heart are not separate things. They're one thing. Love and thinking are one thing. Both the mind and the heart need to be freed from the perspective of the physical world. The heart is freed from object relations by arriving at nonattachment.

So we see, the task is not easy. It's immense. But so what? What else are we going to do? If we're going to find out what the truth is, then we're going to find out what the truth is. How big or difficult or long doesn't matter. For a long time, the student cannot help relating to the teaching and to essence and to truth in terms of object relations. You cannot help but do that. Seeing through object relations is hard, but that is the path. The path leads to the truth, you see.

The resolution of the dilemma, how to live in this world of objects and see objective reality, I am calling the resurrection. The resurrection means seeing the world of objects from a new perspective, as infused and united with and by the fourth dimension. Truth embodies the world. So instead of a world constructed of discrete objects that are inert, the world becomes a living world of harmony and oneness. Things are differentiated, but they are not separate.

Functioning and doing and living life, then, is not some unusual thing of flying here or there, materializing or dematerializing. You live a normal life, but it's a life of truth, of harmony, of fulfillment, a life that is unencumbered. There's a freedom of how you see the fourth dimension. You live in harmony as a unique individual connected with everything else, and you see yourself as the oneness, or you see yourself as the ultimate ground and source of everything. The human consciousness goes through all of that and that becomes life.

All these are possibilities for a human life. This is life. So the usual human life is still there. You shop, you push carts, you feel disgruntled. All of that is there, but it participates in a bigger wonder, where the range of experience is wider and doesn't contradict our ordinary life. Our ordinary lives become integrated into something bigger and freer, more boundless.

So the resolution of the Basic Fault, which is seeing the physical world as the reality, is not elimination of this world. The world becomes more open and real. We don't eliminate the three dimensions; we simply see a fourth one. When your perspective shifts, nothing is gone. If from the perspective of the third dimension you say, "I move my hand," from the perspective of the fourth dimension you say, "The universe moves this hand." You see that your hand doesn't belong to you. The universe's hand moves. The shape of the movement does not appear different, but your perception of it is different. That is life awakening.

TEN

Christ the Logos

Today we will talk about something appropriate to Christmas, which is in a few days. I've been thinking for a while that much of the contemporary understanding of Christ's message does not adequately represent my understanding of Christianity's true contribution. And I think this is one important reason why many people in Christian countries are turning toward other traditions, especially Eastern traditions.

The way I see it, Christ's message is not simply another way of stating our spiritual situation, not simply a different version of what traditional spiritual paths address. Christ's contribution is actually a unique and specific understanding of the reality of the human being. This contribution is part of the evolution of our understanding of human beings. So Christ's thought about reality is different from other traditions, not in the sense that it's an alternative to other understandings, but in the sense that it is a new development.

Christ's teaching doesn't contradict other teachings but presents us with a more complete picture. It brings forth a new dimension of our understanding of human beings. Many statements attributed to Christ point to the truth of this new understanding. For example, Christ says, "I am the Way, the Truth, and the Life. No one comes to the Father except through me," and "I am the light of the world." What is Christ saying here?

Understanding these statements will help us to see what Christ's unique message adds to the global realization of our spiritual nature. We'll begin with his statement that "no one comes to the Father except through me." If we understand this, we understand what Christ is. So what does it mean that we have to go through Christ? What does it mean to go to the Father? The Father here is obviously the ultimate truth, the most absolute reality.

Here we need to introduce another factor important to Christianity. As far as I understand it, Christian belief involves the notion of original sin. In fact, the idea of original sin is specifically Christian. What is original sin? Original sin is not something that we do in our life. We have it the moment we are born. It is the fabric of being a human being. Although the doctrine of original sin first appears most prominently in the Christian theology of Augustine, the notion is derived from Paul's letters in the New Testament.

Original sin is the fundamental problem that all human beings have from the beginning, a problem that is not dependent on whether we are good or bad, whether we do the right thing or the wrong thing. Although Christian scholars explicate the notion in various ways, in my view original sin is the belief that we are an independent entity, that we are a separate human being. So the belief in separateness, the belief in entityhood, the belief in being a separate entity and having our own will and mind and choice is the original sin.

We grow up believing we are an individual with our own mind and will and so on. If we accept that sense of separateness, that sense of isolation, that concept of complete independence, we are not Christian. To be Christian is to recognize that sense of separateness as the biggest problem; it is to recognize our original sin. So original sin is not something to feel guilty about or something we can remedy by trying to do good. It doesn't work that way. Original sin can only be resolved through Christ's help.

It is said that Christ came to release Christians from their original sin. That is his help. If you turn to Christ, you are cleansed of your original sin. Christ does not cleanse you from the cardinal sins, the seven deadly sins. That is your own work. You have to do that work, the work of purification. To work through the original sin, you need Christ's help. You can't do it on your own. The way I see it, a Christian is not simply someone who is born to a Christian family, but someone who recognizes original sin, understands why it is a sin, and through this understanding sees that the only way out is through Christ.

Simply saying that you are a Christian is not enough. The Christian path involves recognizing original sin, and recognizing Christ's role in freeing the soul from that sin. It is not a question of belief but of truth. Christ said, "I am the Way, the Truth, and the Life." Christ is the way in the sense that he is the way to go beyond original sin. Christ is the way to overcome original sin. But what is Christ? Why is the Christ the only possibility for the release from original sin, from the sin of believing that you are a separate soul? This question points to a very deep truth of what Christ is.

In various traditions, especially in Eastern traditions, the world is seen as illusion. The whole world you see and experience is of the nature of dreams. This is true from the perspective of the Absolute, the deepest reality. When you are aware of reality as the Absolute, you see the ephemeral nature of the thoughts and images that are normally taken to be the world. The normal perception is revealed to be a thin, insubstantial film over true reality. Traditions that emphasize this view are oriented toward leaving the world, toward penetrating this external facade and going toward the true reality. This is liberation. In Hindu, Taoist, and Buddhist paths, this is a basic notion. Liberation is seen as a release from the cycle of birth and death; it is freedom from the human condition, freedom from being a separate human being. We see that all we experience, all of life, all of the universe, is ultimately an illusion, what Hindus call Maya, what Buddhists call mind. We realize the truth that we are something much more substantial, something beyond the mind, beyond the world.

The realization of the truth from this perspective involves seeing the world as unreal and valuing the escape from human life. Our life is as unimportant as our thoughts, and is part and parcel of the overall illusion. The value of life is as a way station where we learn something and depart. Human life in itself has no intrinsic value, nor does the material world. To be spiritual is to go beyond life and the world. Most traditions ascribe to this general view.

I believe that Christ understood this view and went further. To know Christ is to go beyond the world to the Father, but there is something new in the story of the resurrection. I think the resurrection is the resurrection of the world. In spiritual realization the world dies and is revealed as ephemeral and unreal. We experience the death of the whole world.

The resurrection of Christ is not simply the rebirth of an individual person. It is the rebirth of the world, of the totality of existence, of the totality of the universe. The resurrection is the rebirth of life and the rebirth of humankind. So Christ is a redeemer in that respect. He redeems not only the individual but the totality of human life. He redeems the world. Christ's resurrection is from the death of the world, from the death of the universe, after we recognize its illusory nature. In that death of the world, there remains only the Father, only the Absolute in its majesty. That death is the complete annihilation of everything else.

But from that death, there is the possibility of a new arising. The world is reborn, but reborn as the real world. Just as an individual can die and be reborn and redeemed, the whole universe is reborn and redeemed. Through this rebirth, the whole universe is seen in a different light, a light that was not seen before the spiritual realization and not seen during the spiritual realization. We do not see the real world when we have not yet seen through the naive belief about the absolute reality of the apparent world. We also do not see the real world when we see the apparent world only as illusion. When we come to see the real world, it's the same world, except now it is redeemed. It is no longer an illusion. It is a new world.

It is true that the world we see every day is not the real world. From the perspective that is more fundamental than our mental constructs, the world we have been seeing is revealed as an empty illusion. Just as our individuality is revealed on the inner path to be an empty illusion—not ultimately real, only a mental construct—so the world that we see is revealed to be a mental construct. We define through the mind not only ourselves but the world. In the course of our realization, as we go beyond ourselves to discover our true essence, we also need to go beyond the image of the world to discover the true nature of the world. Just as the soul is reborn with its essential qualities when the ego dissolves, when the world construct dies, the world, too, is reborn as an oversoul, a universal soul with essential qualities. This is what Christ represents. So what I see in Christ is not the rebirth of an individual but the rebirth of the totality of all existence as reality.

This perspective is different from simply looking at reality from beyond the mind and seeing the whole world as an illusion. From this perspective the world is not exactly an illusion. Although the perceived world is not the absolute reality we have naively assumed it to be, it is nevertheless animated by the absolute reality. With the understanding of Christ, the world can be known as the expression of the Father, or the face of the Father, or the heart of the Father, or the manifest part of the Father. The world is the Father appearing as the universe, the ultimate truth manifesting in form.

And the ultimate truth manifesting as or in form is not simply a new illusion. It can be seen as a new illusion, but it can also be seen as a new creation. Out of nothing comes something. It is true that in some sense nothing is the ultimate, the most pure, but out of that, there is something new. To say that the Ultimate Truth is absolute and beyond form, beyond concept, is true, and this is felt to be the deepest or highest perception. But to say that this perception is the final goal of the soul's realization is like saying that the ultimate nature of the body is atoms, to the detriment of all the other levels of life, thought, and feeling.

If we recognize and experience the atom as part of us, we realize that we are not bodies, that everything in us is atoms. So you could say that the level of atoms is a deeper reality than the body. And it's true that on the level of atoms there are no organs, no person, no other people; everything is atoms. But can you say that this level is more real? Can you say that the atoms are somehow more real than the body? It is true that the self-organizing forms of the body are not in some sense more fundamental than the atomic level. The forms constitute a creation out of that undifferentiated sea. So part of the Christian revelation is that the body itself is no longer seen as form moving away from the Source, but rather that the body never departs from the Source. The body never leaves the reality that "I and the Father are one." This is a new development in the understanding of the human being. Some other teachings have included this insight, but I think that Christ gave it a central place.

This is how I interpret the message of Christ. Christ is the redemption of the form of the world. The manifest world is a new creation, arising out of nothing, out of purity, out of absoluteness. Here, "out of" doesn't mean "separating from," it means more like "made out of." When we contemplate the manifest world from the outside, so to speak, and believe that is all there is, we fall into error. We take ourselves as an object separate from other objects. We take the surface to be the ultimate reality. This perspective obscures the true perception of how things are. However, the alternative is not to see this obscured way of considering manifestation to be an illusion. The Christian revelation shows us that the world with all its forms, including our human form, is an actual creation, as if an artist had created it. Raw materials create beautiful forms. We could value the raw materials over the forms, because that's the most pure level, but the form itself has value; the fact that it has form has value.

So this is the redemption: In the course of our path of realizing what is beyond mind, the forms that came to be seen as only conceptual, empty, and unreal, now become full and real, filled with the truth. Here we can speak of a whole dimension we call the Cosmic Christ. In the way I understand Christian revelation, the person Christ, or Jesus, taught and embodied this perspective more clearly and more completely than anyone else before him. Christ taught that the kingdom of heaven has arrived here and now. When we go through the redemption, when the original sin is released, we realize that the kingdom of heaven is here. When we release the original sin, we experience the resurrection, and not only are we resurrected without the separate self, but the whole world is resurrected. Human life as a whole is resurrected, including the human mind, including the human heart. So Christ's contribution to the understanding of the human situation is to show the truth and thus the value of the world, of existence, what in religious traditions is called creation.

At the beginning of the spiritual path, the world is a big problem, being an individual is a big problem, the mind is a big problem. And from the perspective of beyond the conceptual mind, these are simply constructed concepts. Christ's revelation teaches us not only to go beyond apparent reality to the knowledge of the Father, but to come back from and with that knowledge, resurrecting all that we had to drop in the course of discovering our fundamental nature. So the revelation shows the value and the truth of human life, of the human individual and of the human mind, which participates in the forms of the world.

Thus our perception of the world goes through a series of transformations. At the beginning, in the naive view, the world is a neutral given, a particular reality full of discrete entities, including us. In the next stage, we come to see that this given world is ephemeral, an illusion of the mind constructed of concepts. In the perspective we are discussing today, we see that the world is made of concepts, but the concepts are felt and lived and known through our living presence. We now see a world of harmony, a world made of truth. We see that the forms are variations of the truth. We understand, for example, that "table" is a concept, but in the redeemed world that concept is filled with truth. The concept simply carves the truth into form, which produces a sense of beauty that is not there without the form.

So all the human things that the ego-self was attached to, all the attachments that were revealed as imprisoning us and that had to be abandoned for the realization of our true nature, now return in their redeemed form. This is the resurrection and the redemption. This is why Christ is called the Redeemer. Christ redeems what we have had to give up in order to be real. This understanding shows us that the things of the world actually do not need to be given up in an absolute sense, but do need to be redeemed. That is, we need to realize the truth and reality of the world, which necessarily entails going beyond the naive mental view of it.

Now we understand more thoroughly why saying, as some traditions do, that the world is only an illusion that we must go beyond just doesn't do it. If the world is only an illusion, why is it here? Is it some kind of cosmic joke? We come here, we suffer, we try to get out of here. Sounds like a silly arrangement. But this is apparently what many teach. I think they hold this view because they do not recognize completely that this world exists in a real way. They don't have the perspective that there is a true purpose and a true reality to this world and to human life, that we're not here to discover that life is an illusion and then get out of here.

We are here to live in a real world, in a real way. The redemption is our recognizing that the world, including all of humanity, is life; the world itself is alive. We recognize that the whole world is made of living consciousness. And we realize also that the nature of the consciousness is love. When we come to a realization of the nature of the soul, we see that it is infused with potential, with all the essential aspects and all the dimensions. We realize that the soul is the cohesion, the integration, and the totality of all of Essence. From this perspective, we realize that the universe is like a universal soul that contains all of the essential qualities. We look around and see the redeemed world, the actual resurrected universe, which means that the world is one and indivisible. The world is not illusory, not a construct, and not a dream. It is a real world that shines with truth, that overflows with love, that transforms with limitless intelligence.

One way many people experience this realization is to perceive the whole world as the living body of Christ. This means the end of separateness and the redemption from original sin. When we see the true reality of the world in its redeemed truth, we see that there are no separations. The oneness we have realized is composed of the various human qualities—composed of love, composed of compassion, composed of strength, of beauty, peace, and harmony. All these qualities are revealed to be what constitute not only our souls but also physical reality. All of physical reality, all of the universe, can be seen then as a harmony, as an expression of love. All the dimensions and all the accidents of life appear in harmonious oneness: Oneness that is peace. Oneness that is love. Oneness that is harmony.

This is Christ's message. For me, when we celebrate Christianity, this is what we celebrate. We celebrate that the actual world, including our true nature and our concrete lives, is goodness, is love, is harmony, is peace. Christ is not bringing peace from somewhere else to some spot in the world. Understanding Christ's message, we see that the whole world has the nature of peace, harmony, goodness, and love. We see that the world as a whole is heart. The Buddha saw that the world is mind. Christ saw that mind and said it is made of love. The world is heart. So the whole universe is revealed as the heart of the Absolute. And that whole universe as the heart of the Absolute is Christ. And to see the universe as heart is to see it as harmony, to see it as love, to see it as goodness, to see it as forgiveness, to see it as beauty, to see it as peace.

So the revelation of Christ brings back—full of life—the concepts, the forms, that we had to let go of to free ourselves from the world. Through this redemption, through that resurrection, we can see the significance of human life, which is not simply a matter of being free from the world but is actually about living in a real way. This realization can bring harmony between human beings, and between human beings and the rest of reality, because we see that we are all made of one thing. We are all made of joy and love and peace, not only light. Everything is made of that.

Our realization of Christ in this way makes sense of the statement that "no one can come to the Father except through me." Only through Christ can we go to the Father because we can't go to the Father as a separate individual. There's no way. We cannot penetrate to the Absolute, to the ultimate nature, believing that we are a separate soul. We have to lose our original sin, to let go of our separateness, and become the Christ. Only then can we realize that the Christ is the first-born, in some sense the only born of the Absolute. We realize that the Christ, the totality of the universe as a harmony of all that there is, is the first manifestation of the Absolute. It is the first Word. Christ is the Word made flesh, the first form that arose from Absolute non-existence.

Here "Absolute" means before appearance, before creation, before existence. And the first thing that appears out of that is the Word. The Word is not just a word uttered by someone; the Word is the totality of all there is. The Word is the totality of all there is in the sense that it is a concept, an articulation. The Word is a concept in the mind of the Absolute. In some sense, the Absolute thinks and the world is created. But the Word in the mind of the Absolute is not like a word in our mind. The Word in the mind of the Absolute is the totality of the universe as complete harmony. One way to see it is that the potential within the Absolute that is not manifest becomes manifest.

When we are in the process of realizing ourselves and reality as Absolute, the emptiness beyond being and nonbeing, at some point we recognize that the biggest obstacle is the sense of our ego boundaries, our belief that we are a separate individual. We feel that we have a separate mind, a separate will, a separate heart. This sense of being a separate entity becomes the biggest spiritual problem and the hardest to surrender.

This belief is difficult to let go of and we cannot let go of it by ourselves. How can we as an individual free ourselves from being an individual? An individual simply cannot free himself or herself. Only Christ can help you. Christ is the resolution.

So we understand the teaching of Christ when we realize that the individual, separate, bounded soul is a belief in our minds, and we relax and realize that the soul is continuous with the rest of reality. That soul continuous with the rest, as that totality, is then the Logos or the Christ or the Word. This is an exact and specific resolution because we don't simply let go of our boundaries and become pure consciousness, pure awareness, or the Absolute or something like that. We let go of our boundaries without losing our uniqueness. We continue to be a soul, to be an individual, but are continuous with the rest of reality. We are an individuation, then, out of a totality. So it's a very specific resolution.

The disappearance of the boundaries is not complete disappearance of the individual. So we lose the sense of bounded individuality as we become that totality of cosmic dynamic presence—the Logos itself, in which there is no individuality. Yet, it is not simply boundless dynamic presence with no individual, even though it has no division or duality. For it is also possible to be a unique individual not separate from that cosmic presence, such that it's hard to tell if you are an individual or not an individual. You are an individual and unique and at the same time you are the totality. That means the concepts are there still: the concept of a person is there, the concept of a table is there, the concept of a house is there, the concept of a tree is there, the concept of life is there, the concept of humanity is there, the concept of the universe is there. All the concepts are there but are not completely separate from each other. They're more like variations in the same substance, formations of the formlessness.

So the Christ is the Way to the Absolute, in the sense of being the oneness of all that exists, which contains all the individuals in their redeemed condition; and at the same time the Christ is the Life of the Universe. The world itself becomes the Life, becomes a living existence. We actually experience the world as animated by living presence. Everything is made of a living, pulsing, breathing consciousness. And it is all one thing—the infinite boundless one existence. That is beauty, that is harmony, that is peace, that is truth. All of it together, all the essential aspects, all mixed together in a harmony: That is the true Life, the true world, the true existence.

So when Christ says, "I am the Life," I don't think he means life the way people normally think of it, as being either animate or inanimate. He doesn't say, "I am life"; he says, "I am the Life." What is the Life? The Life is the Absolute, the Ultimate Truth, becoming living. One of the most significant of the ninety-nine names of God mentioned in the Qur'an is "the Living." The Life is when the Absolute, the Ultimate Truth, manifests as a living existence, a living conscious existence. You can't say the Absolute is the Life. You can't even say the Absolute is conscious. But as the Christ, as the Logos, as the first manifestation, it is Life, it is Living. So the Christ is a Cosmic Life, a Universal Life. And the life that we know is a particularization of it, a very specific perception of it, a development of it.

But we can experience the whole universe, all that exists, including the inanimate, as Living, as Life. We can experience the whole universe as the consciousness of love, as the consciousness of harmony, as the consciousness of peace. We can experience the whole universe as the Life, not in the sense that it has aliveness but in the sense that it is functioning. Part of being alive is functioning. A human being functions, moves, does, and thinks. So to see the Christ is to see the universe as a functioning oneness rather than as a static oneness. The whole universe is one unified existence that is in a constant state of transformation and change and movement and functioning. So the change of seasons, the transformation of forms, death and life, and all the rest are the functioning of that oneness. It is a seamless flow of forms, as the continuous creation of all.

When we see the universe as Oneness without perceiving the functioning, we're looking at a deeper reality in some sense. We're seeing the Supreme dimension of pure presence or maybe the Nameless dimension of pure awareness, and we're seeing it as a state where there is no time, where it seems there is only eternity. But when we see the universe as Oneness on the level of Christ, time is there, but redeemed as real time. Then time is nothing but transformation, change, and functioning. So we redeem the human mind by resurrecting its concepts as real. The concept of time, the concept of space, the concept of an object, the concept of humanity, are resurrected as made of consciousness, made of the truth, made of reality. All forms are a direct manifestation of the Life of the Father as the Son.

This is my understanding of the contribution of Christianity, a contribution that no other tradition so clearly and definitely makes.

So let's see if there are any questions.

STUDENT: How is this Christ perspective connected to the Absolute?

ALMAAS: When the Absolute is realized, is really established, you can see the whole universe emerge again, but in a more real, more living, more organic way. The mind comes back, but comes back in true thinking. For the first time, you understand what thinking is. The thinking, the mind that we thought was a problem for spiritual realization—which it was—is now redeemed and functions in a real way. We realize that there is true thinking, liberated mentation, in which the thoughts themselves are an expression of love and peace and harmony. Then there is true feeling. There is true action. True thought. All redeemed.

The dream of the human soul is to live in the real world, with joy and compassion, with harmony and peace and love. The dream of the human soul is to live a human life where life, world, and what is thought of as spiritual aren't separate. We don't liberate ourselves by leaving the world. We liberate ourselves by living the world.

So it's as if the shell is redeemed. The shell that is the ego, the empty shell, the fake one, is redeemed as the soul. When we see that the ego is not separate, when we recognize its original sin, the shell becomes connected, continuous with the whole. And that very shell, now made of essence and love and truth, we now realize is the soul. In the Christ perspective, the shell that is the apparent world, the empty world, the fake world, is resurrected as the Cosmic Logos, the true living world, the universal soul.

In this resurrected world, heaven is on earth, heaven is the world. Christmas, with its sparkling tree of many lights and colors, is the celebration of this heavenly life on earth, the resurrection of this new body.

STUDENT: What's the difference between the Christ perspective and other teachings about separateness and loss of boundaries?

ALMAAS: Different people look at it in different ways. Some people talk about the separateness; some people talk about leaving your identity. Some teach about nonduality. There are all kinds of ways to look at it. It's true that most traditions speak about going through that experience of loss of boundaries. But the loss of boundaries can happen in many ways. The experience of the Logos, in one way or another, is a loss of boundaries in a state of oneness. But that is not the complete experience of the Logos.

Not all traditions know the complete experience of the Logos, but they experience it in one manifestation or another. So you could experience the oneness without experiencing it as a functioning oneness, as a living oneness. That's one experience of the Logos, as a way you pass through the experience of oneness. But Christ says he is the Way and the Life, which means there is more. He is the oneness that is the Life that happens after one dies into the Absolute.

So the movement from original sin to the Absolute is not specific to Christianity; all traditions have that in one form or another. Christianity emphasizes original sin as part and parcel of being human, having nothing to do with being good or bad. And only Christ can redeem you from that original sin. Although many theologians tell you that you have to believe in that person Christ and to believe in Christianity to be redeemed, I don't think it works that way, although the belief might help. What needs to happen is the actual perception of the original sin of separateness and then the actual perception of the nondual dynamic oneness. So believing in your mind in Christ does not do it; you actually have to perceive the Christ.

So being both the Way and the Life is important,

but being the Life is the specific contribution of Christianity that's not talked about much in other traditions. Christ's message is the redemption of the totality of all existence, seeing the Logos as the Cosmic Logos, as the Cosmic Christ, giving existence a true value. Christ happened to be a complete embodiment of that level of consciousness in being a person. So you could say that the Logos itself, true nature as a dynamic, creative, active, living, indivisible presence of realness, got incarnated as an individual. And that's the sense in which Christ is the Son of God, because the Logos is what first comes out of the Absolute. The Logos is the first radiance, the first light, the first intelligence. Think of the resurrection as happening all the time. The Logos is the firstborn, the first emanation of the Absolute. Christ the Logos is the oldest of the old.

ELEVEN

The Unfolding Pattern

It's a common delusion of students that they will gain something by doing practices over time. We believe that who we are and what we do continue and change in the course of time. But seeing things more as they truly are brings a radically different picture.

Take the movie *Casablanca,* which we spoke of earlier. We know that a movie is simply a series of light phenomena moving on a screen, and yet we are convinced that Bogart is doing something at the end that produces a consequence: allowing the fugitive couple to board the airplane and escape the Nazis. And we are also convinced that what he is doing is a consequence of what he has done and felt, of all that has happened since the beginning of the film. The story is engaging; as the music plays, you begin shedding tears. You are inspired or touched—you're not thinking, "What an interesting pattern of light and sound phenomena." You can view the whole thing as the story of Casablanca and yet you also know it is the transformations of light that produce the appearance of changing forms.

You are told to do a certain practice that will lead to a certain realization. However, being told to do a certain practice is actually simply the instantaneous flow of reality, like the instant-by-instant flow of light and sound in a movie. Whether you do the practice or not, what happens is also the instantaneous flow. If you do the practice, then that flow has a pattern. The flow deepens and changes. All of these phenomena appear to happen in time, but actually we don't need our assumptions about time to see the flow and harmony in the pattern of what happens. Logically, you could see that flow happens without time. If you remove the word "time" from the *Principia Mathematica*—one of the mainstays of Western logic, written by Bertrand Russell and Alfred North Whitehead—the book becomes a mystical work, like the *Bhagavad Gita*.

All of our ways of looking at the world involve the concept of time. The world we usually see emerges from our assumption that there is such a thing as time. The moment your mind is not conditioned by the concept of time, you realize that things really are different from what and how you think they are. The world appears as it always has, but your understanding of it is completely new. So, in some sense, you have no choice in the matter about whether to be deluded or not. Absolutely no choice. The light chooses, you don't. Like Bogart in the movie, you are being projected, manifested by light.

Although the flow of reality is spontaneous, it is not chaotic or haphazard. The flow is lawful. Reality flows in a pattern. Considered over a span of time, the flow of the pattern appears as cause and effect, as if one action leads to another. When the movement is done correctly in the doing exercise we have been practicing, it reveals the flow of being, and is an initial perception of how the universe as a whole is flowing out into existence. That flow can be seen on many levels, depending on how complex your mind is, and on what concepts underlie your perception of the universe. If you use the concept of time and space, and you use the concept of being an individual entity, then the flow of being appears as the flow of essence within you.

As you practice the doing exercise, you will feel a flow, an emergence, an unfoldment of one state after another, one manifestation after another. But what you perceive arises within the stable concepts that you believe in, for example the concept of being an individual entity that is continuous in time and space. These concepts do not change; something inside you changes so that you experience a flow. This is called the realization of the soul, which leads to the realization of Essence. However, eventually you might eliminate the concept of being an individual entity continuous in time and space. Then, reality changes. You realize that the flow is universal, that even your body is a flowing out of being, as is the totality of your environment. So how we perceive things depends a lot on the beliefs and assumptions from which we begin. What I'm saying is not unscientific. Many scientific discoveries have established that what you perceive depends a great deal on what you believe, that perception is not independent of belief. The way I see it, at every instant the totality of all that appears to our minds flows out spontaneously; at every instant what we see has an unmanifest, unseen source.

From this perspective, there is no difference between

one person and another, because their source is identical. Neither is there really a difference between ego and enlightenment; neither has anything to do with you. If you are ego, then ego is what's being generated. If you are enlightened, then enlightenment is what's being generated. If you are ignorant, then ignorance is what's being generated. We get scared sometimes when we think of things this way, when someone points out this deep truth. This truth confronts your deepest convictions about yourself, about your life, and about reality. But that fear itself is simply the flow of the pattern at that moment. There's no escape, you see. Whether you surrender or you revolt, you have nothing to do with it. You are being produced at every moment. Your resistance is being produced, and your surrender is being produced. Your knowledge is being produced, and your ignorance is being produced.

STUDENT: So how does will fit into this?

ALMAAS: Will is also produced.

STUDENT: So when we exercise will to break some small habit, what's that?

ALMAAS: That is the unfoldment of the pattern. You see, what I'm saying does not contradict everything else we do. Perceiving the flow is simply a particular way of looking at reality. Sometimes you might feel as if you were applying your will, with great consequence. When you investigate further, you realize that the application of the will, the decision to apply the will, is not initiated by you. What initiates will is the Source. The result of applying the will is identical with the application of the will. The flow of the pattern is lawful, as nature is lawful. When the temperature and pressure coincide in a particular way, clouds form. Then there is rain or snow or fog. Unfoldment, too, happens according to the laws of the truth. Because we don't see these laws, we adhere to the smaller perspective of cause and effect, of time and space. So we understand reality in terms of the limited laws of time and space. But truth has its own laws. Creation exists as lawful pattern. The pattern of reality could be understood from within—through the usual reasoning in terms of time and space, cause and effect—or the pattern could be understood from outside the perspective of time and space, in which case it appears as lawful movement, transformation and flow.

It is possible to see that the two points of view are equivalent in terms of the phenomena. The phenomena are identical, but the perspective, and thus the experience, is different. If you are watching *Casablanca*, you might be completely engrossed in it; the story, the setting, and the characters all appear real, and one event follows the other. Or you might be aware of the light projecting images onto the screen and creating what appears in each instant. Part of enjoying a movie, of course, is forgetting about the light and believing the story. If you're always looking at light, after a while movies appear as the imagination of the projector. But the two points of view are equivalent in terms of what appears on the screen.

STUDENT: My point of view about time has a lot to do with the aging of my physical body. I know I have less hair than I had fifteen years ago. So if you consider your body, is there a different perspective on the flow of time in terms of human physiology?

ALMAAS: Yes, that's definitely the case; your body and my body are aging. That's a valid way of viewing time. But there is another point of view. You could see that your body at this moment is not in a continuum with your body from ten years ago. Your body at this moment appears right now, and your body from fifteen years ago doesn't exist here and now. How can something that doesn't exist produce something that is here right now? That's actually the less logical perspective. We skim over that illogic because we believe the concept of time and, hence, of causality. If you apply logic completely, you have to question how something that doesn't exist could produce something that exists right now. How could that be? Conventional thinking is far less logical than the point of view I'm presenting. I'm saying that there is something real, the ground of all that is here, that is at this very moment manifesting things spontaneously each instant.

STUDENT: Does that mean that if your point of view changes, your physiology will change?

ALMAAS: No. As I said, everything happens according to a lawful pattern. The flow, the manifestation, the emergence, occurs in a pattern according to certain laws. The pattern is exactly what you see. The body appears to grow and change. Just as in the movie, one frame after another; here Bogart drinks and here Bogart talks to the policemen. Change and transformation happen. But is there really something that changes and transforms, or is it one frame after another, images that are being projected by the light? Is each frame, each image, caused by the image before it? No, each image is created by the light. The speed of the projected images encourages you to perceive change as a continuous chain of causes and effects.

STUDENT: My usual perspective seems directional, in the sense that I want to see things moving laterally, tied together in time and space. But actually there's no lateral movement, there's only projection.

ALMAAS: That's true. Lateral movement means

movement in space. Movement in space appears as the passage of time. The mind cannot think except in those terms because the mind uses images in order to know and to think. Images are pictures in space, and the movement of images gives the sense of time. So, as you see, I'm not saying that anything is different from how it appears. I'm not saying that what appears to everyone is not the way it is. Everything appears and happens as usual, meaning that the pattern of the changes of shapes that we attribute to movement continues to be the same. You could interpret what you see according to the usual point of view, or you could perceive it directly and realize that what's happening is something completely different, even though it appears to be the same. This direct perception of reality brings a sense of freedom, a sense that there's no need to worry anymore. What you're doing now has nothing to do with what's going to happen next! So what is there to worry about? You completely surrender to the flow. And if you surrender to the flow, the pattern of the flow will appear in terms of greater freedom and realization.

STUDENT: So, in looking at things, it's either patterns or natural laws that are operating that make things look like a continuum in time?

ALMAAS: Yes. We can actually see that the natural laws are abstracted from the perception of the patterns.

STUDENT: How would you explain, for example, the explosion this year of the space shuttle *Challenger,* which killed everyone on board?

ALMAAS: It's like anything else! Why is what happened to the space shuttle different from your talking right now?

STUDENT: Because I'm not clear about it.

ALMAAS: The thing that made the shuttle explode is

making you talk to me right now. There's only one cause, what is sometimes called the Prime Mover. From within the perspective of manifestation, where we take appearance to be the ultimate reality, there seem to be causes and effects. The space shuttle exploded because there was a mechanical malfunction. That is true. But the malfunction was not a result of what happened at the docking station. The malfunction was produced instantaneously at that very moment. And the explosion was not a result of the malfunction, but was produced instantaneously at that very moment. The explosion is like anything else: moving your arm, saying a word, snow falling, catching a flight, seeing God, taking a shit, a war happening, a murder, a marriage, an orgasm.

There is no need to consider one incident greater than any other. No matter what it is, each and every thing happens one way. Things appear different but have an identical source. We assume cause and effect because that provides an accurate description of our usual point of view. There's another way of seeing it. You can watch a movie and completely believe it, and explain what happens. You can see that Bogart is depressed because Bergman's character came back into his life after many years, or you could see that whatever is happening, every part of it—her reappearance, his getting drunk, and so on—is all being produced by the projector. Both points of view are accurate.

STUDENT: But one point of view is truer than the other, isn't that right?

ALMAAS: You see, that question was also produced by the light.

STUDENT: So from that standpoint I have no responsibility . . .

ALMAAS: Absolutely none.

STUDENT: . . . for why I'm here instead of sleeping in on Sunday morning . . .

ALMAAS: Absolutely. You have no responsibility.

STUDENT: So to the extent that I could allow the flow of being, that too is part of the light?

ALMAAS: Whatever you do is being produced by the light.

STUDENT: That makes me feel less guilty about things.

ALMAAS: That is the flow of the pattern, of the manifestation. When you hear that you have no responsibility, it is lawful that the next frame is less guilt. I'm not doing anything and neither are you. It is all happening. Spontaneous manifestation. Sometimes referred to as display, sometimes as continual creation, sometimes as the *lila*, the play of Maya.

STUDENT: So there's no free will?

ALMAAS: From within the manifestation, it appears as if there were free will. If you look from the Source, no free will exists. So it all depends from where you look. Whatever you see is produced by the flow. It does not get you off the hook, though. As long as you experience yourself as a separate self, it is best to take responsibility. If you do not take responsibility, the flow will manifest in darker and more difficult patterns. However, if you take responsibility in a real way, not by feeling guilty but by being responsible in your dealings with the world, the more that responsibility will manifest the flow in a lighter and more illuminating way. Authentic responsibility is our way of experiencing the illumination of the flow that culminates in its revelation of the true nature of the pattern, as the creative outflow of the Logos, the Patterns.

STUDENT: The real difficulty for me seems to be trying to reconcile the two viewpoints.

ALMAAS: They're completely reconcilable. The phenomena are identical. You're just looking from different directions. Either from this direction or from that direction. That's all.

STUDENT: So it is almost like cause and effect, actually, if you turn the words around. You're just being caused, and the effect is just what's happening.

ALMAAS: Yes, you could say there's only one cause that is causing everything all the time. You could call that the Absolute or God or Truth or the Prime Mover—something that is always and completely cause. There's only one mover that moves everything, instantaneously, universally, cosmically. So when you take a breath, then exhale, the exhalation is not the result of the inhalation. The exhalation is completely independent of the inhalation. Independence, though, does not mean arbitrary chaos. Law and harmony are in the movement. After I inhale, the next thing that appears in the flow is an exhalation. My mind might focus and decide, "I am doing it, and there is a cause and an effect." The direct perception is that my chest rises and my chest falls. But I'm not seeing that one causes the other. Like the movie, one frame materializes instantly after the other. In this perception, there isn't a sense of causation.

STUDENT: My question has to do with the concept of time as it relates to memory. If there were not a memory, there would not be a past. So is our memory being re-created all the time?

ALMAAS: All the time. There's no memory.

STUDENT: So why do we not experience a break of some sort? Is memory also a flow? Is that why memories are incorrect from time to time? How does memory function in what you're talking about?

ALMAAS: The memory is images appearing in our

minds. The images that appear in your mind are created instantaneously all the time, as are your mind and your head and your body. They're all being generated spontaneously together. So you don't remember in the sense that you recall something that happened at some other time and space. Thinking is creative. Something entirely new is brought to life. Our usual mode of thinking relates what is being generated now to something similar or familiar and calls that memory.

STUDENT: How is that different from delusions?

ALMAAS: Delusions too are created.

STUDENT: So delusions and memories are inactive?

ALMAAS: What you're not getting is that nothing is excluded. When I say nothing, I mean absolutely nothing. Anything you conceive is being produced instantaneously. If each and every thing is not included, then there would be a contradiction with normal, everyday perception. Spontaneous manifestation is absolutely total. And because it's absolutely total, there is no contradiction. The perceptions of the two points of view are exactly identical, in terms of the patterns of form and change. They are different qualitatively, though. One is the normal conventional experience, and the other is the beautiful luminous harmony of reality.

STUDENT: That sounds like there's no difference between someone who's crazy and someone who's not.

ALMAAS: There might be a difference in the way they appear, but there is no difference in terms of how they happen. Both are generated by an identical source. If you judge one as better than the other, there is a thought being generated in your mind that one is better than the other. Your judgment that one is better than the other is neither caused by nor the result of your perception of the two people.

STUDENT: Regardless of what I think about two people, it's what they're experiencing that's really not different if you look at it from the point of view of the flow?

ALMAAS: Two people are different in the sense that they feel differently, they appear differently, they respond differently. But they're not different in an ultimate way. You over there are not different from this chair. You are both generated instantaneously, with neither any prior cause nor any future consequence. The flow is like a magician who pulls a rabbit out of an empty hat. Next he pulls out an apple. That's how reality happens, like a magician pulling things out of a huge hat. One thing after another. And this perception has no utility. It's not good for anything, but is simply a way of seeing things. When you perceive the pattern of the flow of the universe, it's not as if you could do something differently. The moment you see the spontaneity of manifestation, you realize that the idea of doing something with it is ridiculous. That idea is itself also produced by the flow. And thinking that it's ridiculous is also produced by the flow. Absolutely no escape from the lawful pattern of reality. There's no exit, not in the Sartrean sense of futility, but in the sense of absolute freedom.

STUDENT: So why bother talking about it when there's no escape?

ALMAAS: Because that is what's happening. The pattern has no why. To search for a reason for talking about it means we've gone back to time and space and causality. We could contemplate the causes and explanations. But from this perspective, the flow of the pattern is like anything else. The explosion of the space shuttle has the identical source as talking about the flow of reality.

STUDENT: Is this the same as when we talk about humans being the sense organs of the universe?

ALMAAS: In some sense, yes. This perspective is a different angle of perceiving reality. Seeing yourself as a sense organ for the universe means that you realize that your base or your ground is generating everything. Although you're connected to the Source, you are aware of yourself as an individual within the manifestation. When you feel you are an individual connected to the Source, you can experience yourself as a sense organ for the universe. But if you recede and look as the Source rather than as the individual, then you realize that the sense organ is also being generated. The flow of being produces all experience, all perception, all action, all events, all thought, all feeling. Absolutely nothing is excluded. Everything comes out of the hat. Even the hat comes out of the hat.

The only value of that realization is that it's fun, like going to a movie. You enjoy movies because you're not that involved in them. You enjoy a scary movie like *Alien* because you're not on the spaceship being eaten by the monster. You know it's a movie, so you're only somewhat involved in it. You enjoy the feelings and sensations and have fun on the ride. Life is also like this. You know that life is being generated, so you could be somewhat involved and watch it and have fun. Because you know that reality is spontaneously manifesting, you could have fun regardless of what's happening, even if you saw yourself being eaten by a monster. You realize that the monster and the you who is being eaten by the monster are what's emerging at that moment. It's one frame of life.

STUDENT: But if he eats you up, you won't be emerging anymore.

ALMAAS: How do you know that?

STUDENT: The light may still be there, but . . .

ALMAAS: When you're aware of the perception of the flow of the universe, you're aware that you are the Source. That's the only way to do it. You're aware both of the Source and of the manifestation; otherwise, you can't be aware of this process of flow.

STUDENT: But if the manifestation gets eaten in one frame, it's hard for it to reappear in the next frame.

ALMAAS: One particular form may not appear.

STUDENT: Right.

ALMAAS: But when you perceive the flow, you realize that the manifestation is not only you. You're not only you. You're also the monster and everyone else. So one body seems to disappear, but another body will appear, just as in the movie. One person has been eaten up, but the movie isn't over. You keep watching the movie.

STUDENT: So something on the screen was eaten, but the projector wasn't eaten.

ALMAAS: Right. The projector doesn't get eaten. The projector is projecting the eating, the eater, and the eaten.

STUDENT: So the only thing that exists is the frame that's being played now. And as you get less steeped in the past and the future . . .

ALMAAS: You have to be in the moment absolutely now.

STUDENT: Sort of like being stoned. What you're talking about brings back memories of the old days when I'd get stoned. The only thing that exists is what is right now.

ALMAAS: That is a fact. Can anything exist logically except what is right now? For instance, as you talk now, my perception is that I don't hear you talking. It is not my perception that you have opened your mouth and talked and that I hear words. My perception is that the words instantaneously emerge right here, and so does the hearing of them. It has nothing to do with you or with me. You did not utter those words. They were uttered by the Absolute. So how does that grab you?

STUDENT: Sounds great!

ALMAAS: So you see, it's fun. Reality provides all kinds of movies—horror movies, romantic movies, adventure movies. Each person is a movie. Each person is movie upon movie, movie within movie. This whole thing is a constant changing show. Instantaneously happening.

STUDENT: When you are hearing that way, do you feel different in your body?

ALMAAS: The more I am in that perception, the more there is a sense of grace, the more there is a sense of love, the more there is a sense of clarity, the more there is a sense of peace. That's why people say that perception of flow is more accurate than the usual perception of physical reality. Because that perception of the pattern of life is more open. You could say there is less resistance in that perception. But, really, whatever you think or say or see is part of the movie. From this perspective there is no value judgment. Whether I'm feeling full of wonder and happiness or I'm feeling sad or angry, it's all absolutely generated by one source. Makes no difference whether I'm complete ego or absolutely God-realized. No difference whatsoever. And if I think they are different, that also is being produced by the one source.

STUDENT: So it's kind of like having a perpetual blank blackboard where everything appears right then.

ALMAAS: Yes. Like in the movie, the frame that appears has nothing to do with the frame before it or after it. The frame appears right now. Everything that is happening now is like a frame, an instantaneous frame. And because the frames move quickly, we think that the forms that constitute their content are continuous in time and space; we think that they operate according to cause and effect. But in some sense the screen is not a flat screen. The screen is sculpted according to the forms you see. Reality is more like a formation, an emergence, a continual outflow, an unfoldment, like how a flower comes out. When you see from that perception of flow, you're aware also of the Source. All the forms that appear are transparent to the Source. And the Source, based in absolute silence and peace, somehow casts an appearance of beauty and grace over everything.

STUDENT: So the difference between experiencing the Absolute and becoming the Absolute is the recognition of that source?

ALMAAS: Becoming the Absolute means realizing that all emergence is coming out of you. And when I say "you," I don't mean your body. "You" means everything, everybody. If you think of "you" as an individual, you're still within the frame of mind that maintains time and space. When I say everything comes out of me, I don't mean that it comes out of this individual. The me that I'm referring to is the me of everybody and everything. It is the ground beyond being and nonbeing, the inexhaustible mystery.

So all of your problems are being produced at this very moment. What your mother did or didn't do to you has got nothing to do with your problems. Within the frame of mind of time and space, your problems are caused by what your mother did to you, what your father said to you, or whatever occurred in your personal life. And it's good to work on it from that perspective. But even when you are working within that usual perspective, you're following the pattern. You have no choice in it. And you have no choice because you don't exist the way you think you exist. That's all. There's nothing dramatic or hopeless in not having a choice. It's just matter of fact. It's like Bogart swaggering around asserting his independence from Bergman. Bullshit. He doesn't have free will. He is being produced, as is everything else. If you believe the movie, Bogart has free will. He has so much free will, in fact, that in the end he sacrifices his love out of the nobility of his heart. However, if you are not engaged in the worldview of the movie, if you're outside it, you realize that he has no free will at all.

STUDENT: Every time the movie is shown, he does the same thing.

ALMAAS: Exactly. In this case it's obvious that he has no free will. He never could change any of it—the ending or the middle or the beginning. He does always the exact same thing. So from this perspective of flow, you don't say there's free will or no free will, you don't say there's a human being or no human being. You say, "It appears that there are human beings. It appears that there is free will. It appears that there is space and time. It appears that someone is talking." Things appear. The perception is that things manifest as an appearance. There's no need to assert, "No, truly there are people." It suffices to say, "It appears that there are people." And that appearance that there are people is all the reality there is, as real as things can be. There's nothing wrong with appearance. It's not bad or fake or pretense. That's how reality is. The appearance is the reality. There is nothing behind or beyond or under or over manifestation. The more that perception happens, the more you experience yourself in the now completely, until only the now exists. This very instant is the only thing that exists. There's nothing else. And it is not even an instant.

STUDENT: In the context of what you've been discussing this morning, what is the function of this work?

ALMAAS: Doing the work is a pattern unfolding. There is the pattern of not doing the work, and there is the pattern of doing the work. If you don't do the work, a certain pattern unfolds. If you do the work, a different pattern unfolds. Your decision to do the work is not your decision. Your decision is produced. Because you're still not awake, you're happy about the decision. Your happiness, too, is part of the pattern. You have nothing to do with it. Your belief that you exist as somebody who still is not awake also is not yours. That belief is being produced too. So one of these days you will see the projector and say, "Aha, I got it! I keep thinking I'm doing this and that, but there is a light over there projecting the whole thing!"

You see, this is not really a new idea. Have you read Plato's *Republic*? Remember the allegory of the cave? There are prisoners facing a cave wall with a fire burning behind them. Workers carry inanimate objects in front of the fire. These objects cast shadows that are projected onto the cave wall and the prisoners think they are real. Plato says that the light of the fire and, ultimately, the sun, is what produces the images we perceive. He didn't know about movie projection at that time, but that's what he's describing. So this perception of one source that generates all of reality is not new; it's ancient. The realization is as Western as it is Eastern.

Plato goes on to say that the best way to know the truth is to leave the cave and discover the source of the light. Get out of the cave and walk into the daylight.

There is a whole sun there. And you see, in this perception all points of view of reality are equally valid in the sense that they are all equally instantaneously manifesting. Whether you experience that realization is the void or God or self or oneness, they are all produced by the light. They are the images that appear.

So in some sense you could say that our life and our action are a matter of perceiving ourselves into reality. We perceive ourselves into existence. The perceiving generates and creates the being. No separation exists between perceiving and creating. As you perceive your hand, your hand is being created. Perception and creation are identical. If you think that you move your hand and that your hand is bigger now than it was when you were two years old, those thoughts are what is being generated. So you're not wrong and you're not right. You're simply being generated. No one is ever right or wrong. No one is ever good or bad. The only thing that ever happens is instantaneous manifestation. And it is actually not even a happening, for happening implies time, while it has no time in it.

STUDENT: It seems the only time that you really take responsibility is when you're awake.

ALMAAS: Even when you take responsibility, that is being generated. If you do not take responsibility, that too is being generated. When you're awake, that happens to be the frame. When you're asleep, that happens to be the frame.

STUDENT: You don't think being awake is going near the film director?

ALMAAS: Going near the film director is the frame that is being generated. This perception of the flow of the pattern corners your mind absolutely. There is no alternative. If you really follow this perception logically, you see that your mind has no exit but to be in the now.

And you realize also that it's not a choice to be in the now but that you are, in fact, in the now all the time. Where else could you be? There's nothing else. Even when you're not in the now, you are in the now. You can't be in the past, right? Even if you're sitting here spaced out, thinking about the past, it's absolutely a new phenomenon. Absolutely fresh. The present is neither the cause nor the result of anything else. Spontaneous existence corners you absolutely. You can't exist on your own. It's funny, no? I mean, what do you do but laugh? You might see and hear the nuclear missiles coming from Russia and you can't do anything but laugh. And if you're scared that you are going to die, you laugh too. Because that fear is being produced as the missiles are being produced.

So the moment you have a theory about anything, your theory is basically a story. Whenever you have a system, whenever you have an approach, whenever you have a terminology, whenever you have a science, it's a story that is being generated. There's no Ultimate Truth other than what's happening right now. You could say this is a school, we do work, people learn to develop themselves and be free and realize who they are and all that. We could say that and that's a good theory, but it's a story. Other people could have a different story— that this is some kind of cult with a secret force that pulls all these people together toward some secret purpose that will not appear until later. Neither story is accurate. The accurate perception is that this is the pattern in which reality emerges right now.

STUDENT: So you really don't care if you die?

ALMAAS: If you die, that is the pattern that emerges. And if you care about it, that is what emerges. I heard a story once about a Zen master who had been teaching for forty years or so. He was going to die, so he brought all of his students around him. While death was arising, he was shaking with fear, which disappointed all of his students. When he saw their disappointment, he broke into laughter. What was being produced was fear, so what's the big deal? Why is being scared worse than being enlightened? Fear and enlightenment have one source. So his enlightenment was beyond judgment. That's made into a Zen koan to reflect our confusion: The enlightened guy gets scared before he dies, and when people start crying, he just breaks out laughing, and then he dies. So what do you say? Do you think I'm giving you an idea, a certain perception to contemplate?

STUDENT: The perception causes less identification.

ALMAAS: You think that's the reason why I'm doing it?

STUDENT: Not necessarily, but one of the things that occurs as you begin to see the pattern of things is that you become less identified.

ALMAAS: But, you see, I didn't give you any idea. You heard a noise near your ears that carries certain images and interpretations. The noise came from the Absolute, not from me. Just as I come from the Absolute. Just as your ear comes from the Absolute. So you see, it's easy to get tricked back into the normal way of perceiving. The usual way of seeing things is so powerful that you can't think any other way. Some people will come to me after this talk and say, "I like this. I don't like that." It doesn't make any difference. That is the pattern. There is only the Absolute and the pattern, and nothing else. The Absolute and the Logos. So you might get tricked into thinking in terms of time and space. But are you being tricked? Who's tricking you, really? Apply your logic consistently and you will realize who's always tricking you.

This does not mean that you have no responsibility. You have complete responsibility. But how you understand responsibility is the product of the mind you've always had. All of that is the flow of the pattern. So it's a matter of looking at things linearly in terms of time or looking at things instantaneously in terms of now. If you perceive things in terms of linear time, you will see the past. If you perceive things instantaneously, you will see the Absolute. So you could observe yourself reflecting on your experience. You could observe your mind, basing one idea on another, thinking one thought after another, constructing a sequence that is held in the memory as the passage of time. If you observe that activity closely, you realize that there isn't really a sequence. The sequence is only in imagination. In reality there is only what exists at that very second. If you look at your thoughts in your mind and are aware that the sequence appears only because of memory and time, your mind will immediately go. Your mind will flicker out like a flame. And when the mind stops, that is true peace. No one is hassling you.

Mental anguish, along with the thinking process that produces emotions, is based on the notions of time and causality. You cannot make yourself suffer unless you think in terms of causality and time. When you suffer, usually you're saying, "Now I'm angry because someone did this to me. Now I'm hurt because such-and-such happened. Now I'm scared because someone did that to me." If you simply eliminate the thought of time and causality, suffering ends. You could be aware of what's right at that moment, know that whatever you're thinking at that moment is actually just happening in that moment. What you feel has nothing to do with what happened yesterday. Just be aware of yourself this very second. Just realize that you are instantaneously emerging. Break the temporal continuity of sensation. Realize instantaneously, right at this very second, that you are emerging. You are absolutely instantaneous emergence. You are not a continuity in time.

Logically it's easy to see, but experientially it's a little difficult. Whatever sensation or whatever feeling you're experiencing, just realize that is what is here at this very second. Forget what it has to do with, in terms of causes and time and all that. Just perceive it as it is. If you're uncomfortable, there is discomfort. That's it. There's a sensation of sorts that feels like discomfort. It doesn't matter why there's discomfort. If there is discomfort, just stay with the discomfort. Let your mind go. Don't listen to the sounds in your mind telling you it's because of this and that, urging you to react. No, just stay with it. If it's discomfort, it's discomfort. If it's ease, it's ease. And you could go even beyond the discomfort and notice the actual sensation that you call discomfort, or you call ease, or you call one thing or another. Stay with the bare consciousness, the bare sensation of whatever it is you're experiencing, without reflecting on it. Whatever you think, however you feel, emerges as instantaneously as the bare sensation. So don't get trapped by the thought or emotion or sensation. And if you realize that you get trapped by it, you realize that this too emerges as spontaneously as everything else.

Your awareness becomes instantaneous. As things emerge, you spot them. The moment the thought emerges, you spot it. The moment the feeling emerges,

The emergence and the spotting are one
low and the awareness of the flow happen
ou see things as they emerge, you see their
you don't need to control anything. You
only need to be aware of what's happening. Aware
without trying to figure out what you're aware of.
When you hear noises, you don't think of their source,
you only hear the noise. Life becomes an awareness of
the flow of the pattern. Anybody know the Tarot cards?
What is the last one?

STUDENT: The World.

ALMAAS: Yes. That is the pattern. The world is the
perception of how the pattern unfolds.

We perceive ourselves on many levels and dimensions of being. Today, we're talking about some kind of
ultimate dimension. But there are all kinds of dimensions, many different levels, from the usual worldly dimension to the boundless dimensions. Reality becomes
simpler the more there's understanding, the more there's
awareness, the more there's realization. Things change.
Your perception changes as your understanding expands. Who you are, what the universe is, what life is,
transforms. So whatever you are, wherever you are,
however you are, is fine. It is all the flow of the pattern.

TWELVE

Attunement
to
Objective Reality

We've been discussing many different perspectives from which to understand reality. Today I'd like to talk about the integrated picture, to see more clearly how the various perspectives we've been learning, the work on purification, the work on doing and being in the world, bring more objectivity and more balance to our understanding.

The work we do in this school is not metaphysics, philosophy, psychology, religion, or science. Although it's none of those things, the Diamond Approach is not disconnected from any one of them. This work is a certain kind of science; it includes a definite body of knowledge and employs a specific methodology. If we could give this science any name, it would be the science of what a human being can be. And the actualization of what a human being can be is useful to many other fields, whether science, philosophy, religion, metaphysics, medicine, or healing. The science of what a human being can be applies a certain kind of knowledge that I call the Diamond Knowledge. By knowledge I don't simply mean information. Although it includes information, knowledge is primarily the direct experience of the content of reality and the methods necessary to actualize that truth.

At the present time, the Diamond Approach consists of three main areas of experiential knowledge: the *knowledge of the soul*, which includes the knowledge of the ego, and the knowledge of the heart and spirit; the *knowledge of Essence*, which includes the knowledge of states, transformation, and realization; and the *knowledge of God*, sometimes called the knowledge of objective reality. Each area of knowledge is an immense field, and all three are interrelated.

Inner work is much more complex, much more vast than we usually imagine it to be. Waking up to the truth of reality is not a matter of having certain experiences or resolving certain issues. Although those experiences are important, actualizing the true human life involves much more of an objective knowledge. It's unlikely that one of these days we're going to have one experience and then become free and live as a complete human being. Many schools and teachings emphasize generating spiritual experiences, which for us is an easy part of inner work. For a work system like ours, the generation of spiritual experiences is not the be-all and end-all of our path; it's only one aspect of the path and has to be understood in relationship to the whole. Some teachings construe one or another aspect of the three realms of knowledge—of soul, of Essence, and of objective reality—to be the final truth.

As we explore the knowledge of the soul, we learn that it is an infinite ocean that no one single individual can encompass. The soul, considered the organ of evolution, has infinite realms and facets. Sometimes the soul is called the organ of experience, the organ of perception, or the organ of action. The evolution of the human soul is the evolution of the human being. The soul's evolution is inextricably linked with the experiential knowledge of Essence, which is inextricably linked with the experiential knowledge of the cosmic realms, what I refer to sometimes as the ground dimensions.

The knowledge of the soul does not mean only experience of the various states and conditions and transformations of the soul, which is the personal consciousness. It also includes the various capacities and functions. To know the capacities and functions of the soul means to know how to operate as human beings should or can operate. The knowledge of the soul includes knowing how to live correctly. The soul evolves through some kind of education. Frequently, while some parts of the soul develop, others remain untouched. Often the development of the soul is not balanced, is askew in various ways. So we tend to go around in circles instead of going straight because of this imbalance in development. But with the development of balance, we learn to move forward, toward greater evolution and expansion.

We can develop the capacities of the soul by understanding that the various techniques of religion, spirituality, and science are based on certain functions and capacities that the human consciousness possesses. For instance, the technique of meditation is based on certain human capacities. The technique of prayer is based on certain capacities of the soul. The technique of scientific research is based on certain capacities. Although we usually don't investigate or discriminate among those capacities, it does not mean that they don't exist. If we are to realize the various aspects of the Essence realm or the God realm, we need to exercise and develop certain capacities of the soul. It's not just a matter of being a good person. That's what I mean when I say this path of inner work is a science. The various realms of knowledge work according to actual laws that we can discern.

So the work we do here has to do with the activation, development, and evolution of the soul, so that it in turn can actualize the various realms of knowledge. The various spiritual techniques we employ are not oriented only toward the experience of Essence or God. Most spiritual techniques are primarily oriented toward a certain education that corresponds with the development of the organ of evolution. That education is a matter of learning how to approach experience. So the spiritual education, which is a central part of our work, is not a matter only of having experience, but also of learning how to relate to and understand the experience. How we approach our experience is what will bring resolution, what will bring actual fulfillment, what will bring the awakening, what will bring the reduction of suffering. The generation of new experiences, no matter how sublime, will not by itself resolve anything. What matters is the attitude with which we approach our experience.

We have been focusing in our work on refinement and development of the soul because that is the organ of experience. Having deep experiences is of little use if the organ of perception and action is undefined, primitive, and still operating according to the animal realm. As long as our attitude to experience remains primitive, our development will not progress in a balanced way and we will not change. There will be no true transformation. We will have experiences once in a while. The experiences are, in some sense, a guidance. They are learning experiences, impacts. The purpose of these experiences is to transform the soul, which is the personal consciousness, so that the soul, in time, will learn how to approach experience.

So the various essential aspects are not there simply to amuse and nourish us, but to teach us how to relate to them so that they will have an impact on us. If in our meditation we experience wonderful love and melting, but then go about being aggressive or attacking other people, then what's the point of having the experience at all? As long as our experience does not actually impact us, does not actually change how we live our life, we are still at the lollipop level of spiritual practice. We want the lollipop; when we get the lollipop, we're happy for a while and we stop fussing. But eventually we start wanting another lollipop and forget the one we just had. Some spiritual traditions call this the honeymoon stage.

But if we want our experience to impact our life, it will have to become something more than a lollipop. Experience will have to be approached as nourishment that will lead to actual growth, actual development, actual evolution. What we need is an education about how to be a human being. We might not have any idea what it means to be a human being. Being human does not simply mean being human in isolation from Essence, in isolation from God or Truth. Being human also means knowing how we are related to other realms. So we need the knowledge of the soul, of Essence, and of objective reality to learn how to be a human being. But what is needed more than anything else is an education that will transform our approach to experience in general. Whether we're experiencing other people, or daily life, whether we're experiencing emotions, essential states, or realizations, we need to approach our experiences in a mature way.

The experience will have to impact us in a certain situation, in a certain circumstance, in connection with other facts and elements for it to transform our consciousness into a consciousness that can relate to experience with more maturity. Otherwise, our experience is wasted. It's a lollipop that tastes good or tastes terrible, and then we have to start all over again. We could learn to approach our experiences, whether negative or positive, whether profane or sublime, with balance, maturity, and sensitivity.

The work we do has many different components. We work on understanding and realization, generating experiences, penetrating obstacles, and resolving issues. We work on doing and development, living what we understand. We continue to refine the work we do and to introduce new elements to balance the development of the soul. If we evolve without balance, our spiritual development moves in tangents rather than straightforwardly, moves coincidentally rather than logically. We could develop tangentially and still experience all kinds of wonderful things, but without the balance of mature development, there will be no meaningful transformation.

If we don't become the human being that we can be, what's the point of having wonderful experiences? The experience of awakening, on its own, is not sufficient. It's like waking up after a night's sleep. You're awake, but if you stay in bed, you're as good as somebody who is asleep. If you don't get out of bed and live your life, what's the difference if you're awake or asleep? What I'm saying is that there needs to be a development and evolution, that the experience is the beginning of something, not the end of it.

So, for example, if you experience compassion while you meditate but you walk around being cruel to other people, your experiences are making you worse, not better. The experiences make you worse because now you know better, now you know compassion even if you are not living according to it. This is what we call unbalanced development. The experience of an essential aspect does not necessarily transform the soul, transform the functioning part of you, the living part of you in the world. That transformation is another step, a more difficult journey.

The knowledge of the work is not simply the knowledge of experiences. We also need to learn how to develop our capacity to function, how to live. Suppose you experience will. That's a good start, but what does that mean? How are you going to relate to it? How is that going to affect your life? Are you supposed to use it? Is it supposed to use you? Or something else entirely? Even if you haven't experienced will all of your life, one day you feel will, you feel solid, you feel great, and you think now it's happened. No, it hasn't happened; it has started to happen. That experience is the beginning. It is a very important beginning, but a lot more needs to happen for you to actualize that experience.

We need refinement, education, and development in our capacity to approach experience. How do we relate to any experience, any dimension, any realm with more balance and maturity? To approach any experience openly, whether it is a difficult emotional state or an essential or divine state, we need to approach it with more and more purity. What does that mean?

It means that whatever the experience is, our attitude has to be pure. A pure attitude includes the virtues of serenity, humility, truthfulness, equanimity, detachment, courage, sobriety, innocence, and real action.

If we approach our experience with the passions of anger or pride, with deception or envy, with avarice or fear, with gluttony or lust or laziness, the experience will do more harm than good, regardless of how essential or boundless the experience may be. Whether we are experiencing hatred, love, the Absolute, pure awareness, emptiness, or God, we need to approach the experience with a more and more pure attitude. We need to approach the experience with the virtues instead of with the passions. The more the passions determine your attitude toward the experience, the less useful the experience will be for you, for the community, for the truth.

The knowledge of essence is needed to bring about the purification of the soul. How will the soul know it is lying if it doesn't know truth? How will it know what courage is if it doesn't know strength? So, in some sense, essence teaches the soul by providing experiences of how to be a real human being. The knowledge of essence exposes the impurities and teaches us the way out, or the way of purification. These experiences are teaching elements, not just lollipops. We need to absorb essential experiences so that we will grow from them and not use them to temporarily fill our stomach. The growth of the soul has to do with its refinement and purification.

The more we understand the perspective of purification, the more we'll understand why all spiritual systems work on the passions, what's often called the "blamable" qualities. Blamable because they are the qualities responsible for the gross, the unbalanced, the immature approach to experiencing life. Some of the spiritual traditions deal directly with the passions, others indirectly. Theistic traditions such as Christianity, Judaism, and Islam work directly on the passions and the virtues, and the work of the purification of the soul is seen as the most important part of spiritual work. The Christian mystic does not pray to God so that God will give him a good experience. The Christian mystic prays to God so that God will purify him of his sins. In the Sufi tradition, experiences of Essence and God are not even discussed until a person works on purification. It's considered dangerous to approach those experiences before the soul is purified, because they could produce an unbalanced development. Other Eastern traditions work on the passions indirectly through meditation techniques and other purification exercises, without necessarily talking about the soul.

The question might arise, "Why go to all this trouble?" We spend all this time purifying ourselves and working on refinement so we can approach experience in a more balanced, more mature, more correct way. Why not just have a lollipop or two a day and leave it at that? That's how most people approach spiritual work. Most people get sort of irritated and mad when you tell them to do work to change their attitude. "No, no, I want a good experience. I don't care about changing my attitude. I want to go about it with my present attitude, because I'm hungry and these things are yummy. Give 'em to me or I'm going to be mad at you! And don't tell me I'm attached—of course I'm attached; how else can I be? Isn't that human? And don't tell me I have to be purified of my animal nature. Are you Lutheran or Catholic? What's wrong with animal nature?"

That's our usual approach to experience. This attitude produces unbalanced development, doesn't work, and creates more suffering than it relieves. Treating our experience like snacks doesn't take into account the relationship of the soul to other realms. The development of the soul does not happen on its own; the soul is not separate from the other realms. We're not an individual soul floating around in the universe, developing for our own sake and acquiring a better life. Things are not like that. We discover and understand what reality is by having more experience, more tastes, more knowledge of the God realm or the realm of objective reality, the realm of objective truth, the realm of what actually exists in the universe.

We cannot separate ourselves from the rest of humanity, or from the rest of the universe, or from the spiritual realms. Thinking that we are separate from our experience, from each other, from the universe, is not objective and lacks balance. In order to approach our experience with a balanced attitude, we need to understand what this maturity is for, what the point of it is. We need balance and maturity in our development so we can live according to the truth.

But what is the truth? We've explored it in many ways. From the perspective we're addressing now, we can say that the work of purification, which is a work of refinement—which is the larger part of the inner work—is to qualify you, is to prepare you, is to make you worthy to serve the truth. Serving the truth means living for the truth. What does it mean to live for the truth? What it means to live for the truth changes according to the level of truth you have realized. From the perspective of purification, to live for the truth means first being worthy to serve the truth. To be worthy to serve the truth, we have to be developed and purified enough to know what truth is and is not. We don't purify ourselves to then live a life of hedonistic pleasure; we purify ourselves to become fit to serve the truth.

The true joy and the true celebration will arise the more we realize that we are purifying ourselves to be more worthy to serve the truth. Being the servant of the truth is part of our soul's nature. The soul is the servant; the master is the truth. Whatever dimension of truth we happen to have realized is the master we serve. This is arriving at the station of servitude. The work of purification leads to that station of servitude, of being a good, worthy, and capable servant of the truth.

One of the requirements of serving the objective truth, of serving God, of serving the Absolute, is to be fit for that service so that we won't be living our selfish needs. We live our selfish needs when we serve our belief in having a separate existence. There isn't a separate existence. We aren't solitary souls bobbing around the universe. We are, as I've said many times, like God's finger. We are an extension, a protrusion, of the truth. And if we don't live that way, we won't live according to the truth that is our nature, that is the nature of existence, that is how things are—the natural law. So one of the ways we can approach experience is through the realization that we're working on developing ourselves spiritually, emotionally, and physically in order to be fit and worthy servants for the master that is truth.

What does it mean to serve the truth? We serve the truth when we act according to the truth, when we express the truth in our life, when we see ourselves as the expression of the truth. We need to be purified enough to be attracted to the truth in such a way that the truth penetrates us. We are the expression of the truth when we have become transparent to it. The most objective sense of serving the truth, serving God, serving the Absolute, serving reality, is to express it purely in life.

So the function of the soul in life is not simply to maximize our pleasure, but to realize our more objective function as an organ of truth, as an organ of realization, as an organ of a much larger being, of a much bigger, universal reality. We come to realize that our happiness, our joy, our fulfillment arise from actually serving the truth. We serve the truth by being as pure an expression of it as possible. God or the truth doesn't need you to do things for it, to walk around talking about it or buying it things, but actually to express it, to bring the truth to life. We serve the truth by manifesting it, because what the truth wants is to move from an unmanifest form to a manifest form. That's why the Sufis say that God needs man in order to express Himself in the world. God manifests in the world through the purified ones.

So our job is to be a servant. And to serve is to express. And to express is to be a clear and unimpeded medium for the truth. For that to happen, we need to be purified of our coarser elements. If we approach experience as if it were a lollipop, the objective function of the soul is not fulfilled. The more our soul is aware of the deeper realms and the more correct its attitude toward those realms, the more we express the truth. The deeper realm, the realm of objective reality, is ultimately the home of the soul—its origin, source, and nature. The absolute reality is the nature and origin not only of the soul but of everything. What better master to serve than the innermost nature of you and of everything! So being a servant is an exalted position.

Purification is necessary, but on its own it is not sufficient in order for the soul to serve. Purification makes us, in some sense, acceptable for service but not yet necessarily capable of service. To be capable of service, there needs to be development of the capacities, development of the knowledge, development of all possibilities of the human soul. So the servant first has to be worthy, and then has to be capable of the service. The purification of the soul allows the attitudes of serenity, humility, and truthfulness toward our experience to arise by dissolving the belief in separate existence. The development of the soul makes the service more objective, more real, more accurate, more to the point. Not only do we express the truth, but we do it exactly and precisely according to the need of the moment.

In developing the capacity of the soul to serve the truth, the realm of action is integrated with the realm of attitude. The doing exercise and our work practice on Sundays develop our capacity to function objectively. We inquire into our deficiencies around functioning, not so we can feel adequate but so we can become capable of service. True joy, true manifestation, true celebration, will actually arise only when we realize that serving the truth is our higher role. As long as we are oriented toward serving our selfish needs, serving our belief in our separate existence, the joy and the fulfillment will be blocked because we will be acting according to unobjective rules, according to unreality.

We are willing to serve the truth because we love the truth. Without the selfless love for the truth, without loving the truth for its own sake, service will still be for selfish reasons. As long as we create a separate self, we are bound to suffer. So the work of purification, ultimately, is the purification from the self, from the identity of the ego, from narcissism. The work of purification frees the soul from self-centeredness. Self-interest does have a function in the sense that we need to take care of ourselves in our lives, but if we regard self-interest as the highest principle, then we love our unreal separate self more than the truth.

So the correct and balanced attitude means one based on the service of a higher principle. If our work is motivated or guided by a lower principle, a more selfish principle, then it will tend to move tangentially or not move at all. At some point on the inner journey, the soul will have to go from the station of servitude to the station of slavery. Now how is a servant different from a slave? A slave doesn't own anything, doesn't possess anything, not even his life, not even his existence. A servant still owns his own existence. Although he serves the master dutifully and correctly, a servant still has separate quarters. A slave has nothing of his own; he is owned by the master. So the station of slavery is a more exalted station than the station of servitude. We're not only humble and truthful and serene and all of that, but we are completely owned by the truth. We are under the complete domination of the truth. We are at the whim of the truth, an absolute extension of the truth. We are completely inseparable from the truth, from the master.

When you are a slave, you can be a true expression of the truth, a true prolongation of the truth. As we see, our attitude continues to refine. The purification of the soul, the correction of our attitude toward experience, leads to the condition of mystical poverty. Being poor in spirit means we not only serve and purify, but also that we realize we don't own anything. We move from being a soul to being a spirit. A spirit is a soul that realizes that its existence is not its own. We realize that our very substance, our very consciousness, is not ours but originates in a higher source.

Not only the love and the will and the value come from a deeper source, but our very existence, our very soul, is owned by the master. We own nothing. We become a slave to the truth when we realize that we are not separate from it. True service arises from the station of slavery. True service becomes our natural state, like becoming the finger of the hand and being moved only by the master.

We find our true position, our greatest fulfillment and joy, when we are at the whim of the master. In the station of slavery, the soul realizes that she is an absolute reflection, a pure expression, of the Absolute. The soul realizes that the Absolute is not separate from her, but is her master, her home, her nature. The soul's relationship to the Absolute is analogous to the relationship of the face to the body. At some point in our development, the relationship of the soul to the Absolute is the relationship of who you are as an individual existence to your ground, to your source, to your creator. The soul expresses and communicates the truth. Is the face separate from the body? Are there two separate things? Is there some kind of a relationship? The face expresses the body of the Absolute, but it is not the whole body. The soul is not the totality of the truth, but an expression of the truth and the expresser of the truth. In other words, as an individual soul, each one of us is the expression and expresser of the truth. When we realize our true identity, we recognize that we are the truth in its majesty and the soul is its organ of perception.

So the work of purification, the soul's essential realization displacing the self-centered ego perspective, transforms us into a transparent face, a transparent window to objective reality. Purification is a process of evolution and growth. Purification is not an experience. Mostly, experience happens suddenly. We're meditating and suddenly we are the Absolute, suddenly we're full of grace, suddenly there's love. Whereas experience is sudden, transformation is gradual. The sudden experience is valuable and necessary, but the impact of the sudden experience takes time to develop. We need a certain kind of commitment to the truth, a certain profound love of the truth, more encompassing than the dedication needed to have an experience, if we are to become transparent expressions of the truth. We have to be willing to allow our very substance, our very life, to transform, so that in time we will not only be a servant but be a slave to the truth.

The more deeply we see our inner nature, the more we love it and the more we want to do nothing else but serve it. We begin to wish and pray to become a slave to the truth. In time, the soul recognizes that that's what it wants in its own heart. Servitude is not imposed from above. Neither is it a decision we make. We have to go deeply into the heart of the soul and see what that heart wants. What makes that heart peaceful and happy? What is its highest aim?

If we look at it that way, we see that the work on the passions is indispensable. We need to discover the realm of virtues: serenity, humility, truthfulness, detachment, equanimity, sobriety. We need to learn not to consume our experiences. That's the attitude of the inner glutton, who doesn't want to feel his empty stomach. With sobriety, we are awake with our experiences and not overtaken by our passions. We are not overrun by our unrefined nature. We are awake to ourselves and approach our experience with some kind of detachment, with some kind of humility and gratitude, with some kind of purity.

And from the perspective of service, our motivation for purification is the pure love of the truth, manifested as our expression of it. We're not developing the capacities so we can be stronger or more peaceful or more loving. We're developing the capacities so we will be better able to serve the truth. At least that's how I see it. You have to find out whether that is the case for you.

So expressing the truth involves more than simply sitting there and radiating. Being an expression of the truth means going about our life, relating to people, doing things with authenticity and fullness of presence. We serve the truth when the purified soul is what is functioning in our life.

We encounter various issues and difficulties in learning to function objectively. Many people go about doing this and that in the name of service. But often we do more harm than good. Sometimes serving humanity might mean leaving things alone. If every human being leaves humanity alone, who knows what will happen? Maybe things would be better. Everyone runs around trying to save humanity in his own way. This person's a Communist, he's going to save humanity this way; this person's a Christian, he's going to save humanity this way; this person's a Buddhist, he's going to save humanity this way. In the end, they fight and everything's a bigger mess than when they started. If everybody leaves everybody alone, maybe things will be okay. Maybe that's the best service we could do.

What I'm saying is that real service is not a simple, obvious thing. We cannot decide from our impure, thick consciousness what service is and how to go about doing it. Service has to arise out of clear guidance and intelligence. And the guidance and intelligence will come about through the work of purification, through the integration of the essential aspects of guidance and intelligence in the soul.

There are many stories about students who want to serve. Somebody goes to the teacher and says, "Why don't you give me something to do? I want to serve." Many times the teacher says, "Go home, take care of your kids. Forget about serving God for now. Just go home, be nice to your wife. When the time comes, you will know how to serve." There is a need for a tremendous amount of experience, for integration of experience, for balancing factors of all kinds for the soul as an organ of action to function correctly. But we don't have to be absolutely purified to function with objectivity. If the development is balanced, there is a tendency for action also to be balanced. We can't be purified all at once, but balance is possible from the beginning. Each one of us will have to allow ourselves to get deeper into our heart and see what our heart really wants. What is the deeper purpose? What is the higher aim? What is the deeper longing for? What does the soul want?

What are our priorities in this world, in our lives? Is pleasure our priority? Self-aggrandizement? Fame? Recognition? Or do we seek something deeper, more intrinsic? The soul will not rest until she returns home, back to where she came from. And once the soul arrives home, life is an expression of that origin, a service of that truth. Without returning to our original nature, it's difficult for us to see what our role in life is, because our minds and hearts are full of concerns and conflicts and problems.

Our blessings and realizations are not simply for our enjoyment, but also for our guidance and transformation. And there is no true transformation unless we recognize the limitation of the lollipop stage and have a real motive to go beyond it. The balanced approach to experience is exactly what is needed to actually do the work. The more we have that balanced attitude, the easier the work is, and the more naturally and spontaneously it happens. We need to remember and be aware that it's not simply the experience that matters, but how we relate to it. If we approach our experience with an attitude of greed, the experience will likely be used to feed an endless emptiness that can never be filled. But if we approach our experience with a balanced attitude, the experience could expose that bottomless chasm without trying to fill it.

So our orientation toward experience needs to be one of learning. No matter how painful, pure, or wonderful, all experiences are good when approached with a correct attitude. Approaching an experience with the attitude of learning is an ultimate attunement to reality. Learning this attunement to reality is a challenging process that requires us to approach our difficulties with humility and detachment.

The work we do here is not religious in the traditional sense. Although religion recognizes, in some sense, the balanced attitude toward experience, our work is more basic. Ultimately, we work from an understanding that is the source of religions, sciences, and philosophies, that is the ground of objective knowledge.

Even the perspective of service is different in this work from religious perspectives of service. Our notion of service has to do more with objective reality, with the laws of how the universe functions. For us, service is more of an attunement to reality, an attunement to the truth, to how things are destined to be, to how they can be in their fullest realization. There's no idea of serving in order to be a good person or to please God. We serve from a deeper kind of love, from an attunement to our objective function in this world.

Our attitude in this work is "I want to serve because I love the truth, not because I'm good. And in serving, I'm quite willing to see how bad I am." So when Christians say, "First you have to see your wretchedness," I take that to mean that we first need to recognize our impurity, our deficiency, our emptiness. And even after we have seen our wretchedness, to be saved we have to believe in the Christ. Seeing through our wretchedness is the work of purification.

But the purification alone is not enough to completely attune us to the truth. In the Christian tradition, we need to be saved through the action of Christ, through the resolution of the original sin. The action of Christ is the action of unification and union, realizing that we're not separate. The original sin is the belief in separateness. To see through the separateness, to realize that we are not separate from the truth but an integral expression of the truth, is true service. We are not only a servant but an actual slave of the truth. When we serve the truth and become God's slave, we don't lose our independence, we don't lose our life; we gain the true life. As Christian mystics say, the true life is the life in the Divine Being, life lived as part of the Divine Being, the Cosmic Truth.

So true attunement means finding the true function of the soul and living harmoniously with all that exists. True attunement is universal in scope. We cannot arrive at attunement as an independent and isolated enterprise. If we think of inner work as developing ourselves and our souls for our own sake, we will not transform in any significant way. The perspective of developing ourselves separately from the rest of the universe reflects a lack of understanding about what reality is. Original sin, which is separateness from the source of reality, is not simply a religious transgression but a faulty understanding. It is the Basic Fault.

Much of the suffering that we experience has to do with lack of attunement to the objective truth, to the true condition of reality. We are not attuned to what is real, to what we're supposed to do, to the perspective of true living. Our lack of attunement to the higher principle that is an expression of objective reality means that we operate in ways we were not made to operate. We're bound to suffer.

What I'm saying about purification and the attitude of service has to become heartfelt knowledge. It's not enough for it to be information in the mind. We need to understand objective reality through the heart, through our soul. What we ultimately want is to live the way we're supposed to live, which means to serve, which means to be an expression of something much bigger than what appears before our eyes.

To be a true slave of the truth, we become one with the truth. The truth lives through us. We live the truth. Fully appreciating this understanding, we realize that the individual soul and the totality of all truth are not two. They are two sides of the same thing, inseparable facets of reality.

THIRTEEN

Divine Quintessence

In waking up to our true nature, we need to see through, work through, and become free from two kinds of ignorance about reality. Our ignorance holds in place the limited view of what we are and what reality is.

Learned ignorance has to do with our previous experience, the accumulated knowledge and impressions and influences from past experiences. We can understand and work through learned ignorance, which includes the beliefs and ideas we have accumulated from having lived. Our past experiences influence us in all sorts of ways. Much of what people work on, in terms of the content of issues, conflicts, and obstacles, is the accumulated ideas, beliefs, and knowledge from our past. It is easy to think that our limitations are caused by difficult things that have happened to us in the past; but actually the simple fact that we have had past experience creates obstacles. The mind solidifies our experience into notions of what we are and what the world is in such a way that we see reality through the veil of the past. This veil is penetrated as we awaken to our true nature.

The second kind of ignorance is called innate, or basic. This primordial ignorance is something we are born with, something inherent to the soul that isn't mature. So waking up is seeing through not only learned ignorance but also innate ignorance, the unclarity or the lack of understanding of what reality is. Innate ignorance has two sides: one to do with recognizing the ground of reality, the other with understanding the relationship of particulars to this ground.

Seeing through and beyond innate ignorance, being free of it, is what some call basic enlightenment. Seeing through innate ignorance first has to do with recognizing true nature in itself. What is it? What are its characteristics? How is it experienced when it's experienced totally and clearly? When we wake up to our true nature, what is the nature of that awakening? What is the waking up? What do we wake up to? What is it we understand?

We have been exploring different ways of understanding true nature. When I say true nature here, I mean the ground of true nature, not the qualities that emerge from it—the source of the qualities, the underlying nature that is always the same, the underlying nature that does not depend on circumstances and time and space. To wake up to reality means to wake up to its nature, to wake up to its true condition. The true condition of reality is the true nature of all the forms of reality, the forms of experience. When we are experiencing sadness, aggression, thought, memory, our body, another person, the dirt beneath our feet, or the water in the ocean, we can also understand the inner nature of all these phenomena.

The inner nature of all forms of reality, of all forms of experience, is inherently empty. That emptiness is the deepest characteristic of true nature, the deepest dimension of true nature. Whatever we experience, if we experience it fully, we recognize that there is nothing there. Whatever we experience is ephemeral; it does not have its own substantial existence. The inner nature of reality is not only transparent and luminous but, when you experience it fully, you realize that there isn't any mass to it. There is no abiding existence, no continuing existence through time. We say that is the emptiness of the ground.

The deepest ontological truth about this emptiness of the ground, this openness, this spaciousness, is nonbeing, which is very difficult for most of us to understand. Nonbeing confounds the mental faculties. At the same time that nothing exists, experience arises and forms manifest. For forms to manifest, they manifest being; they manifest presence. Forms are not simply constructed by our individual mind; they are truly manifesting in the field, as a kind of beingness that we experience as presence, as a subtle fullness of the luminosity. The subtle nature of reality is not only radiance, but radiance that has fullness and thereness.

The fullness and thereness of the ground of reality, which we can call Being, is not being in the sense of a being that continues in time. The Being of reality is not like a bird that emerges in space, that exists on its own, as its own identified existence. Being is simply an appearance in the ground. The bird is simply a form that the ground takes. And, as it manifests, the form has a sense of presence. The form is there. If we experience it immediately, we experience its thereness. But how can that be? We've just said that the deepest truth about the nature of reality is complete emptiness and nonbeing. Now we say that the form is actually there.

The intriguing mystery is that the nature of forms, the nature of the body, the nature of consciousness, the nature of all phenomena, include both emptiness and presence, both Being and nonbeing, in a mysterious juxtaposition. This interpenetration of Being and nonbeing in reality is even more mysterious than pure or nonconceptual awareness. Pure awareness is an aware ground, an aware medium that doesn't know what it is aware of and doesn't discern one thing from another. By nonconceptual I do not simply mean not mental, not constructed. I mean the barest minimum of sensitivity, the ground that is simply the capacity to be aware, to perceive. Therefore, by nonconceptual we mean noncognitive. There is perception, but there is no knowing, no cognition of any kind.

Although we see that nonconceptual awareness is both emptiness and presence, both Being and nonbeing, we cannot say this in the actual experience of nonconceptual awareness. We cannot say anything, because pure awareness lacks recognition, lacks knowing.

But enlightened awareness is the true nature of all manifest phenomena. I am making a distinction between nonconceptual awareness, which is the ground of all experience, and what I call the Kernel of the Kernel, the Quintessence. I use the word "Quintessence" to mean Essence of the Essence, Ground of the Ground. The word is used in ancient Greek philosophy as the fifth element; *quint* means five. The ancients thought all matter exists in one of four elements: water, air, earth, and fire. The fifth element was the underlying *prima materia* constituting all celestial spheres. That is the original meaning of the word. But now, in

English, "quintessence" means the most distilled essence of something.

Kernel of the Kernel, a translation of the Arabic *lubb al-lubb*, which means the Essence of the Essence, the cream of the cream, is the title of a celebrated Sufi book by Ibn 'Arabi. Whereas pure awareness is spacious, clear, and transparent, almost like colorless light, Quintessence is that and also profound and deep and vast. Quintessence unifies the day and the night, the sky of the day and the sky of the night. Emptiness distills to utmost profundity as total peace and stillness, pure privacy and intimacy.

Quintessence is the Inner of the Inner, totally inner, totally private. The absolute intimacy of Quintessence is emptiness that lacks distance between one thing and another, between awareness and experience. Between our awareness and what we experience is complete nonbeing, so we are completely our aware experience. Quintessence is total intimacy, which we experience as an utter silence, stillness, and imperturbability. At the same time, it also has a sense of fullness, of gracefulness, of presence, a sense of beingness explicitly there as we experience its total absence. Quintessence is at once an inscrutable mystery and a bright clarity.

The Kernel of the Kernel has the clarity and the freshness of pure awareness, the nowness and fullness of presence, and the depth of the intimacy of emptiness. They are all present distinctly, explicitly, and yet there is absolutely no separation between them. They are completely one, completely indivisible, and nevertheless explicitly discernible. Even though they are all one explicit thereness, we can feel it as complete absence, completely nothing there and everything there at the same time, in the same shot, in the same perception. This is the paradox of enlightened awareness.

The lack of obstruction of the emptiness, of the non-beingness, makes transparent the actual presence. The absolute emptiness allows the perception or the feeling, allows whatever is there, to be so, fully and clearly. So the absence or the nonbeing doesn't mean there is an empty space between you and what you experience. Emptiness means that space is gone, distance is gone, you and your experience as two separate things is gone. The intimacy between you and what you experience is total. At the same time, the emptiness is completely private; it is the innerness of your awareness and consciousness. Nothing penetrates the emptiness, because any thought, any feeling, any state that faces the emptiness instantly dissolves. You can only enter the privacy by giving up your being. And yet, thoughts and dimensions and forms manifest in presence and in clarity, in a clarity that is a graceful fullness.

By seeing through the innate ignorance about the underlying ground of what we experience, we arrive at this paradoxical mystery of the totality and the fullness and the emptiness of this ground. Enlightened awareness, the Kernel of the Kernel, seamlessly includes everything we know about our true nature, all of what we know at once together, without its being a collection of things or qualities. The complete stillness and privacy of the emptiness add to the clarity a searing, sharp, smooth quality. And the clarity and the fullness add to the emptiness a kind of brilliance, a kind of shine—a shine made more intensely luminous by its total emptiness. This full, luminous emptiness has a kind of lightness, a kind of freedom that is beyond the idea of freedom, a kind of total relaxation and ease.

The paradoxical juxtaposition of qualities creates a sense of delight and wonder. The true nature of all manifest phenomena is at once both full and empty, both completely substantially manifest and absolutely light and not there. At the same time as it's clear and brilliant and shiny, it's also dark and deep and profound. So the delight is in seeing how this awareness is paradoxical, how it doesn't make sense and yet it is completely so. You experience delight because of how light and empty you feel, as if there were no gravity at all, and yet you are the depth of the universe, the most real and the most substantial truth.

We can experience Quintessence as the body of reality, as the medium that manifests everything. Enlightened awareness is a medium that explicitly is, where the feeling of "isness" is singularly clear. At the same instant as the singularly clear isness, we can experience singularly clear "it is not." Mind and no-mind are seamlessly together. This paradoxical nature of reality becomes playful delight. Enlightened awareness completely confounds the conceptual categories, easily pushes them to their utmost possibilities, plays with them so clearly, so fully, and with utter abandon.

You may be wondering how this is related to the Absolute, the Logos, and other boundless dimensions of reality. What I am discussing has more to do with the journey of descent. The journey of ascent has to do with realizing all the boundless dimensions. In the journey of descent, all of the boundless dimensions are integrated as one living being. I usually think of Quintessence as the nature of manifest phenomena. Just as the nowness is how timelessness appears in time, and the spaciousness is how emptiness appears in space, Quintessence is how the Absolute appears in manifestation. So we can consider it the manifest Absolute, and the Absolute in itself can be considered the unmanifest. Some schools of Buddhism make a similar distinction between the unmanifest *dharma-kaya* and the manifest *dharmakaya*. Quintessence is more like the manifest *dharmakaya*, the manifest body of truth, the true body of manifestation.

The Kernel of the Kernel can be seen in various ways. As the Essence of the Essence, it is the underlying nature of all the qualities of Essence we experience. And if we see the Kernel as the manifest world, then the Kernel of the Kernel is the Quintessence. The Kernel is the manifest world in its clarity, in its unobstructedness, without the accumulation of learned and innate ignorance. Quintessence is the nature, the essence, of this manifest world of clarity. Quintessence is the utmost elegance of manifestation, a beauty that is wholly clear, and whose clarity is utmost because it is totally empty. The whole perception has an exquisite elegance—the emptiness is elegant, the awareness is elegant, the beingness is elegant. The absolute nature of all manifest phenomena is a seamless coincidence of freshness and intimacy, of a fresh winter day and the deep, dark night.

What we're exploring here is the nature of reality, the nature of all experience, the inseparability of forms and formlessness. Quintessence is the nature of the underlying ground of all forms. This mysterious yet simple truth is both the freedom and the promise of freedom.

As we've been working this week, many questions and issues around doing and functioning have come up. How do we conduct ourselves given this understanding? How do we live life from this view? So far we've been dealing with the side of innate ignorance that has to do with the actual nature of the ground of reality. The true condition of reality is at once empty and full and clear—a searing kind of isness and notness at the same time. We've also been exploring the ignorance having to do with the relationship of particulars to this ground of reality.

Seeing through this second kind of innate ignorance is especially difficult because it entails not only perceiving that the particulars are inseparable manifestations of the ground, but also accounting for change, transformation, and the movement of reality. How does it happen that the particulars are manifestations of the ground? How does appearing happen? These are questions about the actual process of manifestation, questions about the happening of all that happens.

When we realize the happening of all that happens, we see the magic and the power of true nature and we understand the question of action and activity. This mysterious ground, this empty presence, this spacious lucidity, this fullness that is at once nothingness, is not a static presence. It's full of energy, full of life, full of dynamism, full of throbbing, orgasmic, convulsive movements happening all the time. This dynamism and power and force are what manifest each and every form, spontaneously every instant.

This simple stillness full of graceful clarity, in its depth and silence, is gently and effortlessly manifesting everything in a process of effulgence and light. The enlightened view includes the process of manifestation, includes this constant effulgence that creates all the things in the world from the void, that materializes each thing from nothing. In that sense, reality is a wizard. Out of complete nothingness appears all that we perceive and experience. And it's as simple and as easy as dreaming something. When you dream, you create a whole universe that feels like solid matter; people get hurt and various things happen, but it's really not taking any effort. You are completely asleep, completely resting, and it is all happening. It is the same with

Quintessence; it is completely still and silent, and at the same time it is unfolding everything with effortless ease and spontaneity.

Recognizing the spontaneous happening of reality, we see the pulsing creativity that instantly manifests the entire world that we see from moment to moment. The world emerges, appears, disappears, emerges newly, appears, disappears—all instantly, all constantly. We can see this in our own experience. Our experience is always a creative emergence of various forms of feelings, thoughts, and sensations constantly changing. In the complete view, our experience, the outer world—everything, including our body—is constantly generated, created, and formed. Only when we see this dynamic creativity do we understand movement and action and change. Each form, including us, is created newly and differently each instant; these slight differences, when seen through the continuum of time, appear as movement—just as the still frames of a movie projected quickly, one after the other, give the sense of movement and change when actually it's instant-to-instant creation.

So even in the still, silent quietness, even in the total, relaxed ease, the all-creating monarch is always creating the totality of all the universes, creating them in an instant and destroying them in an instant. The all-creating Quintessence does not need seven days. In an instant the whole universe is there completely, everywhere distinct. Just as in an instant you can create an entire world in your mind, the Quintessence creates you and that entire world in its mind; and it creates far more than that too. The Quintessence creates all that we experience.

Different teachings capture different parts of this mysterious and rich process of manifestation. Each emphasizes different aspects of this property of reality.

Although each teaching adds great insight and understanding about the happening of all that happens, I don't know whether any one teaching can encompass its totality in terms of all of its implications. That includes our teaching.

Some teachings emphasize the dynamism. Some teachings emphasize more the emptiness, the stillness, and the clarity. Although these can be distinguished, they are actually interpenetrating and inseparable: the stillness, the depth, the clarity, the presence, the beingness, the dynamism, the force, and the power are all one thing. Reality is a living presence. Just as we realize that our individual experience is this living, dynamic wonder, we see that in its completeness the whole universe is this living wonder. All of reality is one consciousness, at once dynamic and still. The paradox is not only between absence and presence, emptiness and fullness, but also between stillness and amazing energetic dynamism. They don't contradict each other.

In the modern world it's easy for us to conceive that the world is really composed of atoms and particles whirling at amazing speeds. We read our physics books and think it's true, even though that's not how we experience reality. Typically you feel yourself as a solid mass of body moving and entering your car, which is even more solid. But you believe it's all dynamism, it's all movement. The spiritual ground is much more inclusive than modern physics; even the electrons are dynamically being created from instant to instant.

The dynamism of true nature is the source of all energies, all forces, all power that we experience and feel and see in the universe. This creative dynamism not only accounts for our movements and actions and thinking, but it also generates the wind and the weather, the movement of the planets, and the creations of the galaxies, the stars, the volcanoes, the hurricanes—everything. Some of them we might feel are beautiful, wonderful things as long as they don't threaten us, and some of it can be devastating. But even hurricanes seem minuscule when you compare them with star nurseries where billions of stars are being created. I am giving you a sense of the amazing sea of energy and dynamism that we're sitting on. It's not just idle energy; it throbs and creates and destroys in a complete, orgasmic kind of climaxing. The Quintessence is constantly climaxing—it's the ultimate Tantric adept. Each instant, creation and destruction discharge the old and create the new with complete abandon and release, going all the way back to the absolute stillness of nothingness.

We taste this dynamism once in a while. Death and rebirth are constant reminders, but the fact that our experience is constantly changing is the primary and ongoing way we experience it. Different traditions give it different names. I like the Indian term *lila*, "divine sport," because that conveys the playfulness, the ease and spontaneity, the joy and delight, in the sense of cosmic creativity. When we are being creative in a playful, easy, and spontaneous way, there is a lot of joy, a lot of happiness, and a sense that our experiences are meaningful and satisfying. The Indian mythology that describes different stages of this process has conceptualized three primary deities: Brahma the Creator, Vishnu the Preserver, and Shiva the Destroyer. We may sometimes only experience the sense of creativity, or only the sense of presence and fullness of appearance, or only the constant destruction, dissolving, and disappearing. But they are all facets of one force, one presence.

The enlightened view includes the recognition that everything is always happening, that happening always happens. Nobody does anything; it all simply happens. The appearance of reality always instantly arises and transforms. From a more limited perspective, we see it as us doing something or as somebody feeling something or as the weather changing. Of course, we can explain the weather as various forces, pressure, and temperature, which makes sense because it helps us understand something, but actually the whole thing—whether it is a hurricane or a gentle breeze or a stillness in the air—is all always the cosmic creativity happening. The Quintessence expends no more energy to create a hurricane than a gentle breeze; it is always one ease.

The important part about recognizing this dynamism in everyday life is that it is ultimately what moves us; it is ultimately what moves our arms and our legs. In limited situations we might experience the cosmic dynamism of reality as a sense of spontaneity, a sense of flow, a sense of ease of movement. So when we understand something and we have an insight and recognize true nature, we don't take it to mean that it is my mind doing it. We take it to mean that it is the dynamism of true nature manifesting through my limited mind at that time and revealing itself to itself. We can see the agency happening without anthropomorphizing it into a figure that comes and teaches me something. It's more that true nature appears within the individual consciousness as a capacity for understanding, for insight, for responsiveness. The dynamism of true nature appears as the functioning of the real heart, the functioning of the real mind, the functioning of real action. These are the ways that the dynamism manifests in individual life.

It's a subtle thing. In our teaching, we see that our normal mind simply does not have the capacity to recognize true nature. When we recognize true nature, it is actually true nature making the recognition happen. From the beginning of our practice, it is true nature that decided to make itself known through the practice. It's not like we practice and at some point we recognize true nature. True nature is functioning from the beginning. The dynamism from the beginning is what is guiding our work, what is moving the whole process. The practice is simply to recognize that we need to get out of the way; we need to suspend our habitual goal-oriented doing.

The magic is not only in the experience of the enlightened view. The magic is anytime, all the time, anyplace, everyplace. Even when we are not experiencing the instantaneous creation of reality everywhere at once, true nature is ornamenting itself, is changing its jewelry. We can perceive the preciousness of reality regardless of what is arising. If we are aware of the Quintessence, then everything appears as jeweled, even the superego and all of that. Perceiving the Quintessential jewels is the pure perception that whatever appears is always an ornament of reality.

We have seen that the true nature of all manifest phenomena, the Quintessence, is at once empty presence and substantial nothingness, at once profound clarity and sheer depth. The effulgent force of cosmic dynamism spontaneously creates instant-to-instant the happening of all that happens.

Human freedom is the freedom of the dynamism of Being to manifest what its intelligence wants it to manifest. Human freedom is the liberation of that dynamism to display the possibilities and the appropriate forms and dimensions of experience in any situation. This living freedom manifests as individuals who have a personal life that is true and authentic, and at the same time infinite. Our freedom is the vastness of Being manifesting its possibilities and its nature freely, without constraints.

The dynamism of our being cannot be liberated fully without freedom from the conventional view; the liberated condition is not possible without freedom from the self, which is the center of the conventional view. So, for our inquiry to come into its own, for our life to come to greater maturation—which means for Being to exercise its possibilities in an open way—we need to have a thoroughgoing understanding of the self. Most of our work here is an investigation and exploration of the self, its dynamics, its structures, its history, its manifestation and underlying forces. So attaining flexibility from the fixation of the self and freedom from the self are the same thing.

It turns out in the work we do here that a thorough understanding of the values, structures, and dynamics of the self is not separate from a thorough understanding of our true nature, its qualities, and its dimensions. In this exploration of our true nature, the more we understand Being, the more we are free from the conventional view. As we understand the nature and dimensions of Being, particularly as we understand emptiness, the freedom of the dynamism is liberated. The beingness of living presence has an eternal partner inseparable from it, which is its nonbeingness. And when we recognize and understand emptiness as the nonbeingness of Being, as the absence of what we ordinarily call existence, we discover the kind of emptiness that opens the liberation of the dynamism.

Recognizing the nonbeingness of Being does not lead to the disappearance of the individual soul; it leads to understanding that the individual soul doesn't exist the way we usually think it does. Then we discover that emptiness of Being is true not just about the individual self, but also about the perceptions of the individual self. In other words, all that we perceive can be liberated from the ordinary conception of existence as a solid something that is really there. We plaster our beliefs and our projections over all manifest forms, all the world, all the universe that we see. And when the world is free from our ideas about it, we see it in its beingness, we see that everything is a manifestation of beingness in its purity and presence and luminosity.

The thoroughgoing understanding of emptiness reveals not only that the world and the individual soul are manifestations of Being, but also that the manifestation of Being doesn't have the kind of existence we attribute to it. Being, in all its forms, is in complete eternal, inseparable embrace with its eternal partner, nonbeing. When we recognize the intrinsic emptiness of everything, then the beingness recognizes not only that the world is a manifestation of Being, but also that the world is a manifestation of emptiness. We recognize that Being is the radiance of emptiness, and that this radiance has variegated colors and multifaceted forms that we experience as the world and as all the content of our experience.

The emptiness that is the source of the freedom of the dynamism is of many kinds and degrees. There are different kinds of spaciousness—from nothingness and openness all the way to absence and nonbeing. The nonbeingness of Being opens up the presence of Being and brings a lightness, a freedom, an expansiveness, and a transparency to everything. We experience that the innerness of presence is its total unobstructedness because there is nothing in it to obstruct, not even a sense of medium. So that dimension of experiencing emptiness as nonbeing recognizes that space is not a medium.

When it comes to nonbeingness, space is no longer a medium. This is a mysterious understanding that the mind cannot readily grasp. But when we experience it, this very precise understanding brings about total transparency and intimacy, and also allows the experience of the unity of Being to reveal its luminosity and radiance. As we know from our experience of the various boundless dimensions, we can experience the unity of Being before we experience the dimension of nonbeing. The understanding of nonbeing shows that that Being can only exist as the other side of nonbeing.

There are further consequences to the understanding of emptiness as nonbeing, which takes the enlightened awareness to new mysteries. For instance, in the perception of the unity of reality, in which everything is at once Being and nonbeing, there can remain the perception of "here" and "there." There are here and there, and the distance between here and there. When we penetrate the concept of space, there is a feeling of no here and no there. We recognize that emptiness is not a medium. Nonbeing does not have extension; it is not a medium. We sense that here and there are one single spot, that here is there and there is here. Space does not disappear in terms of perception; as long as there is a distance between here and there that can be measured, there is a concept of space and a perception of space. Even if space as extension is perceived, in the realization of nonbeing it disappears as a felt sense. Manifestation always manifests in space; true nature is beyond space, and our realization can reflect that.

Another example is that of radical nonlocality, where the meaning of unity of existence goes through a profound transformation. It becomes nonspatial unity. This nonspatial sense of unity recognizes that each form of manifestation is at once all the other forms. Each form of reality is totally united with all other forms—not in terms of perceived space, which has the sense of all forms being differently located waves of the same ocean, but absolutely, in the sense that all the waves are actually the same wave, all the points are actually the same point. So the feeling of unity is that I am everything, not because I am a medium that manifests everything, but I am everything in a much closer, more intimate way. We can experience it as: "I am one with you not because we are all parts of the same thing, but because I am you. Your heart and my heart are the same heart, and not figuratively."

The thoroughgoing understanding of emptiness is, as far as I can tell, the same thing as the thoroughgoing understanding of presence. Emptiness reveals itself to have mysteries upon mysteries. The realization of emptiness keeps moving and revealing itself, because the dynamism and the emptiness are not separate. We can experience dynamic emptiness, dynamic nonbeing. The identity of emptiness and dynamism is freedom. This freedom that ceaselessly creates the totality of reality is what I call runaway realization.

Let's see now if you have any questions.

STUDENT: The question has to do with functioning. I'm aware that in either the fullness or the stillness, I wouldn't want to get my hands on any piece of equipment or drive a car. Could you speak to the bridge between where I am and how to function from here?

ALMAAS: Are you talking and interacting now from the fullness and stillness?

STUDENT: Yes.

ALMAAS: So it is possible to function to some degree. You are seeing that some kind of functioning is possible, and if your self is gone, then obviously it is not you that does the talking. You thought you were the one who does the talking, and now you are discovering something else. Part of the bridge is to find out who is really doing things. As you see, functioning happens even though the usual sense of self might be gone and the mind might not be operating in the usual way.

As you become more acquainted with the sense of stillness and functionality and as you see through the beliefs of needing the old sense of self to do these things, something new can happen. It is a development, a kind of ripening and maturing. In the past few years I've been teaching about living your realization, which means living the truth you know. The emptiness is what lives, and to live means to function, to do, and to drive a car. A lot of it is a process of discovery—just as you discovered right now that there is talking even though it is not the usual self that is talking. The difficult thing is how to be this presence while there is functioning. Most people revert to their old self to function because they strongly believe that that self is what does. The practice is how to be this stillness, this kind of consciousness, as you move from one step to the next.

STUDENT: This teaching thrills me all the way to my empty core. All week I've noticed this movement appearing and I see that the whole world—the sky and the trees and the ground—just dissolve into this swirling. And when I inquire into what is actually moving, what are the particles, what is the substance that moves, there is nothing there. There is a kind of charge and discharge, a sort of contraction and the relaxation of essence, and then there is the dynamism and the relaxation, the Shakti and the Shiva.

ALMAAS: This is the teaching about movement and how movement happens. The whole universe is in constant movement, constant flow, so when we are beginning to experience this flow, our movement becomes more spontaneous and easy. And even though everything is flowing, there is nothing. That is the interesting thing. Even though the Quintessence is the source of all manifestation, is what is making everything happen, at the same time there is not something there that is making things happen. We cannot find it if we look for it. It is more like the underlying nature of everything that moves, the nature of movement itself.

STUDENT: I hate to be a downer to the concept of "we are all one wave," but what are we going to do about the preverbal structures or the nonconceptual structures of the soul?

ALMAAS: Yes, what are we going to do with them? Seeing through nonconceptual structures is a subtler kind of work than dealing with the cognitive structures constructed by mind. Understanding these earlier structures is not a matter of seeing your beliefs and ideas. Preverbal structures are like deep impressions on your soul that profoundly affect your experience. We work with these structures as we work with inquiry in general; as something arises, we experience it, stay with it, feel it as much as possible, and question it. Because they are nonverbal, these impressions are difficult to understand. They appear vague and difficult to know.

The understanding of these impressions will happen as we become open to recognizing that this is something we cannot understand with our mind. That allows our being to manifest in a way that is beyond mind, that is nonconceptual. So the nonconceptual qualities of Being, those beyond the recognition of mind, will tend to open up and reveal these structures. As these preverbal impressions and how they affect us are brought to experience, the cognition and discernment of them become possible. We can begin to understand them in a way that we didn't see before.

The understanding happens in the same way as with cognitive structures: insight and presence arise. Since there is often a layering of these structures, many people are dealing with nonconceptual structures without knowing that explicitly. They might be arising, but we deal with them in a way that we can understand and conceptualize. That means we end up dealing with later developments of them. As we deal with the later accretions, the structures tend to regress backward until we recognize at some point that we don't understand them. As we stay with what we're not understanding, we open to the qualities of Being that go beyond mind. Working with these early precognitive structures is a whole teaching that I will be doing at some point.

STUDENT: As I got into the emptiness, it was vast, it was boundless, it was soft, it was dark. And then this question came up: Can emptiness be solid? And it was like there was a war—why can't emptiness be everything? Solidness seems to obstruct emptiness, and yet emptiness can be everything.

ALMAAS: Yes, so emptiness can be solid. Solid space is one of the experiences of space. Emptiness is an effervescent total nothing, complete lightness that sometimes feels like it is also solid at the same time.

Completely light, completely not there, but at once more solid and substantial than anything else. That is actually the experience of the Absolute. Many people experience the Absolute as solid absence. How can absence—which means that nothing is there, everything has vacated the place, and even the place is gone—how can that be solid? Being and nonbeing are not separate, are not two realities but one reality seen in different ways.

STUDENT: I wanted to ask you about something that comes and goes. There are times I feel this very rapid oscillation between being and nonbeing; I'm not here, I'm here, all very quickly.

ALMAAS: So if you allow the oscillation to go as fast as possible, what happens?

STUDENT: Sometimes I feel it amplified in the physical body, but I think it is related to the mind disappearing, even though the awareness is still continuous.

ALMAAS: Yes, awareness continues as the thinking mind disappears.

STUDENT: It seems impossible that it can come and go that fast. That's what makes me think it is something else.

ALMAAS: What is happening now?

STUDENT: There is awareness of that oscillation.

ALMAAS: So you are aware of the oscillation. That is what happens. For a while, we can experience either presence or emptiness, either fullness or nothingness, because that's easier in some sense for the mind than experiencing both at once. The oscillation is normal in the sense that in the experience of realization, which one of the two sides dominates is constantly changing. Sometimes it is more the presence, and sometimes it is more the absence. Sometimes they are both equally there; they are two sides of one thing.

STUDENT: I experienced something that felt like I was "notness," and at the same time everything was very vivid.

ALMAAS: Notness sounds good. It is a nice word for the emptiness, and of course, everything becomes vivid. That's part of the experience we have been discussing. The presence, the nowness, the awareness, the emptiness, all of those characteristics of true nature—when they dominate the field, everything becomes more vivified.

STUDENT: And there is a feeling of "never-been-this."

ALMAAS: Yes, that is what notness is. Not only "it is not," but also "it never is." That is a nice insight, actually. There is a simplicity to it; that is what I like about it. So the point is to see that you are taking a peek into reality. This is not just a cloud passing through and giving you some rain. What we are working with, what we are learning, is not a changeable experience. We are trying to understand the ground that is always present, that underlies all experience, all manifestation, all the forms. When I say it is the nature of all forms, I don't mean just physical forms. I mean mental forms too: thoughts, images. It is the nature of essential forms: aspects, vehicles, dimensions. Whatever form experience takes, Quintessence is still the underlying nature.

BOOKS BY A. H. ALMAAS

Published by Shambhala Publications

Facets of Unity: The Enneagram of Holy Ideas

Facets of Unity presents the Enneagram of Holy Ideas as a crystal clear window on the true reality experienced in enlightened consciousness. Here we are not directed toward the psychological types but the higher spiritual realities they reflect. We discover how the disconnection from each Holy Idea leads to the development of its corresponding fixation, thus recognizing each type's deeper psychological core.

The Inner Journey Home:
Soul's Realization of the Unity of Reality

The Inner Journey Home is the centerpiece of the Diamond Approach literature, providing a complete overview of the teaching with references to the author's other books for more details on certain topics.

Luminous Night's Journey:
An Autobiographical Fragment

In *Luminous Night's Journey*, Almaas shares excerpts from his personal journal, which describe a certain thread in his own journey of realization and the processes involved in integrating that realization. This book clarifies how the unveiling of Being and the exposure of ego structures constitute one process, leading to the soul's integrated realization of absolute nature and the manifestation of the human being as a personal embodiment of that nature.

DIAMOND MIND SERIES

Volume 1. *The Void:*
Inner Spaciousness and Ego Structure

In this book Almaas brings together concepts and experiences drawn from contemporary object relations theory, Freudian-based ego psychology, case studies from his own spiritual practice, and teaching from the highest levels of Buddhist and other Eastern practices.

Volume 2. *The Pearl Beyond Price:*
Integration of Personality into Being:
An Object Relations Approach

Here, Almaas demonstrates that healthy ego development is part of the continuum of spiritual development. He also establishes the possibility of attaining inner realization and developing our essential being— "the pearl beyond price"—in the context of living a normal human life.

Volume 3. *The Point of Existence:*
Transformations of Narcissism in Self-Realization

In this book, the author explores the underlying spiritual understanding of narcissism. He presents a detailed map of the steps involved in working through barriers that prevent us from recognizing the most essential nature of our true identity.

DIAMOND HEART SERIES, BOOKS ONE THROUGH FIVE

Book One. *Elements of the Real in Man*
Book Two. *The Freedom to Be*
Book Three. *Being and the Meaning of Life*
Book Four. *Indestructible Innocence*
Book Five. *Inexhaustible Mystery*

This five-volume series presents a collection of talks given by Almaas on topics such as faith, commitment, nobility and suffering, truth and compassion, allowing, and growing up. Through these talks, Almaas offers valuable guidance and advice for those on a spiritual path, and he explores the challenges and psychological barriers faced by those seeking self-realization.

DIAMOND BODY SERIES

Spacecruiser Inquiry:
True Guidance for the Inner Journey

In this work, Almaas uses the metaphor of a "spacecruiser" to describe a method of exploring the immediacy of personal experience—a way of investigating our moment-by-moment feelings, thoughts, reactions, and behaviors through a process of open-ended questioning. The method is called the practice of inquiry, and *Spacecruiser Inquiry* reveals what it means to engage with this practice as a spiritual path: its principles, challenges, and rewards.

Brilliancy: The Essence of Intelligence

A. H. Almaas introduces here a radically different idea of intelligence—one that recognizes an actual quality of consciousness as the source, which he calls the Brilliancy of our true nature. His presentation of this notion is followed by in-depth dialogues with his students on the various barriers to recognizing and embodying this essential quality.

The Unfolding Now:
Realizing Your True Nature through
the Practice of Presence

In his most accessible work to date, *The Unfolding Now,* Almaas shows readers how being present and aware in the moment leads to the discovery of our True Nature. As we begin to embrace the truth of the moment, we feel more like ourselves, and this leads to greater self-acceptance, contentment, and harmony.